SILENT ECHOES

JASON MCGRATH

<u>Disclaimer:</u>

The events and conversations in this book have been set down to the best of the author's ability, although some names and details have been changed to protect the privacy of individuals. Any resemblance to persons, living or dead, should be apparent to them and those who know them, especially if the author has been kind enough to provide their real names. All events described herein actually happened, though the author has taken certain exceedingly minor liberties with chronology on occasion.

First Edition 2024

CONTENTS

Introduction   7

1. THE BASTARD CHILD   9
2. CROSSROADS TO DESTINY   21
3. VEILED BEGINNINGS   33
4. GOING THE DISTANCE   47
5. HOMEBOUND RUNAWAYS   65
6. A JOURNEY TO SELF-DISCOVERY   79
7. BETRAYED BY BLOOD   89
8. OPEN CUSTODY. BOYS TOWN AND
   BATHHOUSES   101
9. BREAKING STRONGHOLDS   121
10. TROUBLE WAS IN MY BLOOD   139
11. NEW FRIENDS, NEW BEGINNINGS   155
12. TRYING TO FIND MY PLACE IN THIS
    WORLD   171
13. PATRICK JOSEPH BROMLEY   191
14. THE WEDDING PLANNER   209
15. BACHELORHOOD TO MARRIAGE   219
16. NEW TOWNS, NEW JOBS   231
17. REST IN PEACE, CHARLES RYLEY   251
18. BLUE HOUSE ACROSS THE TRACKS   267
19. SEPARATION AND RECONCILIATION   281
20. NEW HOMES SAME STRUGGLES   297
21. EMBRACING THE UNKNOWN DOWN
    UNDER   319
22. FOREIGN AFFAIRS TO FOREIGN SOIL   333
23. UNEXPECTED CHINESE CULTURE
    SHOCK   349

24. BROKEN HEARTS AND SECOND
    WEDDING   363
    Epilogue   383

Dedication to my brother Jimmy, whom I could not protect from the streets, and my biological father, whom I met too late.

In loving memory of my brother
James Anthony McGrath

and my father
Patrick Joseph Bromley

INTRODUCTION

"At what point do we entrust our children to government agencies like the Catholic Children's Aid Society for their safety and future when we cannot provide it? Hoping to influence their life, a better life, or is it?…"

This memoir seeks to immerse you in the depths of my journey, to engage you with the raw emotions and turbulent memories that have shaped my existence. It is a tale of loss and resilience, of a young soul navigating the complexities of a life interrupted, yearning for a sense of belonging and the warmth of a family's embrace. It's about a child abused in the system, a crown ward of the province and a victim of the Catholic Children's Aid Society. It's about a coverup to keep their status quo.

If you wish to continue this journey with me, know that the road ahead is fraught with challenges but also with a promise of growth and the hope of redemption. Let us turn the page together and see where the story leads.

1

THE BASTARD CHILD

The bell rang, echoing through the narrow school corridors. I was six years old, a mere whisper of existence in a world without deciding what to do with me. Grade one—a place where innocence collided with reality and where the playground held my secrets as ancient as time. Outside, the other kids streamed toward the metal swing playground; their laughter echoed back against the steel doors. But I lingered, my gaze fixed on the teacher's desk—an altar of temptation. There, stacked high, lay boxes of chocolate bars in their glossy wrappers. Fundraisers, they said. But to my hungry eyes, they were forbidden treasures.

I could not resist. The chocolate bars beckoned like sirens, promising substance for my empty stomach and a fleeting escape from my mundane existence. So, with the stealth of a seasoned thief, I slipped my hand into the box. The foil crinkled, yielding to my touch. I pulled out six to eight bars—my pockets bulging, my conscience hushed by the promise of sweets.

But fate has a way of catching up with little thieves. The teacher materialized, her stern gaze locking onto my guilt-laden face. "What do you think you're doing?" Her voice sliced through the air, severing my illusions of clandestine indulgence, caught with my hand in the cookie jar.

She marched me to the principal's office, my heart pounding through my chest. The room smelled of polished wood and authority. The principal—a stern figure with sunken temples—studied me. "Your father," he said, "insists you go directly home from school," "take those chocolate bars home and sell them all by the weekend. Otherwise, your parents will pay."

I nodded, my skin turning ashen. Home meant my mother's remarriage—a union that birthed not love but my wicked stepfather, Shane Bradley. His anger was a storm, his belt a weapon. I knew what awaited me—the sting of leather against my skin, the taste of fear, and the echo of Hitler's madness in his eyes.

As the school day ended, I stepped outside, my footsteps tentative. Most students had vanished, leaving me alone with my dread. "What am I going to do?" I whispered. Going home was unthinkable. So, I did what any desperate child would: I ran. I fled from the school, the chocolate bars, and the looming shadow of my stepfather.

The city streets swallowed me—a labyrinth of concrete and glass. Behind stores and buildings, I became a phantom—a nameless child seeking shelter in the alleyways. The sun dipped low, casting long shadows across my path. I never made it home. Instead, I wandered, my pockets empty, my heart heavy. The city held its secrets—the murmur of strangers, the graffiti on walls, and the distant wail of sirens.

And so, my rebellion began—a silent protest of a world that had branded me a bastard. At that moment, I vowed to leave more than footprints behind. I would etch my story into the city's Concrete heart—a testament to survival, defiance, and the indomitable spirit of a child who refused to be defined by lineage.

I slinked behind the plaza, seeking refuge behind a fortress of garbage bins. There, I huddled, shivering not from the cold but from fear, as I nibbled on my candy—the only sweets to my bitter reality stolen from the plaza convenience store. A familiar voice sliced through the silence as the sun dipped below the horizon. "Jason, Jason, where are you?" The voice grew louder, more insistent. My brother, Charles Ryley, was on a mission to retrieve me. "Please don't find me," I whispered, willing my presence to vanish into the shadows.

The footsteps intensified, a drumbeat to my racing heart, then halted. "Jason, what are you doing here? Papa is waiting for you at home and sent me to find you." Charles's voice was tinged with a mix of concern and command. "Charles," I pleaded, "I cannot go home with you. You know what awaits me there." His apology was a whisper as he lifted me from my hiding spot. The candy—a small token of defiance—was discovered and discarded. As we trudged back home, I saw something unsettling in Charles's eyes—a flicker of satisfaction that it was my turn, not his, to face the impending storm.

Ascending the steps to the kitchen was like approaching the gallows. Shane loomed there, clad in his signature sweat-stained attire, white briefs, and a white sleeveless child beater undershirt, a uniform of neglect. "Charles, fetch my pants," he barked while my mother, Wendy Bradley, looked on, a silent spectator to the unfolding tragedy. The belt came off with a hiss, a prelude to the pain. "Get over here and take down your pants," he commanded. I lay prone on the floor, bracing for impact. The beating was relentless, his sweat mingling with my tears.

I became numb, a shell devoid of sensation, save for the sobs that escaped me. "That's enough," Wendy finally intervened. He retreated, panting from his exertion. "From now on, you ask me for what you need," he declared, his breaths laboured. I crawled from the ashes of my humiliation and retreated to the sanctuary of my room.

The years under my stepfather's roof etched a blueprint of dysfunction within me, or so the school psychologist opined. My public school days are a blur, punctuated by moments of rebellion and a cry for attention. I was the boy who stole kisses in forbidden places like the girl's bathroom and donned his shirt as a cape, proclaiming himself a superhero in a world that felt like a supervillain. I yearned for acceptance, for a place in this world.

Endless tests and countless meetings with educators painted a picture of a boy lost in the system, a square peg forced into a round hole. Eventually, I was cast adrift to another school, my journey beginning with a solitary wait at the bus stop for the yellow minibus that would ferry me to my new reality.

The bus ride was an ordeal; each day, it was a journey past the lake, where we would pick up other children from their towering concrete buildings. Bullies lurked behind me, their cruel games of hair-pulling and hitting a daily torment. I would step off the bus, tears staining my cheeks, wishing for the familiarity of my old school.

For one summer, I found myself in the backyard with my sister, Ashleigh Ryley, who was close in age and spirit. Curiosity led me to Shane's prized garden, hidden behind a gate. I could not resist the temptation of a plump green pepper. As I bit into its flesh, my sister's cry of warning echoed, but it was too late. She had alerted the sleeping giant— our stepfather.

Unaware of the atom bomb about to explode, relatives were visiting as Shane, mid-renovation, was in the basement, charged outside. I imagined him as a giant from a fairytale and I as a thief caught in his garden. His anger was swift and fierce; he dragged me by my hair into the house and down to the basement. There, he wielded a leftover 2x4 plank with a fury that shook the very foundations of our home. My screams filled the air until my Uncle Mark Davis intervened, pulling him away from me.

Shane's garden was his sanctuary, where he could escape his troubled past. He cherished it so much that he would drive us to the lake, where we would collect smelt from the rocks, their stench overwhelming. We would return home, reeking of decay, to bury the fish in trenches he had dug in the garden, a gruesome fertilizer for his beloved plants. The neighbours next door complained, and city inspectors brushed it aside.

One day, the air was pierced by Shane's bellowing voice, demanding we gather in the backyard. He stood, a pear core in hand, seething with rage over the stolen fruit. Charles and I had been the culprits, secretly feasting on the pears and tossing the cores over the fence. We made a silent pact not to confess. In response to our silence, Shane lined us up and, with a baseball bat, delivered a punishment to our bare feet that echoed through the neighbourhood. Onlookers watched from a distance, yet no one intervened. Back then, you kept your eyes and ears shut to the things happening next door in our family. What was it with this man and his produce? He was trying to win first prize at the local fall fair.

Shane had a room filled with guns, rifles, and knives —a locked chamber in his bedroom where he would spend hours tending to his collection with care; he never showed his wife or family that kind of commitment. Our camping trips to Albion Hills were a brief escape from this Reality. The journey down the hilly slope to the quiet lake was always bumpy, but there, at the water's edge, a sense of peace would settle over us, if only for a moment where a picnic table awaited in the shallow embrace of the water.

The serene atmosphere by the lake was abruptly interrupted by the sound of rifle shots, breaking the calm like thunder on a cloudy day. I hurried up the hill, driven by a mix of dread and urgency, only to be met with the sight of Charles, rifle in hand, aiming at the innocent creatures of the woods. The sharp echoes of the shots rang out as he and Shane collected their trophies. They emerged from the bushes, hands filled with the still bodies of squirrels and chipmunks, a grim display of my stepfather's twisted sense of pleasure in dominating the defenceless.

This harsh reality contrasted with the carefree moments earlier when my siblings and I had stripped off our clothes and dived into the lake's chilling waters. We swam to the picnic table, our laughter and splashes a brief respite from our troubled lives. The table became our diving board, and for a moment, the deeper waters enveloped us in a world where we could forget.

One drive home was marred by an encounter with a giant painted turtle, which Shane unceremoniously added to our cramped car. Its smell of fear and urine was nauseating, adding to the heavy atmosphere as we returned. At home, the turtle was in my mother's laundry sink, a new 'pet' that took precedence over her needs and our clean clothes. It shows where my mother fits in behind the turtle and Pepper, the German shepherd dog we had as a pet.

The memory of our trip across Canada to Newfoundland and Labrador is etched in my mind. All of us were packed into the station wagon, a tight fit with little room to breathe. The journey was marked by new experiences, like my first taste of Dr. Pepper and the Big Gulp, but also by discomfort and our stepfather's strict rules.

One such rule led to a humiliating incident for Charles, who, after being denied bathroom breaks, had an accident. The car filled with a foul smell working its way to Shane's nostrils, and Shane's reaction was rage and cruelty. The vehicle came to a sudden halt as he pulled Charles out of the car, removing his pants and underwear, forcing the feces and underwear into his mouth, a punishment so degrading that it left us all in silent horror, too afraid to speak up in fear we would be next to partake in that meal. The expression "brush your teeth because your breath smells like shit" must have originated with my stepfather.

As we waited to board the ferry the following day, I was filled with adventure despite the previous day's events. The ship felt like a vessel of discovery, and as we sailed towards Newfoundland, I imagined myself as an explorer of old. The island awaited us, promising adventures and a chance for new beginnings, much like the stories of 'The Swiss Family Robinson' I had always adored.

In the heart of a secluded village, nestled high in the mountains, I found myself in a world that seemed untouched by time. The whispers of my Irish ancestors seemed to echo through the winds, instilling in me a sense of belonging to this rugged island. My mom's relatives' house stood atop a hill, a solitary beacon on a dirt road flanked by the vast ocean and a sparse scattering of homes on the other. At the hill's foot lay a small store, the last outpost before the wild embrace of the cliffs and sea.

Charles and I, young adventurers at heart, roamed the rocky edges, peering down at the ocean's expanse. We discovered remnants of history—a car surrendered to the elements, now a rusted relic on the rocks below. We frolicked alongside shaggy-coated beasts, their woolly forms resembling mythical creatures from old tales; as they wandered the dirt road, we became their shepherds.

Shane spent his days in communion with the ocean, casting lines into its depths. I recall a boat ride around the harbour, the taste of salt on my lips, and the thrill of the catch. A photograph immortalizes that moment: me, a young boy with a mackerel in hand, standing on the rocks, with Shane and Ashleigh, a backdrop to this scene of youthful triumph.

Yes, not all memories are cast in the golden light of adventure. One such memory is sharp with pain: a rusted nail piercing my heel as I played on the swing set. The agony was only matched by the sting of salt-water my mother used to cleanse the wound. But even this could not quiet my spirit; by afternoon, I was back to exploring, a testament to the resilience of youth.

As much as I longed to remain in that haven, reality beckoned us back to the mainland. The home was a place of contradictions, where Shane, a figure who loomed large, presented a complex puzzle. Behind closed doors, he demanded secrets to be kept and unspeakable sexual acts to be performed, rewarding silence with money from his sock drawer. His duplicity was confounding as he mingled with churchgoers on Sundays, his smile belying the darkness that lurked within.

Despite the shadows, I clung to the brighter moments—the thrill of flea market finds at the Dixie Outlet Mall, the taste of Kentucky Fried Chicken, and the excitement of sneaking into drive-in theatres. Like rays of sunlight, these memories offered a respite from the darker undercurrents of my childhood. I was closest to my stepsiblings, Chris and Laura Bradley, who were from my mother, and Shane. Chris was two years younger than me, and Laura was four years younger, so we had a closer bond together as the other siblings were older.

In August of 1979, at the tender age of nine, I faced a heart-wrenching goodbye. The old brown station wagon became a vessel of separation, taking away my siblings as my mother wept, a sacrifice to keep her family from splintering further. The truth about my sisters' bond with their stepfather and the hold he had over them would only become known years later, revealing the full extent of his influence.

2

CROSSROADS TO DESTINY

The engine hummed to life, and as we pulled away, I clung to the last glimpse of my childhood home before it disappeared into the distance. The journey felt endless, a blur of highways and cityscapes, while a single thought haunted me: what had I done to be cast away by my mother?

Eventually, the car halted, and Shane's stern voice ushered us out. We ascended a steep driveway leading to a towering green building that pierced the sky. Uprooted from my suburban sanctuary, these alien structures now dwarfed me.

The door swung open, revealing Mr. Bob Ryley, the estranged patriarch of half my siblings. It had been years since my mother's divorce when I was but two. Inside, I surveyed what was to be my new world. To the right, a narrow passage led to the kitchen, a confined space that allowed passage for only one. A modest round table occupied the kitchen, its edges brushing the walls, while its gaze returned to the living room. An aged pull-out couch rested against the wall, crowned by a black velvet painting of an enigmatic woman. Opposite my makeshift bed, an antiquated stereo system stood sentry, its speakers still echoing the strains of Blondie's "The Tide Is High." To the left, a corridor stretched out, bedrooms lining one side, a bathroom at its end. Six souls in such a cramped space—how would we manage?

Kathy Ryley, the woman I was to call stepmother, was a slender figure with large spectacles perched on her nose and unkempt ginger hair. Her peculiar, high-pitched, monotone voice carried an accent foreign to my ears. Once settled, I ventured outside to acquaint myself with this new chapter: my school, Golf Club Rd. Public School lay just beyond the apartment's shadow, a mere stone's throw away.

The school brought a mix of nerves and anticipation for new friendships. Yet, the shadow of Shane's abuse, the upheaval of my home, and academic setbacks led me down a path of mischief for attention. My memories of that place are sparse, save for the disgrace of standing, sign-adorned, a silent warning to my peers. The sign became a familiar weight, a constant companion through the corridors and playgrounds. In those moments, I felt a kinship with a figure of history, misunderstood and mocked. "If you talk to this person, you will be standing beside them," wrote the sign to warn other students not to talk to me or they would be next. During those daunting moments, I felt what it was like to be Jesus hanging on the cross. Mr. Bickerton, a middle-aged man with a full beard and glasses, was the most excellent teacher who showed interest in me, and I felt like he cared about what I was going through and my learning abilities.

Post-school hours were spent with Johnny Reed, my neighbour, in our secret haven behind the plaza—a wooden fortress that shielded us from the world. It was our refuge, our escape from the complexities of our young lives. Our secret fort, nestled behind the plaza, was a sanctuary until the day older boys invaded it, their smoky haze starkly contrasting with our innocent games. They seemed like titans, their high school stature towering over us. But the fort was ours, and I was not about to surrender it. With a surge of adrenaline, I seized a wooden shard that barricaded the door, and with Johnny at my side, we fled from their angry shouts, our hearts pounding in our chests.

The home was no refuge. Bob's temper flared over trivialities, like shoes on the wrong feet, his slaps stinging more than the skin. His sharp and cruel words left deeper marks than any physical blow. One quiet evening, lying on my pull-out bed, "Jaws" flickered on the screen, and a sudden nosebleed turned into a torrent, leading to a hasty hospital visit. The diagnosis was simple: dry air. But the fear that filled that pail was anything but. The doctor cauterized my nose to stop the bleeding.

Johnny's mischievous grin beckoned me to a new adventure in the basement the following day. Our plan: transform the mundane laundry machines into a fiery spectacle. We stuffed them with paper, struck a match, and waited. But the anticipated chaos never erupted; the fire trucks remained a figment of our imaginations.

My solitary wanderings took me miles along roads, into stores, and through plazas. A Bi-Way store became a playground of fantasies where I gathered Star Wars heroes, pocketing them like treasures. In hindsight, their value lay not in their intact packaging but in the stories they could have told had they not met a destructive end at my young hands.

The Maverick, a 1972 relic, sat abandoned in the underground parking across the street in my sister Janet Ryley's apartment, a dusty testament to forgotten journeys. When Johnny and I were told it was ours, it became a beacon of hope, a dream of future escapades. I even outfitted it with a stolen compass and air fresheners from Canadian Tire, a small rebellion against a life that felt increasingly out of control.

That same night, the superintendent's visit with Marry Brennon, a Catholic Children's Aid Society case worker, cast a long shadow over my makeshift dreams. Mary's presence became constant in my life; her monthly visits and lunches at Swiss Chalet were a brief escape from the chaos at home. Yet, her kindness was a prelude to the upheaval that was to come.

It was an early morning awakening, not by the shrill of an alarm but by the soft murmur of conversation at the kitchen table. There sat my mother, her voice a gentle hum in the quiet of dawn, accompanied by Bob. Shane's presence completed the unusual assembly. Bob caught my stirring gaze and announced it was time to dress; an outing was on the horizon. Kathy, with her keen eye for style, chose for me a crisp white dress shirt, black slacks, and a black wool vest adorned with whimsical purple elephants. The attire was a silent herald; today was no ordinary day.

March 7, 1980, marked the calendar, and our destination was the Scarborough Family Court House. Outside the courtroom, my mother's words fell like autumn leaves, telling of change; Bob and Kathy could no longer offer me shelter at their apartment: a man awaited inside, a gatekeeper to my future abode. Bob's testimony to the court echoed the superintendent's decree: the condo was brimming, and I could no longer be part of its count. Accusations flew like arrows in the courtroom, painting me as a troublemaker within the apartment complex. My mother, a figure of quiet strength, took the stand, only to be met with the Judge's plucking inquiry: why couldn't I reside with her?

The tension in the air was palpable as Shane Bradley stood up and yelled to the Judge, his ultimatum ringing clear: my return would render them homeless. I was beckoned to the stand, a child in the spotlight, just nine years old, as the Judge laid bare the gravity of the situation. Mary, a Catholic Children's Aid Society representative, presented her assessment of me, a report that would tip the scales of my fate. Her recommendation was clear: a special treatment foster home would serve me better than any regular placement.

That day, the gavel fell; with it, my life and future were entrusted to the Catholic Children's Aid Society. A solemn promise was made to my mother and me: a crown ward, the province would safeguard my best interests and shield me from harm. The journey back to the apartment was a silent procession, the car's hum contrasting the day's earlier cacophony. A tender kiss on my mother's cheek was a soft epilogue to our parting, her promise of reunion lingering in the air.

In the shadowed stillness of the underground garage, my pent-up frustrations found their outlet. A piece of the turmoil within me escaped with each window they shattered. Rocks became messengers of my anguish, denting the car's body, marking it as mine in destruction. It was a silent declaration: if I could not keep it, no one would.

Now a tableau of ruin, the car bore witness to my sorrow. I sat there amidst the echoes of my actions, allowing tears to carve rivers of release. It was a moment of raw vulnerability, a private farewell to a chapter closing too soon. With a heavy heart, I ascended the stairs to confront Johnny. Our friendship, like the car below, was another casualty of circumstance. Through the weight of imminent departure, I explained that our paths were diverging, and the bond we shared must be untangled with my move.

Mary's assurance was a gentle anchor, promising to return once my possessions were gathered. The basement awaited a trove of memories guarded by a caged door. Bob's key turned, and we stepped into a sanctuary of cardboard and collectibles. Amidst the treasure trove, Bob handed me a stack of hockey cards, a parting gift mingled with the artifacts of my past. They were added to the collection of belongings that would journey with me, a mosaic of my history in tangible form. Days later, the fateful knock echoed through the halls, and Mary stood at the threshold, ready to guide me into the unknown. The loss was all-encompassing—

father, brothers, sisters, friends—all the anchors of my young life were now memories in the making as we drove away,

Mary spoke of a kind new family, but my thoughts were consumed with escape, with returning to the family from which I had been torn. My mind is so confused for a nine-year-old. I have lost my entire family in such a short time, and things are not going to get better for me. They get a lot worse. The car pulled away, leaving a trail of dust and uncertainty behind. Mary's voice, tinged with optimism, assured me that the family awaiting my arrival was kind. As we cruised down Golf Club Rd, the familiar landscape whispered promises of proximity to my true home. The thought comforted me; I could almost feel the embrace of my real family, just a stone's throw away.

The house that greeted us was a mirror image of my mother's, a 1950s relic with a backyard oasis. A pool shimmered like a blue jewel amidst the green, beckoning me to forget, even for a moment. Temptation lurked down the street, where a variety store stood to guard opposite a quaint fruit market. There, amidst the mundane, I committed a silent rebellion, pocketing a pack of wine-tipped cigars. Lighting all five cigars was foreign to me, as was the smoke that soon filled my lungs behind the store.

The aftermath was as bitter as the act itself. I

returned to the house, seeking solace in the calm waters of the pool, but the sickness within could not be quenched. My room became my refuge, where I succumbed to the weight of my actions and the world. Awakening to a throbbing head and the aftermath of my indiscretion covered in vomit, I was met with the gentle concern of my foster mother. I lied, claiming illness from dawn. The shower washed away the remnants of the day, and I found peace in the embrace of clean sheets, a small comfort in a world turned upside down.

The adventure at the Ontario Science Center unfolded with the promise of discovery. As I wandered through the halls, my mind danced with thoughts of future inventions and possibilities. The gift store beckoned, a treasure trove of wonders, where a particular flying airplane caught my eye. It was a simple thing, powered by a wound elastic band, but it held the allure of flight.

The act of taking it was swift, a decision that weighed heavily on my conscience. Yet, there I was, assembling the wings with a sense of urgency, the wingspan impressive in its breadth. The elastic band stretched to its limit; I released the plane into the open sky, chasing after the freedom it represented. But liberty was not mine to claim. Confronted by the foster son, I lied about the plane's origins. He cast it to the wind in a swift act of justice, a lesson in facing the consequences of my actions. The first foster home left but a faint imprint on my memory, a transient waypoint on the road to an uncertain future.

The second foster home, nestled in the East end, was near a school that now escapes my recollection. The foster home was an alien landscape where my reflection betrayed me in the mirror. Exploring my surroundings, I found solitude in the sanctuary of the woods. It was a realm where I could don the cloak of any character, free from the world's script. The trees stood as silent witnesses to my imagined adventures, a comforting constant in a life of change.

One day, the earth beneath me betrayed my trust, and I was trapped in a mud hole. Childhood fears whispered tales of quicksand, and I envisioned a lonely end swallowed by the ground where I sought refuge. Though kind, the family that housed me could not fill the silhouette of 'home' etched in my heart. Their faces, their voices, they were all foreign echoes, never quite aligning with the memories of my kin.

The mirror revealed a boy whose skin did not match the expectations of others. Placed in a family whose hues were darker than mine, I grappled with the reflection that stared back a constant reminder of the mismatch between the world's perception and my inner identity.

A family where the patriarch's nightly ritual of removing his prosthetic legs became a dreadful performance that haunted my evenings. My solace was found in the animated tales of "Fables of the Green Forest," where I lost myself in the adventures of woodland creatures. Yet, one morning, as I walked out on one of my adventures, something seemed remarkably familiar with my surroundings. As I passed the forest area and kept walking, reality beckoned at the sight of Ferndale Baptist Church, the spiritual haven of my early years. It stood as a testament to a life once lived, a weekly pilgrimage where I could bask in the presence of my family, if only for a fleeting moment.

The thoughts started twirling in my mind; I would now be able to see my family every Sunday and convince them to take me back home with them. All I had to do was tell them how bad it was, that I missed them and wanted to come home. Each Sunday, I sat amongst them, cloaked in the warmth of familiarity, cherishing the illusion of inclusion. But as the congregation dispersed, I was left behind, a solitary figure in an empty lot, my hopes of returning home with them dissipating like mist. Things were not going to change overnight. I did not care about how Shane treated me and everything he did to my siblings and me; I just wanted to go home.

My wanderlust led me beyond the church to a strip

plaza where the thrum of bowling alleys promised new alliances. I became a cartographer of the streets, charting my way back to the apartment that once was home. Yet, my visits stirred discontent, and soon, the whispers of disapproval reached the ears of the Catholic Children's Aid Society. Complaints came from Shane and the Ryleys, who said I was spending too much time hanging around the building and wanting to move back in with my family.

Their solution was swift and decisive—to sever my ties to the city and transplant me to rural unknowns. The prospect of farm life, with its pastoral scenes and livestock, was as foreign to me as the stars in the sky. As I bid farewell to the urban jungle, I pondered the life that awaited me—a life among cows and open fields, a stark contrast to the German Shepherd and pet turtle of my city days.

Goodbye, city; hello, country. The next chapter of my life was about to begin on a farm where the future was full of green pastures, farm animals, and manure.

3

VEILED BEGINNINGS

Once more, my life was packed into bags, and as Mary drove me away from the foster home, a sense of relief washed over me. The destination was unknown, a mystery foster home nestled in the countryside, promised to be a haven with kind parents and fellow foster kids. Glancing back, the city that cradled my childhood faded into nothingness. My social worker's voice, a constant drone, buzzed in my ears, her words melding into a monotonous hum that pounded at my temples. A cocktail of frustration and anticipation bubbled within me. The journey stretched on, and to my young mind, it seemed an eternity.

The urban sprawl gave way to open skies as the roads shrank to two lanes, sometimes down to one. The worker spoke of reunions with my parents, a future glimmer of hope, but my gaze was fixed on the endless fields of corn, wheat, and cows dotting the pastoral landscape—scenes I had only encountered in library books. After what felt like an odyssey, we reached the abode, an unassuming brick house with a quaint metal barn sitting on a vast fifty-acre canvas of fields and woods.

The house was located between Parkhill and Grand Bend, about twenty kilometres apart. With its wooden fence and three horizontal planks, a solitary horse lazily nibbling on hay. My memory served images of pigs, rabbits, chickens, and more horses residing within. Inside the house, I met my new foster parents, Scott and Holly Burke, a couple in their forties with warm smiles that belied the uncertainty of first impressions. Their family included three children—two girls, one my peer, Heidi, the other younger by two years, Blake, and a toddler boy, Alex. An older man, Don, a permanent fixture, occupied the basement, a testament to the house's gravitational pull.

The household was a mosaic of eleven children, a blend of biological and fostered, a number that seemed a Herculean task for two adults. My arrival marked the twilight of summer, the cusp of autumn. I recall the ritual of school preparations and shopping trips with the foster mother and siblings, where K-Mart and Bi-Way were the sanctuaries of frugality. I often ponder whether frugality was a virtue they held dear or merely a facade to hoard the government stipends. The scent of those stark white, no-brand sneakers from Bi-Way still lingers in my memory—our feet shod in the spoils of bargain bins.

Our transport was a trusty brown Datsun pickup, its rear adorned with a canopy and sideways seats that folded outwards. We, the young adventurers, would huddle in the back, the unforgiving steel of the wheel well beneath us. One harrowing day, an accident sent the youngest of us, Blake, tumbling from the truck bed onto the unforgiving asphalt, escaping with mere scrapes—a testament to both luck and resilience. Over six years, several trucks came and went, as did fragments of my memories, some deliberately buried, others jumbled in time.

The return from our London escapade, laden with exquisite attire, made me yearn for a Value Village in those bygone days. I sat cross-legged on my bed, assembling the school supplies from our shopping spree. Holly's efforts to impress were palpable, as if each penny spent was a bid to make me feel cherished. The aroma of the new brown plastic pencil case was Intoxicating, a precursor of friendships yet formed. Adorned with my name in shiny gold and black letters, it cradled freshly sharpened crayons, a ruler, pencils, and an eraser, each item a promise of a fresh start.

On the inaugural day of school, I dawned. Alongside my foster siblings, I stood by the roadside, the anticipation palpable. Moments later, the bus trundled to a halt, its doors yawning open. Ascending the steps, I surveyed the domain of the eighth graders at the rear—custodians of the coveted back seats by the bus driver's decree. The driver, a kindly woman with a halo of curly grey hair and spectacles, greeted us—our destination: Stephen Central Public School, the proud abode of the Panthers. Amidst a sea of unfamiliar faces, I contemplated potential alliances and adversaries.

My gaze settled on a slim figure, his denim garb bearing the marks of countless adventures, untouched by soap or water. His wild, untamed locks might have been an ode to Rastafarianism, but his solitude drew me in. Ernie, as he was known, soon dubbed 'Dirty Ernie,' was the school's enigmatic recluse.

I approached him not out of necessity but out of empathy. In befriending Ernie, I unwittingly branded myself, accepting the invisible boundaries it drew around us. Yet, it was a choice I embraced willingly. Grade four ushered in new challenges, not least of which was Mrs. Gill, our diminutive teacher whose stern demeanour belied her fragile frame. Her voice, capable of piercing through corridors and around corners, soon revealed the steel beneath her delicate exterior.

In Mrs. Gill's domain, she reigned supreme—a stern warden overseeing her educational penitentiary. Her meter stick was her sceptre, wielded with a fearsome authority that cracked not just upon the desks but the spirits and backs of those who dared defy her. The school's budget for these wooden instruments of discipline must have been as strained as the silence she commanded.

Surviving the first day felt like a victory, a hopeful glimpse into a future that might shine brighter. As the bus rumbled homeward, I bid farewell to Ernie with a wave. His home, a mere stone's throw down a dusty path, stood as a red-brick testament to his father's vocation—the local dump. It was a museum of the discarded, where treasures salvaged from society's refuse adorned the yard like bizarre trophies. The daily grind at the foster home starkly contrasted the school's rigid structure. Assigned the task of purging the garage of its daily detritus, I could not help but feel like a cog in a relentless machine, my sustenance hanging in the balance of my compliance.

The farm tour revealed a menagerie of life and labour: six majestic horses, a cacophony of pigs, and the quiet watchfulness of chickens and rabbits. One harrowing incident etched itself into memory: Blake's foot ensnared by the stirrup, and her body dragged mercilessly until the horse relented. She emerged with a bruise that blossomed like a dark flower—a stark reminder of the farm's unforgiving nature. Everything was about Blake and sports.

The basement walls were a gallery of equine triumphs, ribbons cascading like a colourful waterfall, each a testament to the daughters' prowess. My interactions with the quarter horses were bittersweet; the laborious task of manure management shadowed the joy of riding. And then there was baseball—the endless cycle of games, the sport that dominated our lives, became a relentless cycle of dusty fields and the monotonous grey of uniforms. With his swagger and makeshift bat sceptre, Scott fancied himself a diamond deity. His gap-toothed grin was a beacon of misplaced pride that often stirred a rebellious fire within me.

Holly's games offered a respite, a chance to escape the echo of Scott's bravado and the stale scent of ambition worn by older men. Our games were a different story—cramped rides in the Datsun, the air thick with exhaust, as we traversed the countryside. My disdain for the game was no secret; I loathed it with every fibre. Despite my competence with bat and glove, my throws were a study in erratic trajectories, much to Scott's amusement.

He would drag me outside to the driveway, insisting we practice before every game. As I stood there, bracing myself, he would hurl the softball with all the force he could muster, trying to replicate the blistering speeds of Minor League pitchers. Though he couldn't quite reach those speeds, he seemed determined to make up for it by throwing even harder at me. Each pitch felt like a test of endurance as the ball rocketed into my glove, the impact sending a sharp sting through my hand. The leather would snap loudly against my palm, a painful reminder of his relentless drive and my resilience. The farm chores were a daily testament to toil. The barn was my morning call, where I gathered eggs and faced the intense reality of manure. The wheelbarrow became my companion, ferrying the remnants of farm life to their final resting place behind the barn. It was a laborious existence that left little room for academic pursuits. Yet, there I sat at the mercy of Holly's red pen, night after night, wondering why excellence eluded me despite my efforts.

Life in the foster home was becoming familiar, a routine that included new siblings and a school slowly feeling like mine. Yet, there were moments when my thoughts drifted to my biological family, wondering if I ever crossed their minds. Amidst this new life, an old problem resurfaced, and I started wetting the bed. "Wake up, time for school," said Sam Davis as my foster brother nudged me. I woke to the unpleasant dampness, the smell of urine clinging to my skin. I glanced at him, hoping my secret was safe. In a rush, I hid my soiled pyjamas under the mattress and made the bed, hoping to trap the smell beneath the sheets.

Breakfast was always the same. "Don't use too much," Holly would remind us as we thinly spread the jam and peanut butter over our toast. It was a small act but a daily reminder of the strict rules governing the house. I left for school, and I could still smell the urine under my clean clothes. "Everything all right?" Ernie's voice broke through my reverie during recess. "Yeah, just thinking," I replied, managing a half-smile.

The school day dragged on, and with each passing hour, my anxiety grew. Returning home, I was greeted by the sight of clean sheets and the lingering fear of another night's accident. The cycle was exhausting, and my secret was a heavy burden I carried alone. Holly entered, her voice soft but firm, "Next time, just tell me, and we'll take care of it together." I nodded silently, the weight of my secret growing heavier.

Each day after returning from school, the garage was my first task, meticulously cleaning every corner to meet Holly's exacting standards. "You've missed a spot," she would say, pointing out the imperfections in my work. The barn was next, where life and death intertwined in the rawest form. Scott stood solemnly by the mare, her stillborn colt, a sad reality of farm life. With a machete in hand, he severed the colt's head, instructing me to assist in removing the lifeless body.

The act was as routine to him as discarding yesterday's refuse.

This harsh introduction to farm life dulled my city-born sensibilities towards animals. The chickens were next; their heads secured between nails on a log, their fate sealed with a swift axe swing. Scott's command to release the bird led to a frenzied dance of death, the headless chicken painting the yard red. "It's the circle of life," he muttered, an attempt to normalize the brutality.

The rabbits were the hardest. I had cared for them, named them, and, in a twisted turn of fate, watched as Don and Scott ended their lives with cold efficiency. The rabbits I had nurtured became mere commodities, their pelts and meat stored away for future meals. It was a grim lesson in survival that taught me to appreciate the sustenance they provided despite the cruelty it entailed. Scott loved his wife's rabbit stew, and the taste for wild rabbit meat grew in me, too.

The chill of the pre-dawn air on the weekend was a harsh awakening as Scott's voice, gruff with urgency, roused me from sleep. "Today, you become a fisherman," he declared. I was leaving no room for protest. I imagined a serene scene, much like Shane's tales of Newfoundland's waters, but as we arrived in Grand Bend, reality hit me like the cold splash of the lake. The town was a relic of the past, where old, shed buildings huddled together as if sharing secrets of the sea.

The boat was a beast, its belly filled with the tools of the trade—massive green nets and bobbers that spoke of a battle with the deep. As we set sail, the land became a distant memory, and the lake, a living entity, greeted us with waves that crashed against the boat's side with primal force. My stomach rebelled against the motion, and I offered my meagre breakfast to the lake's depths.

When the boat's engines quieted, a mechanical symphony began above. I ascended to find the nets, heavy with the lake's bounty, being hauled aboard. Scott's voice cut through the noise, "Grab hold and pull!" he commanded. Together, we wrestled the catch onto the deck, a cascade of White Fish amidst the unwanted—catfish, eels, pike, and suckers. The suckers, worthless to our cause, were mine to cast back into the watery abyss. Meanwhile, I assembled wax boxes, a monotonous task made bearable only by the rhythmic gutting and cleaning of fish by Scott's skilled hands. This was my summer, a relentless cycle of box-making and beer bottle-collecting; each cent earned a small victory in life's labours.

Adventure seemed a scarce commodity in the sprawling quiet of the countryside, where the nearest town of Parkhill lay ten to fifteen kilometres away. Yet, down the highway in the quaint village of Greenway, a little stream trickled under the road, beckoning those with a penchant for discovery. Dwayne, a lad from the neighbouring farm beside ours, agreed to join me in this simple quest. With sticks, string, and hooks in hand, we fashioned our fishing rods, a testament to our resourcefulness. The creek, adorned with burs, became our gateway as we ducked under the road to claim our spot on the cement ledge.

Armed with only slices of bread stolen from the kitchen's bread box, I crafted bait from doughy spheres, each promising potential. The line, weighted by a modest sinker, plunged into the stream's embrace. Anticipation hung heavy in the air, a palpable force that seemed to still the very flow of the water. Then, the line sprang to life with a sudden tug, a silent battle waged beneath the surface. With a swift pull and an upward jerk, victory emerged from the depths—a small fish no more than a few inches long. They were minnows, but to me, they were a treasure, a symbol of success against nature's odds.

A long-absent smile found its way to my lips, born of a simple joy that had eluded me for too long. This was more than a merc hideaway; it was a sanctuary where I could bask in solitude, reel in dreams, and ponder the vast tapestry of life. I found a slice of peace where I could truly belong in this unassuming nook. The act of fishing, once a serene contemplation, had morphed into something primal, reflecting the stark lessons learned in the shadow of death. Each fish that met its end against the concrete walls or beneath the jar's twisting pressure was a testament to the indelible mark of the rabbits' fate. It was a silent struggle, played out in the quiet under the road, where life and death danced in my hands.

Yet, it was in Dwayne's company, within the hollow spaces of his barn, that a different narrative unfolded. Here, the pigs grunted their greetings, and the loft brimmed with bales of straw and hay, a golden sea waiting to be shaped by youthful imagination. Fortresses and mazes wound their way into secret corners, and I was the architect of my wonderland.

With its towering stacks of straw, the barn became a realm of endless possibility where time stood still. The mazes I crafted were more than just paths through the hay; they were corridors to other worlds, secret passages that led to adventures yet to be had. The pulley system was my vine, and as I swung from the loft, I was not just a boy in a barn—I was Tarzan, Master of the jungle, calling out for Jane and the adventures we would share.

In those moments, suspended between earth and sky, I found my Neverland. It was a place where the world's worries could not reach me, where the only limits were those of my imagination. Each swing was a flight of fancy, each landing a chance to start anew. In the barn, among the straw and the echoes of laughter, I discovered the joy of dreaming, the freedom of play, and the pure magic of being a child in a world all my own. This was my dresser chest into another world's Chronicles adventure.

I hollowed out a large cavity and had a window and door on the side leading through to other tunnels going to another section of the barn. Inside my room, I made a table and chairs and brought posters from my room to attach to the walls, so I built my private hideaway that was better than the garbage-holding areas at the old apartment I shared with Johnny.

4

GOING THE DISTANCE

I climbed the front yard tree or explored the nearby creek in an era devoid of computers and video games. School was a challenge, and by the end of the year, my foster parents and the school decided to hold me back a year and place me in special education. They believed I needed to focus more on my surroundings and perform at a lower grade level.

The Children's Aid Society did not consider the possibility of diagnosing me with A.D.D/A.D.H. D and prescribing medication like Ritalin to see if it improved my school performance. That would have been too simple and against their status quo. The easiest solution was to place me in a particular education class they called Special Ed with other slow learners so I would not disrupt the regular flow of the system. I interacted with a regular group of friends during the day, but most of my time was spent playing with Ernie.

One night, I woke to the familiar smell of a wet bed. I got up, stripped off my clothes, and pondered where to hide my pyjamas. I lifted the top mattress and shoved it as far into the center as possible. After making my bed and getting dressed, I headed upstairs for breakfast. Holly soon discovered my mattress hiding spot, forcing me to devise more creative ways to hide my clothes. I had yet to consider the sheets and blankets or my limited number of pyjamas. Sometimes, I wore my clothes to bed, waking up in urine-soaked underwear and pants.

It was either January or February when I was outside, playing in the snowbanks in the ditch, waiting for the bus. Suddenly, I fell through the drift and into the ice-cold water up to my waist. My boots filled with water, and I felt like I had fallen into a pond. I quickly ran back to the house, through the door, and into the kitchen where Holly stood. The bus horn echoed against the walls, and I was told to run to the bus as it was my fault for playing in the ditch. I sat down on the bus, my jeans dripping onto the floor, and my pants froze stiff from sitting. I could not bend my knees when I got off the bus and headed toward my class-room. My teacher sent me to the principal's office.

The secretary's gesture of providing gym shorts and

a T-shirt was a small comfort as I removed my soaked attire and placed it over the iron wall heater. Being barred from recess was a blessing in disguise, as the chill had seeped into my bones, leaving my skin a fiery red and my toes numb. The warmth of the indoors was a welcome reprieve. After the day's school routine, chores, and dinner, I faced the nightly ordeal of concealing my wet pyjamas and blankets. Ingeniously, I discovered a new hiding place within the wall's wood panelling, secured by small finishing nails. My secret was safe, tucked away beyond the reach of prying eyes.

Summer ended classes, and I began laborious work on a farm, earning a meagre penny for each milkweed pulled from the soybean fields. The fall season was marked by the arduous task of baling straw and clearing boulders from the fields, leaving my skin lacerated and raw. Yet, it was not without its rewards—I learned to drive a tractor. The culmination of my summer toil was the purchase of a mountain bike, a symbol of my perseverance and hard-earned independence.

With my new mountain bike, I could travel a few kilometres to visit my friend, Ernie. My explorations took me to numerous places. On Sundays, we attended services at Grace Bible Chapel in Parkhill, where I met a kind couple, the Ostranders. Neil, the husband, took a liking to me and taught me how to drive a manual car in the parking lot. I often cycled to their house, where Neil, a photography enthusiast, introduced me to the art of developing black and white pictures in a darkroom. That summer remains a cherished memory.

January 14, 1983, began a new school year with fresh faces. My foster sister Blake was assigned to Mrs. Bates, known among students as Scallywags, the sternest teacher in the school. Her reprimands were loud and public, and Blake endured most of her harsh discipline on multiple occasions. I was relieved not to be in her class.

I was growing wiser and managed to arrive at school dry. Sitting at my desk, my thoughts drifted to Holly at home, scouring my room for the missing sheets. I had covered my bed with a blanket, but the absence of sheets was conspicuous. I knew it must have been frustrating for her, unable to locate where I had hidden them. It would take a couple of weeks for my clothes to dry out in the wall before the smell would permeate the room. I was running out of hiding places for my soiled clothes. I started with them under my pillow, then between my mattresses, under my bed, in my closet, under other garments, and finally, behind the wall.

When lunchtime arrived, I decided to run away from school. I ventured along the bush line at the edge of the school property. Crossing into a cornfield, I began to distance myself from the school, following a creek and emerging onto a dirt road about two kilometres away. My escape was short-lived as a brown station wagon pulled up beside me. My principal, Mr. Binder, had come looking for me when I failed to return to class.

During the drive back to school, he inquired about my home life. I confessed my discontent and expressed my desire to return to my family in Toronto. He assured me our conversation would remain confidential and returned me to class. That day, my respect for him grew, and I realized he genuinely cared about my well-being. However, there was an incident that assessed this newfound respect. My Special Ed class taught us arts and crafts, which led to an unfortunate event.

One day after lunch recess, while hanging out with a few guys in the boys' washroom, a classmate named Frank showed me how to make a dart gun using a plastic pen, elastic band, and a pin taped to a toothpick. He instructed me to pull back on the elastic and toothpick and let go. I aimed it toward the bathroom door, expecting another student to enter since the teachers had their bathroom. To my horror, the door swung open just as I released the elastic band, and the principal walked in, the pin from my makeshift dart gun embedding itself in his forehead. His yell echoed through the school as he dragged me toward the office.

Seated alongside Frank and a few other boys, I watched Mr. Binder brandishing a six-inch piece of cowhide leather, a discipline tool for those unfortunate enough to find themselves in his office. In the eighties, teachers were permitted to use physical punishment. Frank was the first to face this harsh discipline. The office door closed behind him, and soon, the air was filled with his screams and sobs. When he emerged, his hand was as red as a boiled lobster.

Next, it was my turn. Mr. Binder invited me into his office, asking me to close the door and sit. He acknowledged the difficulties of adjusting to a new family and school and the need for time to make new friends. By the end of our conversation, I surmised that my status as a ward of the Crown and being in foster care protected me from physical punishment, as he would not want any negative complaints reaching the school board.

He had already informed Scott about the incident and asked me to wait in the office area for Scott to pick me up. After half a day of school, I was apprehensive about going home. When Scott arrived, he discussed with the principal before I was called back into the office. During my wait, Scott convinced Mr. Binder of the loving Christian family environment they provided for me. We left the school and drove home, where I was sent to my room for the rest of the night. I did not notice any disturbance in the wall, so I felt safe knowing Holly had not discovered my hiding place.

That night, I wasn't called for dinner and was told to stay in my room, only allowed to leave for the washroom. It felt like a cruel punishment, withholding food because of something I did wrong. As hunger gnawed at my stomach, I decided to sneak out to the food hamper beside the stairs. I tiptoed through the basement, carefully opening the door to avoid any squeaks.

Inside the cold room, shelves were stocked with food from the latest grocery run. I grabbed a box of Nabisco biscuits and a bottle of maple syrup and quietly retreated to my room. I mixed the biscuits and syrup using my fishing tackle box until they were soggy.

I hoped my daring bathroom escapade would earn me popularity, but it only became a joke at my expense. When I got home, Scott called me to the kitchen table, where my tackle box sat open. He ordered me to sit down and eat the mushy mixture for dinner. The fibres of the biscuits had broken down in the syrup, turning it into a glue-like substance that made me sick. This was supposed to teach me a lesson about stealing food when I was forced to starve.

The next day, a classmate was hosting a birthday

party at his house, complete with tobogganing and dinner. Despite not asking my parents for permission or having a gift for him, he insisted that I enjoy the festivities. With the end-of-school bell ringing at 3:30, I was apprehensive about returning home and whether Holly had discovered my hiding spot. To avoid going home, I decided to attend the party.

Boarding my friend's bus, I informed the driver that I was heading to my friend's house and had given the necessary letter to my teacher. As I settled into my seat and looked out the window, I saw my foster sisters boarding the bus ahead of us. I ducked in my seat as the bus pulled away from the school. The half-hour ride felt like an eternity as I contemplated the consequences of my actions and the potential outcomes of attending the party.

Upon reaching our stop, we disembarked in the small town of Crediton, where my friend's house was on the main street. We entered his house, met his parents, and played in his room while waiting for his other friends to arrive. After dinner, we prepared to go tobogganing at a local dam. The thrill of sliding down the hills temporarily distracted me from my worries about home. As darkness fell and the weather turned unpredictable, I told my friend my parents would pick me up. However, the thought of returning home was too daunting, and I chose to run away into the unknown darkness instead.

The cold seeped into my bones as I walked along the main road, causing me to shiver. I stared into the night sky, my legs growing numb. Not knowing the time, I noticed a tree fort in the backyard of a house just off the main street. With the lights on, I quietly made my way around the side of the house to the back. I climbed up the tree and into the fort. It was no five-star hotel, but it shielded me from the wind and offered a hiding place. I curled into a ball on the floor, resting my head on my bicep, and fell asleep. The freezing weather woke me up intermittently, my bones shivering.

A few hours later, I was jolted awake by a voice calling my name. I heard someone climbing the tree and backed up into a corner. A beam of light pierced the darkness, momentarily blinding me as I tried to focus on the figure at the fort's entrance. Recognizing the uniform, I realized it was the Provincial Police. The officer asked if I was okay and urged me to come down so he could take me home. We pulled into the driveway, where the officer met Holly at the front of the garage. She approached the vehicle, and the officer asked if I recognized her. I acknowledged her but was reluctant to live with them or enter the house. He insisted that I had to return to the house. As I walked towards the house, the cruiser pulled out of the driveway and disappeared.

Just as I was heading to my bedroom, Holly came downstairs and instructed me to return upstairs. Dressed only in my pyjamas, she led me outside into the cold and told me to shovel off the ice rink that Scott had made in front of the barn. It had been snowing long, and high snowbanks lined one side of the barn. I began shovelling the snow under a clear, star-filled sky. My breath formed clouds in the frigid air as I worked to clear the rink. After about an hour, my hands and feet had gone numb. Holly came out and told me to go to bed. Slipping into fresh sheets felt terrific; I pulled the blankets over my head and filled the space with warm breath. Soon, I was fast asleep.

On February 6, 1983, as a twelve-year-old, I sat on my bed after school, contemplating how to run away again. Scott and Holly had gone away for the night, leaving Don in charge. I was exhausted from the constant assaults by both the Burke and the other foster boys. I could not take it anymore. I decided I would keep running away until someone would listen to me and get me out of this harmful environment.

My roommate, Sam, came into the room and saw the resolve on my face. I told him I was planning to run away and not return. He said he was coming with me. I could understand his feelings; he was being abused like me. We planned to wait until everyone was asleep. I put on extra clothes, two wool socks, and a sweater. Sam also got dressed, and we both put on our coats. I slowly opened the bedroom door, trying not to make it squeak. I could hear Don upstairs watching TV. The lights in the other bedroom were out, and I could not hear the girls talking. We slowly walked across the basement to the stairs on the far side of the house by the garage.

I climbed the stairs and slipped on my winter boots. Sam and I quietly opened the garage door and sneaked out by the deck. We bent past the sliding windows and looked through; I did not see Don on the couch or chair. I climbed over the fence, down the ditch, and into the field towards Dwayne's barn next door. There was no looking back now.

The twisted feeling in my stomach increased with each step and became excitement. Finally, I could get away from this house of torture and have someone listen to me without turning their head in the opposite direction. We crossed many fields and farmhouses before I slowed myself down to a slower pace. I bent down, grabbed a handful of snow, and ate it to quench my thirst. It was a beautiful night; the sky was clear, and the stars shone brightly. My breath was crisp, and I could not feel the cold because of the adrenaline pumping through my veins. I did not have a watch, but we walked for hours. We went past the one-leading corner and headed towards Parkhill. I wanted to avoid walking along the road in case the police were out looking for us.

On our journey, we came across a house with two snowmobiles in the front yard. I suggested to Sam that we check for any keys in the ignition, thinking it could speed up our escape. We stealthily approached the snowmobiles and climbed onto the seats. As I tried to start one of them, the house's front door opened, and a man started yelling at us. Seeing this, Sam and I jumped off and started running through the fields. Two men started the snowmobiles and began chasing us. We managed to evade them by jumping over a couple of fences, after which they could not follow us. I did not dare look back or listen for any sounds; I just kept running faster and faster.

Suddenly, I flew backward through the air and landed on my back. I initially thought I had been caught by a rope and pulled back by the snowmobile. Sam stood there, laughing at my predicament. As I slowly got up, I felt a stinging sensation on my face. I put my hands over my face and pulled them away to find them covered in blood. Sam told me that blood was running down my face. Then, I realized I had run face-first into a barbed wire fence.

The twisted feeling in my stomach returned as I

realized my journey was over and I would need to seek help. We walked along the road to the nearest house. I rang the doorbell, and a lady quickly ushered us inside. I lay on a couch with a towel over my face while Sam asked the lady to call home. Don answered the phone. Since the Burke's had not returned home yet, Don came to pick us up and drove us to the doctor's office in Parkhill.

At the doctor's office, I lay down on the table. The doctor told me I would need about six stitches. He said I was lucky not to have lost my eye because one of the barbs had gone in beside my eyeball. He administered a local anesthetic to different areas of my face before stitching up the wounds near my eye, forehead, nose, lip, and chin. He then placed a bandage over my eye to keep out dirt and prevent infection.

We returned home, and I quickly fell asleep in the comfort of my bed. However, I knew to stay comfortable. The door burst open, and the light came on as Scott pulled the sheets off my bed. He was yelling at me, pulling me out of bed. Sam just looked over at me and stayed quiet. Scott told me that if I liked running away so much, he would kick me out of the house and let me leave. I did not have my coat; it was about three o'clock in the morning, and I was stunned by the abrupt awakening. He opened the door and threw me out of the house in my pyjamas.

I stood outside, freezing and shivering, as I wrapped my arms around myself to stay warm. I must have been outside for about half an hour when Scott came outside and told me to leave if I wanted. I told him I did not want to go and wanted to return to bed. He sent me back to bed. I woke up and headed upstairs for break-fast. The girls just looked at me, and the older boys were laughing at me under their breath. Scott was at the table. I had removed the wrap from my eye so I could see. My eye had swollen and turned black. Scott just looked at me and said he had thought it was much worse. It showed me how he felt about my safety while throwing me around the room and outside into the snow.

March 1983: I grew stronger in my confidence and ability to run away. I would not let this house destroy the person I was meant to be. I remember on a few occasions standing in front of the mirror in the down-stairs bathroom, staring at all the bottles of prescription medicines in the cabinet. I opened some of the bottles, pouring about four or five diverse kinds of pills and capsules into the palm of my hand. I wanted everyone to notice only a few missing from one bottle. I did not know what the prescriptions were for or what they did. They belonged to the older boys in the house. I opened my mouth and popped them in a few at a time like jelly-beans, swallowing each one with a mouthful of water. I lay on my bed, staring at the ceiling, waiting to see what would happen. I soon fell asleep, only to wake up the following day. The pills did nothing; it was the hand of God's divine protection over my life.

Sam and I shared a room, and across from us were two other bedrooms. One room housed the Burke daughters and two foster girls, while two older boys occupied the other, around seventeen or eighteen years old. These older boys would enter our room at night, leading to uncomfortable situations. They threatened us with physical harm or got us into trouble if we did not comply with the sexual acts.

This went on for some time until one day, one of the older boys, John, had a confrontation with Scott and was kicked out of the house. Somehow, Scott discovered what was happening and questioned John and Frank. Then, it was Sam's and my turn to answer questions. We both told Scott that the boys had coerced us and threatened us. Scott told me it was my fault and I had instigated the situation. I could not understand how a thirteen-year-old boy could force two eighteen-year-old boys to do anything against their will. He told me that the boys said I started it and that I was causing the trouble. Sometime later, a couple of workers from Children's Aid came to the house to question all those involved.

I remember being called to the front living room

and sitting in the recliner chair as Scott, Holly, and the other workers sat facing me. I told the workers about the issues at home, including Scott's harsh treatment, the lack of food, and the forced labour around the farm. They told me they would investigate the allegations and left after talking with Scott. I did not hear anything back from them other than Scott, and Holly was a little more careful about how they dealt with me.

Years later, I discovered in a report by the Catholic Children's Aid Society that it was their Quid pro quo policy for me to remain in the care of the Burkes and the Narin group homes until I turned sixteen. I was a source of income for their group homes from the government, so why waste a good thing? Despite being labelled as a troublemaker, I was allowed to share a room with other boys and live across from their daughters. I suspect they were trying to conceal their negligence. I continued to run away, experimenting with different routes and timings.

The Catholic Children's Aid suggested I had no apparent reason for these escapes, as if I enjoyed the hardship of surviving in cornfields and ditches. They claimed I negatively influenced Sam by giving him ideas about running away. It never occurred to them that the inappropriate actions of the older foster boys might have influenced our behaviour. Society decided it was best to separate us, so they removed Sam from the house.

I could not understand their reasoning; if I were the problem child negatively influencing Sam, why would they remove him from the house instead of me? With their own three children and all the other foster children, why would they risk my negative influences rubbing off on the rest of them? I was saddened the day Sam left. We had a lot in common and understood each other. He always had a big smile on his face, even though I knew he was dealing with much pain deep down inside. Later, after my time in foster care, I learned the heartbreaking news that Sam had taken his own life.

5

HOMEBOUND RUNAWAYS

Records show my repeated attempts to flee in May 1983. It baffled me how Society could ignore the turmoil within the foster home. The truth was conveniently ignored, never to surface. The records noted my restlessness by October, even after four long years. The message was clear—I yearned for escape.

Home visits began, and there was a bittersweet reunion with my mother and Shane. Scott, my escort to Toronto, would sometimes accompany me to the Catholic Children's Aid for meetings. Weekends with my family were a temporary relief from the foster home. Despite the past's shadows, I focused on the present, reuniting with my mother, brother, and sister. I harboured a faint hope that my mother would want me back, but her marriage to her volatile Shane cast a long shadow over that possibility.

One memorable visit took us to Canada's Wonderland. As the day waned, Shane's directive was clear—return to the front gates by eight. With my sister Laura in my mother's care, my younger brother Steward and I ventured through the park, indulging in the thrill of rollercoasters and water rides. Time slipped away, and soon, we found ourselves amidst the crowd, all converging towards the exit. Shane's temper was notorious, yet I wondered how it would manifest publicly. With his favoured son by my side, I hoped for leniency.

We returned to the park entrance, swallowed by a sea of people. I thought finding anyone in this crowd was impossible, but Laura found us within minutes. "You guys are in so much trouble. Dad is looking for you," she warned. I spotted him through the crowd, the same man I had grown to fear, his temper flaring.

Pulling me into the crowd's center, Steward trailed behind, "Get down on your knees, both of you and repeat after me," he commanded, "I promise that I will never be late again." After repeating his words ten times, I realized the echo was not from the buildings around us but from the crowd. The park chanted, "I promise I will never be late again." I hung my head in shame as Laura and my mother watched Shane humiliate us before a thousand spectators. My mother finally shouted at her husband that enough was enough. She took Laura and retreated to the car. He allowed us to rise and follow as the crowd began to disperse.

On another occasion, while playing outside the house, I vented my anger at our neighbours, a single man and his mother, who never intervened despite witnessing Shane's abuse. I defecated on a piece of paper and threw it onto their lawn. Steward, a younger version of his father, ran inside to report my actions. I remember getting into trouble a few times during my visits home until Shane declared he did not want me to return. I was sent back to the foster home, not fully comprehending the ticking time bomb of emotions within me.

Back at the foster home, I was introduced to a new roommate, Doug, an older boy with long, greasy hair and a face full of pimples. Kathy and Rachel, a few new girls, also joined us. It felt like a revolving door—children in, children out. To me, it was all about profit. Why was I still in this home after everything that had happened? One afternoon, I found myself in the barn with Kathy and Rachel, playing Truth or Dare to affirm my sexuality after enduring abuse from Shane and the other foster boys. I asked to see their breasts, and Kathy had enormous breasts that she pulled out from under her shirt to allow me to touch them. I also exposed myself to them and let them touch me, too.

In the foster home, boundaries blurred, and confusion reigned. One evening, Scott confronted me about an incident with the girls after I persuaded them to remove their clothes. He questioned me, his anger palpable, about why I had asked to touch and kiss the girls. His reaction puzzled me; they were not his daughters. We were exploring our sexuality. I was finishing my shower and standing there in the bathroom, water dripping off my naked body during his interrogation. I did not have any say in that uncomfortable moment as he pulled me out of the shower by my male genitalia.

He then made a strange proposition. If I ever wanted to kiss another girl, I should come to him and kiss him instead. His words left me bewildered. I was not attracted to men, so why would I want to kiss him? His actions only added to my confusion and frustration. We went upstairs to the living room, and he disappeared down the hallway to his bedroom. When he returned, he was holding a miniature wooden rowing paddle. He asked if I wanted him to beat me with it, claiming I needed to be disciplined to learn my lesson. Defiantly, I told him to go ahead, confident that as a ward of the CCAS, he wasn't allowed to hit me.

To my shock, he bent me over his knees and began stroking my buttocks with all his might, delivering half a dozen blows. The pain was excruciating, and I couldn't hold back my tears. As I cried, I couldn't help but think of my stepfather and wonder how this was any better than being back home. The sting of each strike was a harsh reminder of the cruelty I was trying to escape.

Next door, during a neighbour's house visit, I spent time with a girl named Beth. We were spending time together in her shed when we shared a kiss and a moment of mutual exploration, a confirmation of my sexuality. I knew then that I was not attracted to men. My behaviour was a direct result of the abuse I had suffered at the hands of my stepfather and the continued mistreatment in the foster home. Without any psychological support, my actions were my only outlet.

Fresh faces appeared regularly at the foster home, each with stories of pain and struggle. Amidst this chaos, I found myself acting out in inappropriate ways. I was seeking attention, trying to understand my feelings in a world where I ignored them. Often, I would change out of my clothes after school, knowing that the girls were sitting on my windowsill watching me as I exposed myself to them. Joining them outside after getting dressed, they pretended nothing had happened.

Curiosity and confusion often led me to push boundaries during my teenage years. I found myself drawn to the girls in the foster home, trying to understand my feelings and sexuality. My actions, though inappropriate, were a misguided attempt at normal adolescent exploration complicated by the abuse I had suffered. I often found myself in the closet overlooking the girls' bedroom while they examined themselves in the mirror, doing their explorations. The group home, however, was quick to attribute my behaviour to presumed sexual abuse before my time in foster care. They seemed unwilling to acknowledge the ongoing abuse I was experiencing in the foster home and the need for appropriate support and intervention.

From 1983 to 1985, I was sent to a summer camp near Sarnia, Ontario, Forest Cliff Bible Camp. I attended the camp for two summers, each lasting a week or two. The camp was a welcome escape from the worries and drama of the foster home. I remember the excitement of finding our cabins, meeting my cabin mates, and the small pleasures like buying snacks and candy from the canteen shop. Those moments of normalcy, of just being a kid at summer camp, were precious to me.

I experienced a mix of freedom, adventure, and unexpected challenges. The days were filled with activities like archery, horseback riding, and canoeing. Evenings were spent in communal dining, singing, and church meetings. One incident at the camp left a deep impression on me. I discovered my flashlight, which I had thought lost, in another boy's bag. Confronting him led to a physical altercation with a punch to his nose and a meeting with the camp staff. This incident was a stark reminder of the survival instincts I had developed in the foster home.

However, the camp was not just about survival. It was also about discovery and understanding. I found myself exploring my feelings and sexuality in a setting far removed from the foster home. These experiences, though confusing at times, were part of my journey toward self-discovery. Our cabin counsellor, known only by his scout name, Superman, was a figure of authority at the camp. One afternoon, he led a group of us boys on a hike through the woods. During this outing, he coerced us into a situation that was deeply inappropriate and abusive by making us perform oral acts. Overwhelmed by fear and confusion, I kept silent about the incident, burying it deep within me like a bad dream. The memory of that day remains a stark reminder of the abuse I endured during those formative years.

Upon returning from camp, I shared my experiences with the Burkes; however, I never received any feedback or apology from the camp regarding the incidents. It felt as if I was a magnet for predators, constantly assessed by circumstances beyond my control. These experiences at the foster home and the camp blurred my understanding of love and morality. They were part of my journey, a wilderness of experiences that shaped me into who I am today.

The Burke's took us on trips across Florida and Western Canada to compensate for their shortcomings. These journeys were filled with awe-inspiring sights - the stark beauty of the Badlands, the fascinating exhibits of Dinosaur museums, and the joy of camping in Florida and picking oranges. We traversed the United States, visiting iconic landmarks like Yellowstone National Park, Mount Rushmore, and Yogi Bear Park. In Canada, we explored the breathtaking landscapes of Jasper, Banff, Lake Louise, and Vancouver. These experiences ignited a deep-seated desire to travel and explore the world.

However, these adventures did little to erase the scars of my past. From the age of ten to sixteen, I endured physical, emotional, and sexual abuse. Despite their efforts, the Burke's could not erase the painful memories etched in my mind. I struggled with bedwetting from the moment I arrived until the day I left the foster home. After that day, the bedwetting ceased.

I vividly remember graduating from Stephen Central in grade 8. With my hair grown long and donning a white suit with a pastel blue shirt, I felt like Sonny Crockett from Miami Vice. I participated in the school choir, was a male cheerleader, and even learned to use the first computer, the Pet Commodore 64. I excelled in sports and won many awards. Those days at Stephen Central will always hold a special place in my memories. My final year in foster care was spent attending South Huron District High School in Exeter, Ontario.

At sixteen, in October 1986, I was informed that I could leave the foster home and return to Toronto. I packed all my belongings and waited by the door for my caseworker to pick me up. The departure felt like a release from a decade-long prison sentence. The only people I would miss were Ernie and some classmates, who would soon fade into distant memories.

Just as I had done six years ago upon arrival, I stood in the driveway, analyzing the backdrop. This time, however, it was with a sigh of relief. The time I seemed to crawl as I waited for my caseworker. Marry no longer worked for the Society, and my new worker, Len, was a man with a mustache like Tom Selleck. When the moment finally arrived, I packed all my belongings into the car. I had sold my bike to another foster boy, knowing I would not need it in the city. After bidding farewell to the other foster children, we pulled out of the driveway and headed down the highway.

Years of running and trying to escape had finally led to this moment; I was free. I took one last look at the house, smiled, and then turned my gaze back to the road, not giving a second thought to the foster home I was leaving behind. As we drove through the countryside, I admired the cows and horses in the fields, realizing that it would be the beauty of the outdoors if I missed anything. As we neared the city, the fields and grass gave way to concrete. The sight of hydro towers and wires signalled our approach to the town. A meeting had been arranged at the Catholic Children's Aid Society downtown to meet with a single family interested in taking in an older child.

The meeting with the young couple, Kevin and Tina, went well. They would let me stay with them in their new home in Richmond Hill, just north of the city. After the meeting, my caseworker clarified that making things work was now up to me. I was of age to be released from care, but I could stay with this family who was willing to help me out.

I got to know Kevin and Tina better after driving to their house. They shared stories of their travels through Africa and India and their experiences sponsoring children from various parts of the world. Their home was in a new subdivision, still fresh with the paint smell. My room was upstairs, filled with the fresh scent of newness and the soft, thick carpet underfoot. Kevin showed me around the house, including his motorcycle in the garage, promising to take me for a ride. Proud of her home decor, Tina had a delicate taste that was evident throughout the house.

Unpacking my belongings into the closet and dresser, I felt a sense of freedom. I was finally free from the control of the foster care system: no more shovelling horse manure or skinning rabbits. I was finally home. I took a walk to familiarize myself with my new surroundings. I noticed an old black house on the main road, its windows boarded up, stray cats everywhere, and what appeared to be large fish parts scattered all over the lawn. Seeing a lady walking around the property, her face covered with a black cape scared me away from that house for good.

To my surprise, a large mall with all the leading clothing stores and food courts was just two blocks away. The following day, I started at my new high school, Don Head Secondary School. It was much larger than the school I attended in foster care and had a more diverse student body. I felt a bit out of place and found myself missing my old school. I was told this was a technical school for those with learning disabilities or those wanting to enter a trade. My classes included auto shops, woodworking, and cooking. Even my standard courses like math and geography seemed too easy, and I was getting marks in the nineties.

I made a few friends, and we started skipping school to hang out at the mall. We would go into the Zellers home electronics section and pocket cassettes of famous heavy metal bands like Iron Maiden, AC/DC, and Def Leppard. At school, I found a way to make some spending money. I filled an empty locker with cassettes and other items we had taken from stores, selling them to other students cheaply. While restocking our merchandise one day, I noticed we were being followed. I managed to evade the man following us, but two of my friends were caught by loss prevention security. That marked the end of our locker store business, and I had to avoid that part of the mall.

I became friends with a West Indian girl. She was different from any girl I had known before, with her dark eyes, long black hair, and brown skin. Our friendship ended abruptly after an attempted kiss. She had this distinct smell, and I felt no sadness telling her I no longer liked her.

Then, there was a skinny, lonely-looking girl in my cooking class. I did not like her, but I knew she had a thing for me. A friend suggested we take her to a secluded area near the school one afternoon. What happened next was a horrific act of violation against the girl. The next day, I was called to the office for a meeting with the principal and my foster parents. I saw the girl and her mother leave the office. As she walked by me, I saw sadness in her eyes and felt a pang of guilt and compassion. I gave my account of what had happened and then returned to class.

I am not sure what the outcome of that meeting was, but I never saw that girl again. Her parents had her removed from the school. The school felt that I was learning typically and suggested to my foster parents that I attend a regular high school during the next semester.

6

A JOURNEY TO SELF-DISCOVERY

The following school, Thornhill Secondary School, was a half-hour bus ride away. It starkly contrasted my previous school, with twice the number of students and more challenging subjects. Frustrated and feeling out of place, I began skipping classes. Those in charge of my education had yet to consider my past reports, indicating that I was more of a firsthand technical learner than a book learner. I found myself in detention frequently for acting out, skipping classes, and getting into fights.

One day, my foster parents were called to the office because I was caught with a kitchen knife in my locker that I had shown to another student. I remember Tina's surprise when she saw the knife on the principal's desk, which she had been looking for a couple of days before, and asked if I saw it, and my answer was no. I was suspended for a few days for that incident and had to deal with the repercussions at home. To keep me active and out of trouble, my foster parents signed me up for a membership at their local YMCA.

An avid racquetball player, Kevin bought me my racquet, balls, and protective eyewear. I quickly picked up the game and started beating some local men. My accuracy and speed surprised me, having never been into any racquet sport. I enjoyed going to the gym and working out.

However, a disturbing incident occurred a few weeks into my gym visits. After a racquetball game, I noticed an older man watching me while I was in the locker room shower. Feeling shy, I turned towards the wall to finish drying myself. Suddenly, the man grabbed my towel and insisted on helping me dry off. I froze, reminded of past abuses, and did not know what to do. The man continued to touch me inappropriately. After he left the changing room, I finished getting dressed and met up with my foster parents outside.

I did not fully process what happened then because I had become accustomed to such abuses. Once at home, after the shock had worn off, I told my foster parents about the incident. However, given all the trouble I had been in, they thought I was making up stories. While at the YMCA the following week, I noticed the same man in the locker room watching me. Feeling uncomfortable, I alerted my foster dad, who was there. He confronted the man, and the situation escalated to the point where the police were called. The man was charged, which made me more cautious about my surroundings.

I applied for a summer job at Canada's Wonderland amusement park in the spring. Although I applied late and ended up working in the parking lot, I enjoyed the job's benefits, like free access to the rides, so I spent more time on the rides than at work. One day, Kevin took me to his office in North York, where he worked for the Ministry of Housing. He introduced me to one of his co-workers, a woman named Ingrid, who was in her thirties or forties and was of German descent. I found myself attracted to her. On one occasion, while we were in the office, Ingrid asked Kevin if I could come to her house and help babysit her two boys. Kevin drove me to the house and dropped me off for the day.

I spent the day with Ingrid and her two boys, walking to a nearby park and having lunch together. Ingrid showed me her hobby of making homemade jewelry. As I was sitting beside her, I had an impulse to put my hand on her leg. She looked over at me and told me that it was wrong. I did not understand why it was terrible, but I respected her wishes. Some would say that she took advantage of me and that this was a form of inappropriate behaviour.

What does a sixteen-year-old who has endured sexual abuse comprehend about the inappropriateness of physical contact? She did not resist when I touched her. I do not recall my reaction; I only remember her leaning in and kissing me. Some might argue that she exploited me, labelling it as sexual abuse. She lay down on the bed under the sheets and removed her clothes. She told me what to do to her as I climbed under the sheets.

The way she eyed me when Kevin escorted me to the office, her request for Kevin to bring me to her house seemed orchestrated. I was in control, doing things that a boy my age should not know. That afternoon, I lost my innocence, becoming infatuated with this woman, yearning to stay with her instead of returning home. She was anxious about me revealing this to my foster father, fearful of the repercussions at work and potential police involvement. When my ride arrived, I returned home that night, a smile playing on my lips, already scheming ways to visit her more frequently.

At that time, my job at Canada's Wonderland was only on weekends as it was still spring, and the park fully opened during the week in summer. I began to despise my career, having to arrive at the park before sunrise and enduring the biting cold and constant spring rain. My emotions started to cloud my judgment around this time, causing issues with my schooling, work, and foster parents. I yearned for autonomy, indifferent to others' opinions.

I was weary of living by others' rules when I was constantly getting hurt. It was time for me to reclaim my life, to live it my way. I persuaded Ingrid to let me move in with her the day I arrived. She seemed fond enough of me to disregard what others would say about her relationship with a sixteen-year-old. I remember packing all my belongings after informing Kevin and Tina of my decision to leave their care.

My social worker visited, and we discussed what they believed was best for me. Even Scott, my former foster father, called to warn me that moving in with this woman was a grave mistake. The audacity of him lecturing me after all the abuse and mental torment he subjected me to! I was done with the Catholic Children's Aid Society, confident that I could manage my life better independently than under their supervision. Ingrid and I became inseparable after I moved in with her. Her city residence simplified my commute to work. I am uncertain about the fate of my schooling, but I left because it was too distant and in a different district. I recall exploring various schools, though the duration of my stay with Ingrid is hazy, around eight months.

Public outings with Ingrid began to irk me, especially her insistence on handholding. I was walking beside a woman who could pass as my mother while girls my age watched, which was embarrassing. As I discovered the joy of companionship with girls my age, I realized my time with Ingrid was ending. I remember our drives, her eyes lingering on engagement rings displayed in store windows, and I could not help but question her sanity if she thought our relationship could lead to that. When I announced my departure, she was upset, accusing me of selfishness.

At sixteen, I hoped I was thinking about myself, not getting entangled with a woman twice my age, burdened with her children, and bidding farewell to my social life. I visited my Aunt Samantha, who lived near the YMCA, where I worked out. I am still determining what guided me to her house, but it was an old Canadian Tire store that jogged my memory of her street. I discussed moving in with her and her family, and she agreed. Sara and her husband Walter resided in the basement, while his family and sister occupied the upper floors.

The basement's chestnut brown panelling reminded me of my previous foster home. Walter worked as a carpet fitter with his father. I slept on the couch before the TV, often joining Samantha for TV sessions, where she would guzzle soda pop and chain-smoke cigarettes —seldom seen without a soda or cigarette in hand. She would send me to the store by the Canadian Tire to fetch her Coke or Pepsi while she indulged in her soap operas. I enrolled in George Vanier Secondary School near Fairview Mall, which quickly became my hangout spot. However, my stay was short-lived due to a disagreement with Sara, leading to my eviction. I suspect my sister or mother advised her against letting me stay.

I ventured to Toronto's east end, revisiting my old neighbourhood and friends. My sister had moved across the street from our old building on Lawrence Ave and Golf Club Road, and my youngest sister was dating a boy from the same floor. We would gather in the stairwell for joint sessions, and my other sisters enjoyed burning hash oil off the stove element with a knife.

Everyone had their unique coping mechanisms for past traumas. I befriended Mike, a lifeguard at the building's basement pool. He was a cool guy and a few years my senior. He owned a police uniform and a two-way scanner, claiming to be a former officer, though I suspect it was a costume store find. I once wore it to my job at Wonderland, attracting curious stares on the subway.

Given my age, it was imputable that I was a police officer. One evening, a security guard at work informed me of an impersonator. I assured him I worked in the division cleaning and showed him my park ID, narrowly avoiding trouble. Mike and I would spend time together whenever he was not on duty. Once, he proposed a plan to borrow a car from a warehouse he used to work at. We took a bus to a commercial area near Sheppard Avenue near a military base. He assured me that if we took a car on Saturday, no one would notice until Monday.

The warehouse we infiltrated belonged to a newspaper company owned by the Toronto Star. We snuck in through the loading docks, with Mike kicking out a thin wooden panel on the bay door. My heart pounded as we crept inside, the silence amplifying every noise and fueling my paranoia. We found a board with car keys in one of the sales offices. I grabbed a few sets, and so did Mike. We retraced our steps, exiting the same way we entered, and approached the fleet of company cars parked out front. Mike found a match for one of the keys, and we drove away in a car emblazoned with the company logo.

Mike wanted to visit friends near Kingston, a few hours away, and I accompanied him. Upon our return to Toronto, he offered me the car to use and discard when done. Despite my lack of road experience, I accepted, dropped him off, and took him to the highway. My driving was surprisingly good, even at 140 km/hour in the fast lane, my only prior experience being with a tractor.

About an hour and a half into the drive, I lost control of the car. It spun across three lanes and slid into a ditch, stopping on its side. Fortuitously, it was late and dark, sparing me from being spotted as I clambered out of the vehicle and hitchhiked back to Toronto, trying to erase the incident from my memory. When Mike inquired about the car the next day, I lied, telling him I had left it in a parking garage. Despite the narrow escape, I broke into the warehouse again, taking another car for a day. I do not recall where I went or how long I had it, but I remember leaving it intact in an outdoor parking lot at a mall in the east end. I spent time with my younger sister's boyfriend, strolling down a creek near Norton Park, fantasizing about producing a war movie in the area.

My friend and I shared a commonality - a strained relationship with our mothers that made home uncomfortable. While playing behind the building one summer day, I spotted Shane pulling into the parking lot. My youngest sister, Laura, was in the backseat. Shane exited the car and entered the apartment, leaving Laura behind. I approached her, but she remained in the car, unable to converse with me.

Shortly after, a police vehicle arrived, parking behind Shane's car. Shane emerged from the building with my older sister, Janet, and they approached the police vehicle. Two officers stepped out and conversed with Shane and Laura. Meanwhile, Janet retreated into the building. The situation was tense, and I was left wondering about the unfolding events.

7

BETRAYED BY BLOOD

Sitting in the car, Laura avoided my gaze when I inquired about the police and her presence at the building. I speculated that her boyfriend might be involved in some trouble. Shortly after, the police officers approached me, leading me to their vehicle. They handcuffed me and informed me of my arrest. Confused and nervous, I repeatedly asked them why I was arrested.

The officer in the driver's seat turned around and asked about Laura in the backseat of Shane's car. When I identified her as Laura Bradly, my younger sister, he revealed the shocking accusation against me - sexual assault on my sister. He informed me that I assaulted her on one of my weekend visits during my stay in foster care.

Shane and Laura drove away, leaving me with the police. Laura avoided my gaze as they passed by. The police cruiser took me to the station, pulled up to a large steel door, and drove inside, where they removed me from the vehicle. Standing in front of a large sign on the wall, the officer read aloud that we were being recorded and explained the steps to take after entering the building.

I was processed and placed in a holding cell. The cold, stark cell was vastly different from any comfort, with a stainless steel bed and matching toilet as the only furnishings. Hours later, I was taken to a room where my personal belongings were bagged, and my photos and fingerprints were taken. I was then returned to my cell to await transfer to the Toronto West Detention Center, a maximum-security facility in Rexdale, the northwest corner of Toronto.

At the detention center, I was stripped of my street clothes and shoes, which were bagged. I was subjected to a public shower and inspection, a profoundly humiliating experience as I was forced to bend over and spread my buttocks while a stranger looked through my hair and mouth. I was then given a brown uniform, running shoes without laces, a half toothbrush, toothpaste, and a comb. I was led to a small cell, which I shared with another inmate.

This chapter recounts a significant turning point in

my life, marked by a shocking accusation and the harsh reality of incarceration. It serves as a stark reminder of the complexities of life and the unexpected twists it can take. The jail felt like a scene from a seventy B movie. The range was rectangular, with cells facing each other and two rows of benches in the center. With the cell doors open, I placed my sheets on the bottom bunk and joined the other inmates at a table where a card game was underway. In the corner of the room, a TV encased in a steel box played a local channel. I scanned the room, assessing potential allies among the thirty inmates, most of whom were under eighteen but appeared older and more robust.

In jail, admitting to being in for sexual assault was akin to painting a target on your back. The two worst labels you could have been 'sex offender' and 'rat.' Upon my arrival, the guards asked if I smoked. Despite my negative response, they advised me to accept the tobacco as it could be used for trading. I took two bails of rolling tobacco, known in jail as 'Daily Stale,' and rolling papers. I quickly mastered the art of rolling cigarettes, which served as valuable trading commodities.

We were allotted an hour of courtyard time daily, whether we wanted it or not. We would line up a single file and march to the outdoor range area. The central section was filled with free weights for the bodybuilders. There were also basketball courts and a general location for those who preferred to spend their time in quiet reflection. That day, I found myself lost in thought, questioning why life had dealt me such a harsh hand and why Laura and Shane accused me of such a heinous act. Despite the trials and tribulations, I never blamed divine providence for my misfortunes.

Dinner was a controlled affair. We lined up for our trays and then sat at the tables to eat the day's cafeteria-style meal. As I ate, a tall individual approached me, took my dessert from my tray, and walked away. I did not retaliate, believing I would be out of jail after the next day's court appearance. After one last snack, we were locked in our cells for the night. The lights went out an hour later, and I tried to sleep. At five in the morning, I was awakened for the trip to the courthouse. I changed back into my street clothes, and they took their clothes back in case I made bail.

I was then placed in a holding cell with about twelve others for an hour, waiting for the court van to transfer us to the courthouse for our bail hearings. Among them, standing beside me, was a tall individual who went by the Slim. I was one of only two white individuals in the cell; the rest were black. I was skinny and nervous, standing beside these full-grown adults. I kept to myself but was cornered by the steel toilet. When one of them asked if I had any money, I told them I did not, leading to a search of my pockets. Slim then expressed interest in my new stone-washed jean jacket. I had just bought it because a modern design had come out, and I was unwilling to give it to this bully.

Despite my reluctance, I let him try it to avoid conflict, and he assured me he would return it. He put it on and asked his friends for their opinion, and they praised it. He then informed me that he was keeping it. I felt helpless, outnumbered, and outmatched. They were twice my size, not their first time in the judicial system. Eventually, the court wagon arrived to transport us to court. We were told to line up with our backs to the wall. The same guard that put me in the holding cell in the morning asked Slim why he was wearing my jacket. Slim claimed I had given it to him because I did not want it anymore. When the guard asked me, I explained that Slim had only wanted to try it on. The guard instructed Slim to return the jacket. As he did, he threatened me, leaving me feeling sick.

We were then handcuffed in a single line, with me between Slim and another large Black individual. We were then led to the court wagon, where we sat on metal benches facing each other. The only other white individual sat directly across from me, and I sat there quietly, contemplating my predicament. The other inmate's gaze was intense, his life marred by hardship. Suddenly, he began calling me a 'rat' and, without warning, kicked me squarely in the face. My head hit the stainless steel and riveted wall behind me. Although I felt no immediate pain, instinct took over. I shielded my face with my arms, pulling my head towards my knees. I felt the impact of kicks on my head and back from the other inmates.

The guards in the van slid the little window open and merely laughed, not attempting to intervene while watching through the opening in the panel. At no time did they try to stop the vehicle, yell at the inmates, or discipline them for assaulting me. Upon arrival at the courthouse, I stepped out of the van, my face bloodied and swollen. When questioned by a guard, I kept quiet, attributing my injuries to a fall caused when the driver hit the brakes. I quickly learned the implications of being labelled a 'rat,' especially among my range mates. The courthouse guards separated me from the rest of the inmates, placing me in a holding cell for protective custody, reserved for sexual offenders and 'rats who were not able to protect themselves in the general population because of the risk of getting assaulted or murdered.

We were given a cold ham and cheese sandwich and a cup of coffee that tasted like dirty water. After about three hours, I was called out, handcuffed, and taken upstairs to the courtroom. I was placed in an accused box with four other males. As the judge entered and began going through the cases, each accused stood up in the box when their name was called. When my name was called, the charges against me were read out. The arresting officers were present, and the crown requested that I be denied bail due to my lack of a permanent residence and a responsible party to ensure my attendance at future court dates. The judge asked if I had legal representation and if anyone would post bail for me. Unfamiliar with the court system, I was remanded until the next day to consult with the duty counsel.

After the court session, I was returned to the holding cells to await transport back to the detention center. Around five o'clock, I was taken back to the detention center in the court wagon for another night. The check-in process and changing into prison clothes were repeated. I spent an uncertain amount of time in detention, a week or a month, awaiting my trial date. After several unsuccessful attempts to post bail, I was returned to the same range as the other inmates that I had ratted out the first time I went for bail.

To pass the time and keep myself safe, I tried to make friends and played card games to win cigarettes, which I could trade for other necessities. Although I did not smoke, having cigarettes to trade bought me some respite from potential threats from those inmates who wanted to beat me to death. My time in detention felt prolonged due to the combined time on my bail for the sexual assault and car theft charges. I am unsure of the exact duration before my trial, but I remember that the police had combined the two dates.

One afternoon, I began shaving my head in the bathroom, thinking it might make me look more intimidating. However, a guard ordered me to stop midway as I could not alter my appearance from when I entered the jail. To look fantastic, I chewed off one of the picks from my plastic comb, melted the end flat, and used it to pierce my ear for the first time. The pain was intense, accompanied by a loud popping sound as it pierced through my earlobe.

Inspired by the more experienced repeat offenders, I attempted to make my first prison tattoo using a mixture of toothpaste and cigarette ashes. I scratched the skin on my forearm until it bled, then filled the cut with the mixture. Although the cut healed over, and the mark faded to a faint grey before disappearing completely, it left a minor scar, a constant reminder of my time in prison. The detention center felt like a death trap. I contemplated self-harm, hoping to be moved to a different range. I attempted to break my thumb using a plastic mug in my cell, but my double-jointed thumb merely bent and swelled, denying me the protection of a plaster cast. As weeks passed, new inmates arrived, easing the tension.

The range leaders, known as 'heavies,' ordered me to fight a new inmate. It was him or me, so I confronted him in the shower room and explained how things had to go down. I swung at him, landing a punch on his face before slipping and falling on the wet floor. He pounced on me, punching me until the guards intervened. I was placed in solitary confinement and then moved to a protective custody range. In jail, I learned to stand up for myself, fight back, and even became adept at playing Euchre to win extra meals. A month into my custody, I was due for a court hearing. After a four-hour wait eating my cold ham and cheese sandwich with coffee, we were handcuffed and loaded into the court wagon.

Fear resurfaced from experience in the wagon as I was cuffed between four black males and a skinny white skinhead attached to more prominent black inmates. I had learned to keep quiet to avoid trouble as my initiation was over. When one Black inmate asked the skinhead about his charges, he admitted to being in for sexual assault on a girl. I stared at him, knowing what was coming. An inmate removed his shoe and began assaulting the skinhead by smashing him in the face with the shoe and burning him with cigarettes on top of his bald head.

They told him to hold his hand out and use it as an ashtray. I kept my head down, mouth shut, and eyes averted. Was this his deserved justice for exploiting the weak? I dared not intervene, fearing more scars. I knew those Daily Mail cigarettes would come in handy for something other than smoking, but it never crossed my mind to use them to torture other inmates. I prayed silently for a swift arrival at the courthouse, sparing me from becoming the next target. My prayers were answered, and I escaped unscathed without any burn marks or footprints on my head. I braced myself for a six-month sentence for car theft and assault. However, my duty counsel lawyer informed me that Laura had corrected the information given to the police.

The revelation came about when Laura complained of groin pain at school. The school nurse discovered a minor tear in her vagina, leading to a call home. Laura's father, Shane, rushed to the school before the police could intervene. You see, Shane harboured a dark secret - he was a pedophile who preyed on his children, both male and female. I initially thought I was his only victim, but I later discovered that he had violated all his children, including Laura, his 12-year-old daughter, and my 18-year-old aunt.

Aware of my closeness with Laura and my foster care status, Shane devised a plan. He instructed Laura to tell the police that I had forced myself on her without her consent. He assured her that as a foster child, I would face minimal consequences, whereas the truth would result in his arrest and her loss of a father. Fearing her volatile and violent father, Laura complied with his instructions when questioned by the police. Years later, Laura confessed the truth to me, revealing the extent of her father's manipulation and the factual circumstances surrounding the accusations against me.

In the same year I was incarcerated, Laura, at the tender age of twelve, found herself pregnant. She gave birth to a baby boy when she turned thirteen. That year, she received a Cabbage Patch doll, a stark contrast to the real-life motherhood she was thrust into. Her childhood was abruptly replaced with adult responsibilities. Questions lingered about the baby's paternity, as Laura had a boyfriend from the apartment complex but was also involved with her father. No DNA tests were conducted to confirm the baby's father.

8

OPEN CUSTODY. BOYS TOWN AND BATHHOUSES

Standing before the judge, my lawyer announced that Laura and the Crown had reduced the rape charges to a fondling charge. I was sentenced to four months in an open custody house, a halfway point between incarceration and freedom. I had to adhere to a set of rules, and any attempt to leave the property or run away would result in an arrest warrant and a return to jail. I returned to the detention center to collect my belongings and waited for the paperwork to be processed and for the van to pick me up.

After changing my street clothes, I was escorted to a dock where a white van awaited. The van bore no signs of being a prison vehicle, and the male and female staff wore regular street clothes. The purpose of an open custody house is to reintegrate criminals back into society gradually. About six other inmates were in the van, including Victor, who resembled Bryan Adams.

We arrived at a large, old Victorian house off Dufferin Street and King St in Toronto. The house, surrounded by high-rise apartments, was a short walk from Dufferin. The fence and gate in front of the house were about four feet high and falling apart. The house, over a hundred years old and well-used, was either a drug rehab or social income housing, evident from the lack of upkeep.

Inside, we were briefed on the house rules. I was only allowed to be in one room at a time and had to be accompanied by staff members whenever I wanted to move to another room. As I complied with the rules, I gradually earned the privilege to move from room to room by simply announcing my intentions. The other guys in the house were decent and just trying to serve their time to gain release. We even drove with a staff member to buy groceries for the house, and I helped with loading, unloading, and storing the food.

After a month, I advanced to stage two, gaining more freedom within the house. By the end of the second month, I was free to roam the house from one floor to the next by just saying, "Jason, going to the second floor," without restrictions. By the third month,

I could get weekend passes to visit my family, go to school, or work. I started job hunting during weekend passes and found work at a Shooters Photo Studio nearby.

The four months passed quickly, and I was finally released. However, I was left with no personal belongings and a family that had disowned me because of my sister. I remembered my brother Charles lived downtown, so I sought him out. Charles often spoke about his numerous girlfriends, but I was unaware that he was also involved with a man named Frank. Despite being only seventeen, I managed to get into some downtown clubs and bars.

I found myself in a part of Toronto known as Boys Town, where some underage boys resorted to unsavoury means to earn money. An expression in the gay community called "Gay for Pay" was a term used by heterosexual homeless boys who sold their souls and bodies for cash in return for prostitution with older gay men, primarily pedophiles. This was a world I never knew existed. This area of Toronto ran from Church Street, Wellesley, and Maitland across to Carlton and covered areas like Younge Street, Bay Street, St. Joseph's Steet around Woman's Collage Hospital, and Grosvenor Steet.

One day, I walked into a bar on Yonge Street called

Trax. The bar was dark, with black lights, and filled with smoke. As a good-looking seventeen-year-old boy, I attracted attention. I made my way to the back of the bar, where everyone was playing pool. During my four months living in custody, I learned much about life, survival, and the world's harsh realities. It was a challenging period, but it shaped me and prepared me for the trials ahead. Despite the hardships, I learned to adapt and navigate through the complexities of life.

I had been sexually abused many times already, and I had no other means of supporting myself and nowhere to live, so what other option did I have at this point? In the bustling bar called Trax on Younge Street, walls painted black and purple with blacked-out windows; I felt a discomforting invasion of personal space.

It was an eye-opening experience, making me understand the objectification women often face. Amidst the crowd, I spotted James, a familiar face from my past, engaged in a game of billiards with a cigarette in his mouth and a Labatt's Blue in the other hand. I remembered his missing tooth, long hair, and black leather jacket. He recognized me, and his face lit up with a warm smile. "Jason," he called out, introducing me as his brother to his friends. He was immensely proud of me.

I was a good-looking seventeen-year-old over six

feet tall with long blond hair and grey eyes. The expression fresh meat was a reference to me as I was new, and nobody had seen me before around the gay village. I also gave off this straight guy vibe, which drove all the pedophiles and gay younger boys crazy when they looked at me. It was like an apocalyptic zombie movie, and I was the last human flesh left on earth, and I was on their menu.

It had been years since I last saw James. Shane had driven him away from home, and we lost touch. He had gone and lived in Vancouver for as long as I was in foster care. He offered me a place to stay with a friend, a temporary solution until I could sort things out. The following day, they took me to a leather store downtown, where I was gifted a biker jacket and boots. It felt like I was stepping into a role, like a character from The Village People or Queen. Charles's friend, who I later learned was one of his benefactors, his Sugar Daddy, gave me money for a favour. It was an effortless way to earn, with no work required on my part. These men, known as Johns, would cruise around Boys Town looking for young boys to pick up.

With my newfound wealth, I decided to change my look. I stopped by House of Lords, a salon on Yonge Street famous for its celebrity clientele. I used my earnings to transform my hair into a style reminiscent of my favourite artist, Billy Idol. It was a drastic change:

platinum blonde, shaved short on the sides, and spiky on top. I also got my ears pierced and adorned them with hanging crosses. I was a younger version of Billy Idol, which became my nickname for the next few years.

My usual spot was on Grosvenor St, across from the Central YMCA. I would head out in the evening, navigating the strip and avoiding the other young men trying to make a living. There were always a handful of us, each with our own story, each trying to survive. You see, the "Johns" always wanted new young blood and would get tired of the regulars; they only used them when it was early morning and nobody else was around.

My first encounter was with John, an ironic twist given the slang term for the men who frequented the area. He was six feet six in his forties, and his nickname was John Little John because he was tall. He lived above a Mr. Sub shop on the corner of Yonge and Grenville St, one block from the YMCA. He was a manipulator, a predator preying on young boys in need of shelter. His payment was not in cash for sexual acts but in food, substances, and a place to stay for the night. After getting me drunk, he then drugged me so he could take advantage of me because I needed a place to stay for the night.

We spent the evening in his apartment, watching TV

and sharing beers. He introduced me to a substance I had never tried before, LSD. It was a popular hallucinogenic drug, d-lysergic acid, in the seventies and eighties, known for its mood-altering effects. It came in many forms and names, such as Purple Mikes, Blotters, Microdots, and Tabs.

As I lay on the bed, I experienced a surreal sensation, as if observing myself from a third-person perspective. The room seemed to spin, the walls appeared to breathe, and I felt like I was losing touch with reality. Little John, my companion for the night, did not ask me to do anything to him; he only wanted to touch me. His appearance began to morph in my altered state, transforming into a beautiful woman with long blond hair. When I woke up the following day, I felt used and discarded, wandering Yonge Street without a penny to my name.

My stay with James was brief. I did not want to intrude on his lifestyle or love life, especially as his roommate seemed interested in me. James and other boys on the street had mentioned that they frequented male bathhouses during the day to earn money, avoiding the risk of being picked up by undercover police on the streets. Intrigued, I found one, The Spa on Maitland, above a convenience store on Church Street and Maitland. The entrance to The Spa was a nondescript door on the side of the building, leading up a dark staircase to another door. Behind the glass of the entrance window was a slender black man wearing glasses and ripped shorts with no shirt.

The establishment offered different packages, ranging from six to twelve hours, with options for a locker or a private room where I could sleep after working. Curious about the place and its patrons, I chose a locker to start. The attendant handed me a key and a white bath towel, barely large enough to wrap around my waist. The establishment's front counter was a hub of activity, with patrons exchanging used towels for fresh ones and ordering refreshments and snacks, including instant noodles. The place had all the amenities needed, including access to pay-per-view and movie channels.

For a modest sum of around fourteen dollars, I realized I could make this place my temporary home, bypassing the need for a hotel. It was a cost-effective solution that also offered the opportunity to earn money. This place, unconventional as it was, became my new home. Here, I learned a new set of skills essential for street survival. Upon my first entry into the spa, I was taken aback by the dimly lit environment, reminiscent of a vampire's lair. I had to rely on touch to navigate the space, feeling arms reaching out from the darkness in all directions. The only light sources were the faint glow of emergency exit signs and the illumination from the movie room at the end of the hallway.

Inside, men lounged on black vinyl couches half naked, some watching TV, others attempting to sleep. The wet area of the spa housed washrooms, a shower room, a steam room, and a sauna. Both the sauna and steam room were pitch black, filled with men in proximity committing sexual acts with each other right out of Michelangelo's painting "The Last Judgment."

I preferred to use these facilities when they were less crowded, as I was uncomfortable with the invading space atmosphere and was not into having free sex with men. During this time, the AIDS epidemic was at its peak, and the behaviours I observed made it clear why many of the original hustlers from Boys Town had succumbed to the disease.

To unwind, I would shower, watch a movie in the TV lounge, and observe the interactions around me. Some men would sit in the chairs, making suggestive gestures and smiling at me. Most hustlers, especially the younger ones, would try to sleep on the couches in the theatre room because they could not afford the room's price and could only afford the locker, so they had nowhere to sleep.

Staff would come by and clean every half hour and check up on people to ensure they were not sleeping or engaging in inappropriate behaviour in the lounge. The staff would kick or tap the chairs or legs of the person sleeping and tell them it was prohibited in the TV room. I decided to explore the dark hallways where the private rooms were located.

Some doors were half open, dimly lit, and inviting as I walked by. Men strolled the hallways, some draped in towels, others completely bare. In some rooms, groups of men engaged in intimate activities while others watched. It was a red-light district where open doors signalled open business. I would often lean against the wall, observing the scene. Some men would invite me into their rooms with a nod, but I would politely decline. They would then approach me, striking up a conversation. I would always respond that I was just there to relax.

When propositioned, I would clarify that I was there for work. The men understood this and offered me compensation for their requests. After each encounter, they generously handed me sixty to one hundred dollars. Over time, I became desensitized to the entire process, accepting it to survive in a world that had turned its back on me.

I found myself drawn into this life that promised easy money. It was a lifestyle that led me down a treacherous path, akin to stepping into the Devil's lair. Yet, amidst the darkness, I clung to my faith in God, hoping for deliverance from this inferno. The world I inhabited was far from ordinary.

I encountered johns- Their acts were explicit, and I played my part, but I knew my truth deep down. I was straight, not gay. When the johns touched me, I would close my eyes and conjure an image—a woman's face, her soft curves, her laughter. It was a mental escape, a way to perform without losing myself entirely.

My journey was survival, a tightrope walk between desperation and hope. It was all about the cash. I established a few regular clients who provided a steady income, allowing me to maintain my stay at the spa without having to work the streets. Once they arrived, I would ensure they spent their money on me before they could engage with the other hustlers.

Then, I could relax, watch movies, and let them come to me. As the nights got late, I would see them pop their heads into the door of the movie room and give me a nod to follow them back to their room. After each encounter, I would take a long, hot shower, cleansing myself before returning to the lounge.

In the spa, I became accustomed to the uninhibited behaviour around me. I kept my distance from the other hustlers to avoid conflicts over clients. During the day, I would hang around the Eaton Centre, Yorkdale Mall, and Yorkville. I was keenly interested in fashion, and Yorkville was the place to immerse myself in luxury.

Hazelton Lanes was a strip of high-end designers like Armani and Versace. My favourite spot was the Bellair Café, where I would sit at the bar, enjoy a meal, and watch for familiar faces in the crowd. I aspired to the lifestyle of the actors and models I saw there. One night, a man named Bill approached me in an old Thunderbird. He was well-dressed and invited me to dinner. Afterward, we went to his three-story brick home, filled with fine antiques and artwork.

He introduced me to a substance I had never tried before: cocaine. After crushing and cutting the cocaine with his credit card, he divided the coke evenly into four lines. Bill returned to the couch with a satisfied smile and handed me the rolled-up dollar bill. He demonstrated how to use it, covering one nostril with his thumb and the straw in the other nostril.

He took a deep sniff across the line until it was gone. I followed his instructions, leaning towards the table and aligning the makeshift straw with the powder line. I was careful not to exhale through my mouth, as it would scatter the substance. I inhaled quickly, moving the straw across the table, ensuring no waste. The sensation was intense, a burning feeling followed by a numbing effect and a warmth spreading down my throat.

As I sank back into the couch, a wave of relaxation washed over me. My body felt numb, and I retreated into my world. The predator took advantage of my state, finding his pleasure. Despite the circumstances, my survival instincts kicked in, allowing me to mentally escape to a safer place I referred to as my Neverland. I had a place to sleep for the night and got to enjoy a fine meal, some whisky, and cocaine. I suppressed the memories, effectively erasing the events of the night.

The following day, he drove me back downtown and handed me a hundred dollars for shopping. It was a pattern I was all too familiar with, a cycle of abuse followed by rewards, a pattern that mirrored my experiences with my Shane.

I spent my time at Eaton's Centre and frequented a restaurant called Mr. Greenjeans on the second floor as I ate. I met a bartender with blond hair and an outgoing personality who was studying to become a registered massage therapist. She invited me over for a discounted massage due to her student status.

We took the subway back to her place. In her bedroom, the massage table lay waiting for me. After the massage, she surprised me by expressing her interest in a more intimate ending. This was a new experience for me but a mutually satisfying one. She did not charge me for the massage because she said I was also happy with her.

While she was in the shower, I went to the kitchen for a glass of water, and to my surprise, her female roommate came out of her room completely naked. She apologized and said she was unaware her roommate invited someone over and went back to her bed, leaving her door open as she spread herself across her sheets, leaving me with an erection, wondering if it was an invitation into her bed.

These experiences confirmed my heterosexual orientation. Despite the circumstances that led me to engage with men, I realized my valid preferences lay elsewhere. I harboured resentment towards the men who had taken advantage of me, but I also recognized that they were my means of survival at that point in my life. My urges for females started in foster care and continued after my relationship with Kevin's secretary.

Being abused by men, now around seventeen years old, I did not find myself attracted to the same sex at all but rather quite the opposite. I felt anger towards gay people after all the abuse but also realized that I needed them for my financial means at this point in my journey with nowhere else to live and no family to turn to.

One evening, as I strolled along Yonge Street towards Bloor, I noticed a lively club named Comrades on the corner of Isabella Street. The crowd outside was diverse, and it took me a while to realize it was a gay nightclub. Interestingly, many straight women also frequented the club, enjoying the atmosphere without the usual advances from straight men.

The door attendant, a towering figure named Henry, reminded me of a modern-day Terry Crews wearing his ripped jean shorts and sleeveless jean shirt. Climbing to the top of the stairs, I paid the entrance fee and entered a large, dimly lit room. The club had two bars and communal washrooms, where patrons casually socialized. That was the first time I went into a male bathroom and had girls smoking and drinking on the top of the sinks while guys were urinating beside them.

Coming from a rural background, this fast-paced, uninhibited pagan lifestyle was a stark contrast. The club was a melting pot of different people expressing themselves freely. Half-naked men fondling other men, kissing and having sex in the dark corners just like in the bathhouses. The only difference was that there were hot, young, sexy girls dancing while being open-minded about what was happening around them. Amid the crowd, my eye caught the attention of one girl. I met Mia, a lively Italian girl from Hamilton. We danced together until the early hours of the morning. She came to the club by herself but had friends in Toronto and enjoyed the atmosphere in this club.

The club stayed open even after the bar stopped

serving alcohol. They called it an after-hours club, attracting a younger crowd who came to dance, socialize, and get high on MDMA. As dawn broke, the club began to empty, with people spilling onto the sidewalks, still caught up in the night's revelry, looking for a companion to take home. Mia invited me back to her apartment in Hamilton. She had classes at McMaster University in the afternoon but offered me a place to rest until then.

We drove to her apartment in Hamilton, a tall brown building just off the 403 and Main Street. Mia was experienced, and I could tell she had previous partners in the bedroom. She taught me a few things that I added to my repertoire. In the afternoon, I caught a bus back to Toronto, looking forward to seeing Mia again the following weekend. I ate salmon and wild rice for lunch at my favourite Belair Café restaurant. The following weekend, I went to the club and met Mia at the front entrance. She told me she was off and had no classes for the weekend. She asked me if I wanted to drive somewhere, so Mia and I planned a road trip. I suggested we drive to Ft. Lauderdale, Florida, in her brown Ford Maverick.

I had not earned any money in a few days and did not have money, but I did not want Mia to know. So, I fabricated a story about my bank card being defective and unable to withdraw money. I told her I would wait until Monday to get a new card. Mia kindly offered to cover the trip expenses, and I promised to reimburse her when we returned. Our journey began with a stop at a gas station before hitting the highway. We filled up the car and set our sights on Niagara Falls, where we crossed into the United States. With minimal luggage and a long drive ahead, we relied on coffee and caffeine pills to keep us awake for the twenty-three-hour journey.

By mid-afternoon, we arrived on the main strip of Ft. Lauderdale. We booked a room at the Holiday Inn on the beach. Our room on the main floor had sliding glass doors that offered a beautiful view of the ocean, the pool, and the beachfront. Exhausted from the drive, we decided to rest on the beach beside our hotel. I removed my jeans and shirt and lay in the sand in my underwear, as we had no swimsuits. Mia also removed her clothes, except her bra and underwear. We fell asleep under the scorching sun, forgetting to apply sunscreen to protect our white, pale skin.

We woke up to an empty beach, and the sun had already set. It was around seven in the evening. The aftermath of our sun exposure was apparent; our skin was severely sunburned. We gathered our clothes and returned to our hotel room to rest and eat. The next day, we had to leave for Canada. The effects of the sunburn became more pronounced, leaving my face resembling an overcooked lobster. My skin was blistered and cracked, making wearing clothes or enduring any touch painful. The drive home was uncomfortable, with the wind from the open window relieving my heated skin. Mia had no air conditioner in the vehicle, so I looked like a cartoon character of a dog with his tongue hanging out the window.

We arrived back in Hamilton early Monday morning and rested. Upon waking, Mia asked for my opinion on dyeing her hair blond. I encouraged her, comparing her potential look to Marilyn Monroe. I helped her with the process, although the result was more orange than blond. Before I left for Toronto, we shared an intimate moment. I promised Mia that I would reimburse her for the trip expenses, which I estimated to be over six hundred dollars for the gas, food, and hotel stay. I kissed her and bid her goodbye, knowing our relationship had concluded.

I grabbed the bus at the terminal, returned to Toronto, and resumed my Maitland Spa and Comrades routine, which was open seven days a week. Some of the other hustlers from the strip also hung out at Comrades with their straight friends who were girls. I befriended a bouncer who was using steroids from the club. Intrigued, I decided to try a cycle to enhance my physique. He came with me to the spa and got a room, and he taught me how to inject into my buttocks. I started using the gym and working out; I noticed significant improvements in my strength and muscle mass in my chest and arms over a few weeks.

Johnny, a fellow hustler and spa employee, expressed interest in trying the steroids and wanted to get a cycle from me. Despite our diverse backgrounds and builds, we shared a goal of self-improvement. I agreed to share my cycle with him, and we began working out at the spa. He was afraid of needles and not sure what to do, so I injected the needle into his buttocks. He was half Chinese and Vietnamese and already had a muscular build, unlike me, so I did not understand why he would want to take steroids. It was me who was in jail and had to learn to fight and look tough and strong.

My stash of steroids was a secret known only to Johnny. I had them hidden in my room, in a small box on the desk by the light switch. After each job, I would return to my room to secure my earnings, as I only had a towel and room key. One day, I noticed my bag of steroids was missing. Johnny was the only one who could access my room cleaning while working that shift. When I reported the missing bag to the front desk, they denied any responsibility for personal belongings.

That marked the end of my experiment with steroids. Despite the abrupt end, I had gained some muscle mass and definition, which made me more appealing to clients and increased my earnings. I noticed Johnny spending a lot of time in the gym during his breaks and days off. His physique was improving noticeably. I confronted him about the missing steroids and said I knew it was him who stole them, but he denied any involvement. That was the end of our friendship.

9

BREAKING STRONGHOLDS

While on the streets, I frequented about four different bathhouses, gradually getting to know the regular clientele. This familiarity assured me that money would come my way whenever I spotted familiar faces at the spa. One such regular was an overweight man who sought nothing more than to sit against the wall, indulging in poppers while I twisted his nipples. Poppers, a legal high available in most adult stores, were his escape, and our encounters were straightforward, fulfilling, and financially rewarding.

Another recurring client was Ricardo, or Ricky, as he preferred, a Filipino man in his forties who lived with his mother in Brampton. Ricky's appearance, resembling a pug with his flattened face and bulging eyes, contrasted with his hidden homosexuality.

Despite his efforts to conceal his true self, his demeanour and mannerisms easily betray his secret.

He was a factory worker, careful to keep his sexuality hidden from both his family and coworkers. For a guaranteed hundred dollars per week, Ricky sought companionship with younger, attractive white men like me. He would treat me to dinners and movies, revelling in the company of someone who fit his ideal image. Despite his quirks and preferences, I did not mind his advances, as he was always a reliable source of income.

One particularly challenging night, low on funds and with a quiet spell at the spa, I found myself in Boys Town near the YMCA. A brown Chevrolet Camaro pulled up beside me, and its driver, David, a man in his thirties, struck up a conversation. Dave seemed amicable, though it was apparent he preferred much younger boys. He offered me a place to stay for the night, and we drove to his apartment complex. The following day, I had breakfast with Dave and his roommate, Roger, a large man standing at six foot three and weighing three hundred pounds. Roger was a rent collector for property owners and the building's superintendent. Dave, however, had a darker side, involved in fraudulent activities like depositing and cashing bad checks, eventually leading him to flee to Vancouver to avoid arrest.

Years later, Dave resurfaced in my life through Roger, who invited me to stay at his apartment. Dave's lavish lifestyle in Vancouver had caught up with him, leading to his arrest and subsequent three-year jail sentence for his crimes. This revelation shed light on the complexities of the people I encountered on the streets, each with their own stories and struggles. Though unconventional and, at times, unsettling, my interactions with these individuals gave me a glimpse into their lives and motivations. These experiences were part of the fabric of my life on the streets, shaping my understanding of human nature and survival in a world where everyone sought their means of breaking free from their strongholds.

While on the streets, I needed clothing, having nothing but the clothes on my back. Roger took me shopping at K-Mart and bought me a couple of pairs of pants and shirts. One notable pair of pants was the popular Parachute pants, made from the same material as parachutes, in a dark grey colour with numerous zippers. These pants were all the rage, especially with singers like Madonna, Cyndi Lauper, and Twisted Sister, and they featured bright neon colours and catchy phrases.

Grateful for Roger's help, I soon realized that every kindness had its price. It turned out that Roger was the manager at Comrades, where I started frequenting again, hoping to avoid Mia. However, I never saw Mia again, and she had no interest in seeing me either.

Instead, I established friendships with a couple of girls I met at the club who lived in an apartment on College Street. One night, after a party, I returned to their apartment, where they slept on the living room floor before the TV. One of the girls was thin with dark to red hair, giving off the vibe of a drug user. The other girl, who took a liking to me, resembled a regular high school girl with blond curly hair and a slightly chubby build.

We sat on the floor with blankets and pillows, watching TV and sharing a few drinks. Eventually, I had sex with the blond girl while the redhead watched, though she eventually went to sleep. Over the next few weeks, I spent time with these girls, engaging in intimate encounters with the blond girl and a few others I met at Comrades. Despite these fleeting connections, the harsh realities of life on the streets were taking their toll. My faith in God was wavering, and I felt my soul being eroded by those who took advantage of me and my circumstances.

One fateful night, as I walked along Yonge Street, a man picked me up and took me to his flower shop in Richmond Hill, where he raped me and subjected me to anal intercourse. After he was finished, he dropped me back off in downtown Toronto, leaving me at my lowest point, feeling broken and ready to give up on life. I was consumed with anger toward God, blaming

Him for everything that had happened in my past and for my current circumstances.

Seeking answers, I turned to the Bible, finding comfort in believing that God only gives you trials that you are strong enough to manage. With some money saved, I prayed for guidance and a way out of the city, away from the evils and harmful influences that plagued me. Without saying goodbye to Roger or any other friends, I made my way to the Greyhound station on Bay Street, determined to leave Toronto behind. Boarding a bus without knowing its destination, I eventually found myself on the other side of London going towards Exeter, where I had attended high school before leaving the Burks in foster care. I still had friends there, and it seemed like a haven from the turmoil of my life in Toronto. However, the bus did not go to Exeter, so I had to hitchhike the rest of the way.

Standing on the shoulder of the highway, clad in my black leather coat and biker boots, sporting a look reminiscent of Billy Idol, I struggled to find a ride. The afternoon sun was beginning to dip below the horizon when a transport truck carrying plastic sewage tiles pulled over near London, Ontario. The driver, Rick, leaned out and asked where I was headed. When I mentioned Exeter, he smiled and said he lived there too. He dropped me off in town, beside the GM dealership, where I stood on the cusp of a new chapter, eager to leave behind the shadows of my past in Toronto.

I wandered through Exeter, passing my old high school and reminiscing about my time there. I made my way to Mac's Milk for a coffee, feeling the weight of curious stares from locals who recognized me as an outsider. Even the town police gave me a once-over. Later that afternoon, I spotted Rick driving through town again. He pulled over and asked what I was up to. I told him I was exploring. He mentioned heading to Quebec and that he would be back the next day, inviting me to join him. I eagerly accepted his offer, but there was nowhere to sleep and nothing to eat.

As we approached Laval, north of Montreal, the roads became treacherous with high snow drifts. We pulled into a gas station for dinner, where Rick generously bought us a meal. After dropping off the trailer at a warehouse for loading the following day, we drove the truck to a nearby motel and slept until dawn. Rick had a few stops in Quebec before returning to Ontario. We fueled up, ate a bite, and stopped at a quaint flea market. I spotted a semi-automatic Glock replica with hollow tip blanks in a glass display case. My eyes lit up with excitement. Rick noticed and asked if I wanted it. I hesitated, wondering about the legality and whether a gun license was required. He assured me it was legal and only sold in Quebec, so he bought it for me.

As Rick and I travelled, a loud bang and smoke filled the cabin, accompanied by Rick's scream. He quickly pulled the truck over to the shoulder of the road, the wheels screeching to a halt. I looked down at his sweater and saw a black burn hole where the gunpowder had embedded into his flesh, causing a third-degree burn. Rick yelled at me for what felt like an eternity before we resumed our journey, Rick holding his side and shifting gears. He took the gun away from me, reminding me to be more careful, even if it was not real. After an hour of silence, he handed me back the gun.

Upon our return to Exeter, Rick dropped off the empty truck in Hensall, where his vehicle was parked. He then drove me back to his place on Simcoe Street, where he lived with two roommates, Paul and Randy. Paul, who reminded me of Paul Simon, was short and had a thin mustache. He often seemed intoxicated and always complained about something or someone. Rick was taking his vacation, and they had been planning a trip together.

Knowing I was not living anywhere, Rick did not want to leave me on the streets with nothing to eat. It was winter and cold, so he took me under his wing like an older brother and offered to live with them. He offered to accompany them on vacation, so Rick, Paul, and I travelled to Miami and Key West. It was my first time in Miami, and South Beach was a new experience. Our hotel was right on the beach, and our first stop was to load up on liquor. Rick was into Vodka and bought some bottles of Silent Sam and Florida orange juice for me, a drink that lived up to its name. Paul, on the other hand, preferred peach schnapps and beer.

After stocking up on alcohol, we headed back to the hotel after meeting a couple of girls at the liquor store and invited them back for drinks. Rick mixed up some strong screwdrivers, pouring half the orange juice and replacing it with the entire bottle of vodka. Unfortunately, Paul's erratic behaviour and mumbling scared the girls away, ending our night on a less-than-ideal note. Unable to drink in public, we finished the bottles of screwdrivers and beers before heading to the beach. The Florida sun was scorching, and combined with the drinks, I began to feel dizzy. The vodka, known as Silent Sam for its lack of smell or taste, hit me hard. I stumbled along the beach, watching women play volleyball, their bodies half-naked and bouncing with the ball, before passing out.

Rick found me and carried me back to the hotel room, placing me on one of the beds. I woke up in the middle of the night, soiling my shorts and waking up in my vomit. I dragged myself to the shower, vomiting and defecating as I sat on the floor, letting the water wash over me. The next day, I was plagued with a killer headache and had no appetite for breakfast. Unsure of how many days we stayed in Miami, we eventually headed to the Keys, driving along bridges that stretched for miles, separating one island from the next. We stopped at seafood restaurants, indulging in shrimp and lobster.

Arriving in Key West, I was struck by its resemblance to a large US military base, with Old Town resembling New Orleans' French Quarter. The bars lined the streets, bustling with people drinking and socializing. Home to Ernest Hemingway and famed for its beautiful sunsets, Key West was a fascinating place to explore, adding another pin to my world map of conquests. We visited flea markets, where Rick and Paul purchased switchblades, butterfly knives, Ninja Stars, and boxes of firecrackers. They made sure to hide these illegal items and extra bottles of alcohol in various sections of the vehicle. However, we did not consider the consequences if caught by Canadian Customs and border patrol.

The remainder of my trip with Rick was incredible, contrasting starkly with my previous experiences in Florida with the Burks, Mia and Roger. Aside from the initial alcohol poisoning incident, the journey was filled with unforgettable moments. One highlight was our visit to Walt Disney World, a stark contrast to my childhood memory of getting lost in the park at

Thunder Mountain and tearfully searching for my foster siblings. Before leaving Florida and heading into Georgia, we stopped by some orange orchards, filling plastic bags with large oranges to bring back home with a sun-kissed tan and not burned. This time, we safely made our way back home.

In Exeter, Rick had two rifles in his bedroom closet that piqued my interest—an M16 semi-automatic and an AK47 semi-auto fired 22 mm rounds from a magazine. Rick's father, Herb, lived on the outskirts of Exeter, and he took me to his house, where we would shoot at cans for practice. One day, when Rick was at work, I went upstairs and took out the M16 to play with, imagining myself in Full Metal Jacket, fighting in Vietnam.

The rifle had bullets in the magazine, and the safety was off as I pointed it downwards. When I pulled the trigger, there was a loud pop and smoke emerged, reminiscent of the incident in the truck with Rick. This time, however, it was with live ammunition, and I quickly dropped the rifle on the bed. Thankfully, nobody was home at the time of the accident. Looking up at the ceiling, I noticed a small hole in the drywall near the light fixture, trying to analyze the trajectory of the bullet's path. On top of the fridge, I saw a microwave, its top corner sticking up. Upon opening the door, I found the plate inside smashed, with another hole at the bottom. The realization of what could have happened hit me hard, and I vowed to be more cautious with firearms in the future.

I knew there was no way I could cover this up. I did not know Rick that well, but I was confident he would be furious with me, as would his roommates, Paul and Randy. When Rick arrived home, I explained that I had been examining the guns and that the rifle had accidentally discharged because the safety was not locked. He inspected the damaged microwave and then launched into a twenty-minute tirade about the potential consequences of my actions. He emphasized how someone could have been killed if they had been in the kitchen at the time. I apologized profusely, and Rick moved the rifles to a safer location in the house to prevent future mishaps.

Paul and Randy were also upset about the situation and did not want me to live in the house anymore. Seeing this, Rick took it upon himself to help me find a new place to live. He assisted me in renting a bachelor room on the second floor of a restaurant on the main street, which overlooked the town. The room was basic, with just a bed and dresser. There was no kitchen, and the bathroom was shared with other tenants. Since I had no income to pay the rent, Rick helped cover it. To combat the loneliness of living alone, I bought two rats from the pet store to keep me company at night.

When the first litter came, I realized the rats were male and female. Before long, I had a dozen albino rats, mostly white but with a few brown ones. As I walked along the main street with rats crawling on my shoulders, people started giving me strange looks. The local police department, driving around in their banana yellow cruisers, took a particular interest in me. One day, a cruiser pulled up beside me, and an officer asked me what I was doing in town or who I was visiting. I felt like the first Rambo, being warned not to return for my own good.

I was now on their radar as a troublemaker, and I am sure they had already run my name through the computer database because I came from the big city of Toronto. I enrolled back at South Huron District High School, and because I was living alone, I did not need permission or a letter to leave school or skip classes. I quickly became popular with some students and earned the nickname Billy because of my punk-style looks, attitude, and disregard for authority figures. One of the popular senior girls, Becky Seldon, also the head of the student council, was attracted to me because of my resemblance to Billy Idol. She would invite me into the student council room, which had a lock on the door, and we would make out on the couch.

Despite her preppy image, she did not want anyone to know she was in public with me. Her parents owned a little chocolate store on the main street near my apartment. One of the school jocks who could not stand me was Dwayne Hayter in high school; Dwayne's animosity toward me persisted from our earlier encounters. He was the quintessential jock, with a posse of cronies trailing behind him like obedient lackeys. I decided to join the football team, partly out of defiance, partly out of a desire to challenge him on his turf. However, his taunts and insults during practice pushed me to my breaking point.

One day, fueled by frustration and pent-up anger, I unleashed my fury, sending him crashing into the lockers with a resounding bang. From that moment on, he kept his distance, his bravado reduced to dirty looks. Despite the occasional skirmish, my focus shifted to more enriching pursuits. I found solace in Art class, where Miss Brown's presence was a welcome distraction. Her youthful allure and the hint of mischief in her eyes captivated me and the rest of the males in the class, where she would sit on the edge of the front desk with her short skirt and unbuttoned blouse.

And then there was Bruce Shaw, the principal, a figure of authority who understood me in a way few others did. His leniency and genuine interest in my well-being earned my respect, especially considering his dual role as the Mayor of Exeter. Encounters with familiar faces from my past added another layer of complexity to my high school experience. Seeing one of Burk's daughters, Blake, reminded me of my former foster care life, stirring conflicting emotions. Meanwhile, the school's track and field competition brought an unexpected reunion with Scott, her father, who seemed indifferent to our shared history.

His presence was a stark reminder of the tangled web of relationships that shaped my past and continued to influence my present. Of course, I can help you rephrase that part of your story to make it more engaging while keeping it within appropriate boundaries. Scott did not seem to care much about our past when he saw me. He delivered the news bluntly, telling me that Sam, my former foster brother, had tragically taken his own life. Blaming me, he insinuated that my troubled presence in their home had somehow influenced her decision.

Anger surged through me, and I wanted to lash out and confront him for his accusations. But I knew I had to keep my composure. I chose to turn the other cheek, masking my pain with a polite nod, and bid him farewell. I met Christine McDonald in high school, a striking girl with platinum blond hair and piercing blue eyes. Our casual hangouts soon took a turn when she expressed her desire to have sex with me.

Now that I had my place, I took her upstairs to my lair, where she undressed and spread herself across my bed. It was another girl and another experience for me, and though fleeting, it left a lasting memory. I think she just used me for sex, and after that, she stopped hanging around me. Years later, I learned she had a child around the time of our encounter, though she maintained it was not mine.

Another person who became a part of my life was Paula, a girl whose demeanour intrigued me. Despite our differences, I found solace in her company. With her father working in a body shop and her mother at the police station, Paula's life differed from mine; she was a quiet loner, and I was a people seeker, yet we connected. Her father took a liking to me, drove us around, and showed me his shop. We all went out for coffee and donuts.

One day, we were in her room; the door was ajar, and our bond deepened as we were intimate. A faint creak of a door broke the silence, jolting us from our grip of intimacy. Paula assumed it was her dad, discreetly closing her bedroom door as he passed. Later, over dinner, her father broached the subject with us. Surprisingly, he acknowledged what was happening between us and offered a word of caution, urging us to tread carefully and avoid rash decisions, meaning don't get pregnant. His calm demeanour and understanding approach struck me as remarkable, a stark departure from the strict authority figures I was accustomed to.

As Paula and I grew closer, our relationship evolved into something akin to dating. Despite being in different classes, we stole moments together during breaks and lunch periods. Her father, an enthusiastic car enthusiast, welcomed me into his world, showing me around his body shop and sharing his love for automobiles. He even asked about my future, though I was uncertain about my path then. Our bond deepened, fueled by the knowledge that her parents accepted us as a couple. Living under the same roof was Paula's older brother, Mark, a rough-and-tumble senior with a love for speed. He did not bother us either, as he had his click to hang around.

However, our happiness was soon overshadowed by a daunting challenge. Paula confided in me one day, her voice trembling with fear as she revealed she had missed her period. Her mother took her to the doctor's office for some tests, and she did not return to school that afternoon. Her parents' subsequent decision shook me to the core without consulting me. They withdrew Paula from school for an abortion, a choice that left me reeling with anger and confusion. In a moment of misguided fury, I blamed Paula for "killing my baby," severing our bond in a fit of rage. Looking back, I realize how wrong I was to react that way. Paula deserved empathy and support, not judgment from me.

The weight of my actions bore heavily on my

conscience, and I hoped that Paula found solace and forgiveness, knowing that I was but a chapter in her journey, not the end of her story. I do not know what happened to Paula after school, as I was no longer attending and did not see her around after that. Later that year, I tried to find her, but she, her father, and her brother seemed to have disappeared from town. Social media didn't exist back then, and the only way to connect online was through AOL email.

10

TROUBLE WAS IN MY BLOOD

Frequenting the local Mac's Milk store on Main Street, I struck up a friendship with the lady who staffed the counter. Though her name eludes me now, the memory of our encounter remains vivid. She was a warm, friendly presence in her late twenties, married to a photographer with a studio just down the street from the store.

I would pop into the store twice or thrice daily for coffee, engaging in friendly banter whenever she was working, and the store would not be bustling with customers.

One afternoon, I entered the store for my usual chat and coffee. It was just the two of us. I had purchased a knife from my trip with Rick in Montreal, and I thought it looked cool. In a light-hearted jest, I pulled the knife from my pocket, opened it, and jokingly demanded that she hand over all the money from the register.

She looked at me, a mixture of disbelief and a hint of a smile on her lips. She must have trusted me, as she did not reach for the panic button under the counter or around her neck. Instead, she asked me if it was legal for me to carry a knife.

I quickly assured her it was perfectly legal and that I was only joking. We chatted for a few more minutes, but then some customers entered the store, so I told her I would catch up with her later that afternoon.

Feeling uneasy, I walked home, stashed the knife in my apartment, and returned to the store. In my absence, the police had visited the store for a coffee, and she had asked them about the legality of carrying a knife.

The police began questioning her, twisting her words. She explained to them that I was a friend and had only been joking. The police were on high alert, eager to make a splash in the quiet town with news of a potential armed robbery.

She seemed distant when I returned to the store to resume our conversation. Moments later, two police officers entered and began to interrogate me, demanding the knife and searching me.

I insisted I had no knife, but they claimed to know

already what had happened and demanded to know where I had hidden it. If I had known my criminal code then, I would have managed the situation differently. Instead, I naively trusted them, and they escorted me back home, intent on retrieving the knife.

After surrendering the knife, the officers informed me that I was under arrest. I was escorted to the back of the cruiser and driven to the police station just off the main street beside the post office. Memories of my time in jail in Toronto raced through my mind, causing my heart to race and my stomach to churn.

Upon arrival, I passed by Pam, Paula's mother, who was seated at the front desk. I tried to avoid eye contact, hoping she would not recognize me. Inside, I was fingerprinted and photographed and then placed in a holding cell for several hours. Eventually, I was transferred to the Exeter Road Detention Center in London, Ontario, where I was to stay until my court appearance on Monday.

The youth detention center in London was a stark contrast to Toronto's, and I recall little about that weekend. Meanwhile, Rick had returned from Quebec and was frantically searching for me around Exeter. An officer spotted him near Mac's Milk and inquired if he was looking for me, to which he replied affirmatively.

The officer informed him I had been arrested for robbing the Mac's store and taken to Exeter Road

Detention Center until Monday. Rick and his parents visited me in London, and he assured me he would be at the courthouse for my hearing on Monday.

On my bail hearing at the Goderich Courthouse, Rick appeared and spoke with the duty counsel, offering to assist with bail. They advised me to plead guilty to possession of a weapon charge, assuring me that the attempted robbery charge would be dropped and I would receive probation.

They also assured me the record would be sealed once I turned eighteen and would not impact my future. Given my existing criminal record, courtesy of my Shane, I agreed to the terms. Rick also assured the judge that he would take responsibility for me and ensure that I attended my probation check-ins at the Exeter police station once a week.

He told the judge he would function as my surety. I was released, and Rick parked his truck in the circle across from the courthouse. The courthouse was in the town center, with a one-way circle street branching onto different streets. A wave of relief washes over me as my feet hit the front steps, knowing Rick was there to help me.

Later, we drove in his beloved yellow Corvette, a car he cared for more meticulously than most things. Rick was particularly proud of it, constantly washing, waxing, and cleaning under the hood. He had a friendship with the Chief of Police in Exeter, and we would sometimes visit their house and chat. The police chief was kind to me, perhaps because I was Rick's friend in need or he had sons around my age. Either way, he was a decent man.

As we drove the Corvette along the town's sideroads, Rick and the police chief sometimes met up. We even engaged in friendly drag races like the Corvette against the police cruiser. Rick also had a friend named Richard, so together, they were the two Dicks. I am not sure why Richard is sometimes called Dick, but that is just how it is.

Richard was a Jehovah's Witness, although he lived in London. We all attended the Witness Hall in Exeter together. Rick was on a journey of spiritual enlightenment and hoped I would join him. I felt nervous entering a new building and meeting unfamiliar people, but seeing some familiar faces from high school eased my nerves. One girl caught my attention. Her name was Leanne, and we started hanging out in a group. Leanne had a brother named Kurt and a younger sister.

I was still considered an outsider since I was not baptized into their faith. To impress Leanne, I bought a black leather briefcase to hold all the books about becoming a Jehovah's Witness and spreading the word about the impending end. On weekends, we would dress up in suits and go door to door, proclaiming the imminent end and the superiority of our religion.

The Jehovah's Witness Bible had over twenty thousand instances where the word "God" was replaced with "Jehovah." They viewed major holidays as pagan and refrained from celebrating birthdays, Christmas, Halloween, or accepting blood transfusions.

It seemed like quite a restrictive religion, especially for teenagers. Once a year, we attended a Jehovah's Witness convention at Copps Coliseum in Hamilton and an enormous hall in Halton Hills, where we were immersed in their theology as the only truth. We also gathered with other halls in our district, including one in Strathroy.

In Strathroy, I became attracted to a girl named Kristy. However, she was good friends with Leanne, so a romantic relationship was out of the question, and we remained just friends. Kristy was slim, tall, and had light red hair and eyes. Despite my attraction, she was always with her parents, and I could not help but admire her from afar during our gatherings.

Rick moved to a house for rent on the main street near the Becker's store and the high school. He replaced his male roommates with two girls who seemed like trailer park hillbillies—Gloria and June. I shared a room with Rick on a set of bunk beds. I expressed my desire to get a dog, so Rick found someone with a

Pitbull mix that we named Spike. Spike became my first pet responsibility, and we built a kennel and doghouse for him in the backyard.

I worked at the Hasty Market store at the other end of Exeter as a cashier but took on the responsibilities of an assistant manager. Working alone, I closed and opened the store, did cash drops, and managed the store independently, which felt empowering. While I was working, Rick's sister Tammy and her daughter visited one weekend.

Unfortunately, Spike bit Rick's niece when she got too close to his kennel. She required multiple stitches and plastic surgery, and the dog was euthanized by court order. I took the blame, but it was Rick's dog, and I felt powerless.

I told Rick I wanted to get my driver's license. He was really into muscle cars and only liked Chevrolet and GMC models. We went out looking for a vehicle, and he found a 1969 Pontiac Firebird with black vinyl and metal interior. Rick picked up the car for about four thousand dollars and took it to his friend's body shop at the end of town.

We looked through a colour code book, and Rick chose a Porsche colour, Fuchsia, which looked like Barbie Pink but was a mix of pink and purple. I thought it looked a little feminine, but he was paying.

A week later, the car was finished being put back

together, and we went to the body shop to pick it up. Surprisingly, the vehicle looked impressive with its fifty-inch BF Goodrich performance tires and traction bars.

The four headlights, chrome, and black honeycomb center made the car look like a pouncing lion ready to devour its prey. It also had a shaker hood scoop and tachometer. I painted all the black lettering and the middle of the grill and polished the interior. We changed the exhaust to cherry bomb mufflers with this loud rumble sound.

I sat in the front seat, adjusted the door and rear-view mirror, and put my seat belt across my waist. The car never came with a shoulder strap. I had been practicing with some of Rick's other cars before getting ready for my road test.

I drove the Firebird into the Ministry's parking lot and went to get my instructor, who was a man in his sixties or seventies who should have been retired. He opened the passenger door, got in, and slammed the heavy metal door. I started the ignition, and the car fired up, roaring, lifting its front, ready to go.

I pulled the car out past the side street, and the car rumbled to a stop. I could tell the instructor was nervous and hoped he would not have a heart attack during my test. We only drove for five minutes through town, and he told me to return to the test office. I pulled into the parking lot and parked at an angle but still between the lines.

He told me I lost a point for not parking straight, but I still passed the test. I waited for my driver's license, which had two pieces, one for the picture and the other for a folded paper with my name and address.

I felt proud that I got my license and was more excited that I could drive the car to the high school and show it off to all the girls while making all the redneck jocks with their Ford pickup trucks jealous. I did not know the positive comments I would get from the guys at school because of the colour, but both the guys and the girls loved my Firebird.

On the weekend, I went to a performance store and bought some bright orange paint for the Chevy engine block. I also purchased some chrome parts and braided hoses for the engine. Once I was done, the car was a classic shiny showpiece.

Rick and I drove the car to Toronto to visit my older sister, the first time I had seen her since she stood there and had me turned in to the police with Shane and Laura. At that time, I did not understand what had happened until many years later. Then I drove back to Exeter, and it was good practice for me to drive on the highway again after my incident with Grand Theft Auto after moving back to Toronto. This time, no looking over my shoulder for flashing lights.

Rick and I frequented the quarter-mile race strip in Cayuga, now known as Toronto Motorsports Park. The car always drew a crowd, and we often displayed it at car shows, scouring for performance parts to enhance its speed. Rick had his collection, including a cream-yellow bumblebee-striped 1967 Camaro SS and a sleek Corvette, which we would cruise around, turning heads wherever we went.

Rick's workplace provided him with a pickup truck, his go-to for winter or whenever he was not behind the wheel of his hot rods. One of our more ambitious projects was a Ford GT 500 kit car mounted on a Volkswagen Beetle chassis. This low-riding beauty resembled a Lamborghini but desperately needed bodywork and interior finishing. Despite our initial enthusiasm, we eventually admitted defeat, and Rick sold it off, headaches and all.

Living with Rick meant being surrounded by an ever-changing array of vehicles. After Spike's loss, Rick needed to cheer me up, so we got another dog. Rick found a Rottweiler breeder nearby, and we chose a female puppy with the makings of a champion.

As we named her, Helga Von Hindenburg came from a prestigious German bloodline, complete with microchips, tattoos, and papers. Walking Helga around town was a joy, though initially more of a drag until she learned to follow the leash. Everyone adored her, including other dogs, and she became a beloved part of our lives.

Among Rick's acquisitions was an old model cream-coloured Mercedes Benz diesel, reminiscent of something from "The Untouchables." We added a boomerang antenna, giving it a limousine-like appearance. We packed the Benz for a vacation to Florida, aiming to cross the Port Huron bridge to the United States. However, customs denied us entry after checking my record, so we rerouted our plans.

Disappointed but undeterred, we set our sights on an all-inclusive resort in Puerto Plata, Dominican Republic, marking my first time leaving North America. The flight was exhilarating, and as we descended, the sight of lush green mountains and palm trees took my breath away. Upon landing, the humid air hit me, and as we navigated customs and immigration, the adventure truly began.

Outside, children and teens offered to carry our luggage for a peso, a chaotic scene as we tried to find our bus. The drive to the resort was eye-opening, passing through villages where swine roamed freely, and emaciated cattle and horses grazed, often with birds perched on their backs. The resort sat atop a hill, offering a stunning view but requiring a taxi ride to reach the village below.

Renting a dirt bike, we explored the area, including

a gondola ride to the top of the highest mountain. Despite my fear of heights, the view from the summit was breathtaking, overlooking the entire island and the ocean beyond. The villages, while picturesque during the day, revealed a different side at night, bustling with activities, including prostitution.

During our time in the Dominican Republic, we explored flea markets and casinos where alcohol flowed freely. While the buffet offered repetitive meals, the abundance of fruits was a redeeming feature. Unfortunately, I fell ill from the water and suffered sunstroke, forcing me to rest for a couple of days. Despite this setback, it was an unforgettable experience, marking my first trip outside North America.

The following winter, we returned to the Dominican Republic to a different part of the island. Rick rented a dune buggy with an open roof and sides, reminiscent of the beach-driving buggies. Lacking Spanish fluency, we hired a local boy from a beach known for its saltwater crocodiles.

He guided us for the day, assisting with translations and securing our needs for a few pesos. Our adventurous spirit led us to drive across the island towards Haiti, visiting the capital and various cities. However, our journey was challenging. We encountered police stops where money was solicited in exchange for a package of small crackers, a peculiar trade.

Following the advice of our local guide, we took the back roads through the mountains to avoid further encounters with the police. As night fell, our vehicle struggled over rugged terrain, eventually coming to a halt.

Stranded in the mountains, we sought help from a nearby village. Sleeping in grass huts with mosquito nets, the night felt like an African safari, with unexpected sounds and sights. In the morning, the town revealed a scene from a National Geographic magazine, with women washing clothes in a creek shared with bony cattle and bathing children.

Eager to return to civilization, we were grateful for the villagers' assistance in turning our buggy downhill and jumpstarting it to charge the battery. Their kindness and the unique experiences of our journey stayed with me, reminding me of the vast and diverse world beyond North America.

After our mountain misadventure, the downhill journey provided the boost our buggy needed to recharge its battery, ensuring a smooth ride back to our hotel. Relieved to be back in familiar territory, we spent the remainder of our trip relaxing in the tourist areas and lounging on the beaches.

The tropical sun gave me a deep brown tan, a tangible souvenir of our Dominican adventure. As our vacation ended, I found myself yearning for the familiar streets of Exeter.

Upon our return, Rick's increasingly busy schedule ended our days of travelling together. I spent more time at home with Gloria and June, although our relationship remained distant and awkward. With Rick's help, I secured a one-bedroom apartment above a variety store owned by a friendly older couple outside Exeter. The prospect of having my own space excited me, and I eagerly decorated it with lamps, paintings, and other personal touches.

To keep me company, I decided to get a dog and chose a Samoyed Husky pup. However, I soon realized that a high-energy breed like hers needed to be more suitable for apartment living. She remained restless and destructive despite my efforts to burn off her excess energy with long walks.

One evening, I returned home to find the apartment in ruins; the dog had destroyed furniture and left a mess everywhere. Overwhelmed, I made a difficult decision regarding the dog and my living situation.

Without saying a word to Rick or Stan, I left the apartment behind and moved in with Leanne and her family at their farmhouse outside Exeter. Adjusting to life there was challenging, especially with Leanne's obvious affection for me and her parents' watchful eyes. Despite the constraints of their strict lifestyle, we formed a small Jehovah group, though our activities were limited.

Living with Leanne's family was a stark contrast to my previous adventures. Still, it taught me valuable lessons about responsibility, adaptability, and the importance of understanding and respecting diverse ways of life.

11

NEW FRIENDS, NEW BEGINNINGS

Making friends with the popular kids was never my forte, given everything I had been through. I am trying to remember the classroom where I met my best friend in school, but it was either art or math. His name was Jack Newman; he was a short, overweight kid with a very vocal demeanour, the heaviest in school. He had a group of friends who were considered nerdy and unattractive. Jack and I became fast friends, hanging out every day. One evening, he invited me to join him at his youth group at the Pentecostal church on the outskirts of town. Despite my reservations, as I was still involved with the Jehovah clan, he assured me it was different – more like a social gathering with a band, trips, and activities like laser tag and camping. Intrigued, I agreed to go, though I made no commitments to him or his pastor.

The atmosphere was lively upon arrival, with a band set up at the front of the basement room and rows of chairs for about twenty people. The youth pastor, Keith, led the band and the group in worship. I recognized a few people from school, including Kate, whose dad was my math teacher. Sitting beside Kate was her friend Margret, a tall Dutch girl with bleach-blond hair and blue eyes, my height. Margret glanced back at me several times throughout the evening, giggling with Kate.

Keith delivered a message from the Bible, and after the service, I was introduced to him. He mentioned attending our high school during lunch breaks for Bible study. While initially hesitant, I decided to try it to make new friends. Margret, who worked as a lifeguard and lived on a dairy farm with her family, caught my attention. Despite the significant age gap between her and her youngest brother, who was only three years old, she seemed friendly and welcoming. She was also only two years younger than me.

Attending the church and youth group with Jack introduced me to a new social circle, including my old friends Luke and Beth Adams from my public school. While I initially attended a few lunchtime Bible study sessions, I decided it was not for me and stopped going. Nonetheless, the experience opened a new chapter in my life, bringing new friendships and a sense of belonging during the transition. As I spent more time with Luke, I learned about his family's struggles. His father was hospitalized with a mental illness, leaving Luke's mother and sister, Beth, to manage on their own. Despite their efforts to renovate their house, it looked precarious, reflecting the instability within their family.

One night, while watching a movie at Luke's house, a disturbing incident occurred. Beth, asleep beside Luke and me on the bed, their mother came on the bed wearing only a thin nightgown. She suddenly climbed on top of me, attempting to initiate intimacy by having sexual intercourse. I quickly pushed her away, feeling shocked and uncomfortable. She argued that she deserved love and affection, but I explained that I had feelings for someone else and could not betray that. This experience brought back memories of my past traumas, and I distanced myself from Luke's house after that.

Another memory from Luke's house involved an unsettling event where we shot a wild cat on his property. It was a wild barn cat that kept getting into their house, so I shot it with a rifle with hollow tip bullets that left nothing of the cat except fur. This act, while normalized in my past experiences with the Burkes, made me reflect on the desensitization to violence that had developed within me. Despite these challenges, our youth group activities continued, including visits to the Stratford Pentecostal church, where Luke was interested in a girl named Kristen, Margret's friend.

I admired Luke's red 1986 Pontiac Fiero, which reminded me of a Ferrari and sat low to the ground like a race car. One day, a frightening incident occurred while driving through a snowy town outside Exeter in Huron Park. A group of girls crossing the road did not pay attention after a transport truck passed them going one way, and we were travelling the other way. The four girls froze in the middle of the road as Luke swerved to miss them but hit the last girl. She reflected off the front hood and over the top of the car. She was projected fifty feet, losing her boots and landing in the snow bank on the side of the road. The Fiero came to a skidding stop in the middle of the road as I grasped my breath, realizing we had just run over a girl. Thankfully, after the ambulance and police arrived, Luke was cleared, and the girl was going to be ok, thanks to the car being made of plastic.

It was December 21, and the youth group was having Margret's birthday party at her house. I felt mixed emotions, including jealousy toward her loving family, something I had never experienced. Her father made a traditional Dutch Christmas treat, Olie Bollen: balls of deep-fried dough with raisins and icing sugar added to the warm and welcoming atmosphere. All her close friends came along with the youth pastor and his girlfriend. I sat beside Margret and her friend Kate on the couch as they played this game called "Broom Broom Sweep the Room," where someone stands up with a broom and points to someone, and they need to guess who they picked. I initially did not get the game until Margret told me they always knew the answer. Despite a snowstorm, Margret offered to drive me home, leading to a meaningful conversation that began our friendship.

During this period, I shifted my religious beliefs, as I decided to stay with the Pentecostal church and leave behind the Jehovah's Witnesses, which had begun to feel like a cult to me. I embraced this new community, feeling more at home and supported. The Pentecostal church gave me a sense of belonging and acceptance I had not experienced before. Unlike the Jehovah's Witnesses, there was no judgment based on appearance, and I could attend services in jeans, feeling comfortable and respected. As I committed myself to this new faith, I needed to find a new place to live, and I was fortunate to rent a room from a senior couple, Norm and Marylou, who lived within walking distance of downtown Exeter.

Working at the Hasty Market on Main Street became my first full-time job. I worked my way up to crucial holder, responsible for closing the store and managing cash drops. During my time off, I enjoyed exploring the town, listening to Christian bands on my Walkman cassette player, and visiting Jay at his parents' upholstery shop behind the White Squirrel restaurant.

Another job I found myself at Huron House, a sanctuary for spirited teenage girls whose lives were intricately woven with quadriplegia. Keith's girlfriend, a beacon of compassion, ushered me into this role—a role that challenged the depths of my empathy. Each day, I had the privilege to nourish, cleanse, and move in harmony with these extraordinary young souls. Yet, the emotional landscape was complex, a tapestry of inspiration shadowed by the weight of reality. It was a profound chapter, albeit brief, that etched a lasting impression on my heart, reminding me of the resilience and grace that blooms in the face of adversity.

One significant event during this time was getting my first credit card at Eaton's in London, which allowed me to make store purchases. Jay, always eager for new gadgets, persuaded me to buy him a Walkman CD player for his van, promising to pay me back, though he never did. Despite this, we continued attending youth groups, forming friendships with

Margret, Kath, and others, and occasionally joining the Stratford Pentecostal youth group for activities.

I also encountered a Dutch visitor at the church whose flirtatious behaviour caught my attention. Despite not being in a relationship with Margret then, her presence made me uncomfortable around her. One evening, while alone at my place, things escalated, and we slept together on the couch. This encounter made me uneasy, especially as Margret and others in the youth group started to assume we were dating. After her visit, the Dutch girl returned home to the Netherlands, and I never saw her again. This experience, while brief, made me realize the complexity of relationships and the importance of communication and boundaries. It also marked a shift in my relationship with Margret as I tried to navigate the aftermath of this encounter while maintaining our friendship.

The weekend Youth Convention in Kitchener/Waterloo was the talk of the youth group, with excitement buzzing about the prospect of staying in university dorms and attending conferences and concerts from various churches across the province. Despite my initial disappointment at being unable to afford the trip, Keith, our youth pastor, produced a solution thanks to donations from generous church members. Sharing a room with Jay and a few other guys, I entered the convention with mixed feelings, unsure what to expect.

However, what unfolded before me was a powerful display of faith and devotion. Witnessing young people being filled with the Holy Spirit, speaking in tongues, and experiencing spiritual manifestations, I was fascinated and apprehensive.

I felt a stirring sensation during an altar call, where hundreds of teens gathered to seek spiritual guidance and healing. As pastors laid hands on the attendees, cries echoed through the auditorium as individuals fell to the ground, overwhelmed by God's presence. It was a surreal scene, reminiscent of something from a cult classic yet undeniably real and transformative. At that moment, as memories of my past trauma flooded my mind, I felt an overwhelming sense of release. Tears streamed down my face as I surrendered my burdens to a higher power, embracing the healing and redemption offered by my faith. It was a profound experience that left an indelible mark on my soul, guiding me toward healing and spiritual renewal.

A profound transformation unfolded within me at the end of the summer of August 1991. I embraced faith with open arms and became a born-again Christian, a milestone that marked a new chapter in my life's journey. I commemorated this pivotal moment by acquiring my first NIV leather reference Bible, inscribing within its pages the date that signified my spiritual rebirth and the memorable youth convention.

That weekend emerged as the most enchanting experience I had ever shared with friends—friends who radiated the warmth and authenticity of the family I yearned for during my childhood. The true highlight of the convention wasn't the insightful conferences or the enlightening seminars, nor was it the solemn act of dedicating my life to Jesus. Instead, it was the simple joy of dining in the hall, exchanging smiles with Margret, whose presence added a sparkle to the moment.

As we reclined on the grassy hillside, basking in the interludes between concerts, laughter echoed among us. For the first time, I was enveloped in the embrace of genuine friendship, a feeling so profound that it imprinted upon my heart forever. On the convention's final day, I wandered through the bustling tents, each brimming with unique treasures. I eagerly collected memorabilia, starting with bracelets inscribed with the letters "W.W.J.D."—a famous phrase that stood for "What Would Jesus Do." These bracelets were more than just accessories; they were symbols of shared faith and a reminder to live by Jesus' teachings.

I also picked up a few t-shirts from DC Talk, the renowned Australian Christian pop band that had taken the music scene by storm. Their energetic performances and heartfelt lyrics made them a favourite among fans. Additionally, I found some cassette tapes of other influential artists like Bryan Duncan and Petra, whose music profoundly impacted the Christian rock genre. After that unforgettable weekend, I was deeply immersed in the vibrant world of Jesus Fest and Christian rock. The experience left me with a newfound appreciation for the music and the community that celebrated it.

During the warm summer months, I often found myself at the Mitchell Lions Club, where Margret worked as a lifeguard. I would visit her, taking the opportunity to enjoy a refreshing swim and meet her fellow lifeguards. They would gather in the back room, chatting and laughing between their rotations on the deck, moving from one lifeguard chair to another. Margret's competitive spirit shone brightly as she joined swim teams, competing against other towns for medals. Watching her strive for excellence reminded me of Julie from foster care, who always tried to fit in, win, and rise to the top. Margret and Julie shared a relentless drive and determination that left a lasting impression on me.

Margret embarked on a new chapter at Wilfrid Laurier University in Kitchener/Waterloo, her heart set on mastering the art of physical education. Our bond, which blossomed beyond friendship during her final high school year, now faced the test of distance. I had been her steadfast companion many a night, nestled on the couch in the quiet sanctuary of her spare bedroom, just a whisper away from where her parents slumbered up the stairs and beside Margret's room on the main floor. In the embrace of her family, I found a second home.

According to scripture, the next step after giving my life to Jesus was to be baptized. Beneath the wooden arches, cradled by the harmonious voices of our congregation, I experienced a rite of passage. Margret's father, a pillar of strength and faith, guided me into the crystalline embrace of the baptismal pool. As I submerged, the Senior pastor's voice cast a sacred spell, weaving scripture into the very fabric of my being. I emerged, not just cleansed, but reborn, my spirit dancing with newfound purpose. In that instant, a bond was forged with Margret's family, as tangible and enduring as the faith pulsing within me—a bond I believed unbreakable.

Yet, as I stood there, drenched in water and revelation, I couldn't help but ponder the path that led me here. Margret, a beacon of purity and devout conviction, embodied the virtues her family cherished. And I, with a past checkered by shadows, was the very archetype her parents had cautioned against. It was a dichotomy that left me wondering—could someone like me genuinely be worthy of such grace? We spent our days walking hand in hand, sharing kisses that she believed were promises of a future together. At night, we'd talk in her room about her upcoming move and how it made me worry about our relationship. I feared losing her once she was at university, surrounded by athletes and her love for sports. So, I started to push the boundaries, trying to hold on to what we had, even though I knew it was wrong.

She told me that her kiss was reserved for her future husband, but I pushed it further, and she let it happen, maybe out of fear that she might lose me and have fallen in love with me already. I removed her clothes, and we engaged in intercourse while she lay on the bed as tears ran down the sides of her cheeks. I felt guilty at that moment, but she was not just another girl I slept with. She was someone who truly loved me to give herself, believing I was the one.

The stairs groaned with creaks, and the washroom door closed upstairs as I bid Margret goodnight. The declaration of our bond to her parents was met with resistance; her father's words, a stark dismissal of my worthiness as Margret's partner, echoed in my mind. There was no turning back from our chosen path, a path of defiance and determination in the face of doubt. The challenge was set, and the night was ours to claim.

The saga of my 1982 Camaro Iroc Z28 reached its twilight as it stood, a silent relic at the farm's edge, its 'For Sale' sign a testament to our shared history. During our courtship, vehicles came and went like fleeting shadows. The latest, a Chevy S10 pickup, awaited transformation under my hands. With dreams of customization fueling our quest, Margret and I ventured across the border in her trusty brown Dodge Sundance, a chariot of determination.

Our destination: a New York State junkyard, a treasure trove half an hour from the Canadian border. There, a classic awaited—a robust eight-cylinder Chevy 327 engine, once the heart of a 1970 tow truck. For a mere five hundred dollars, it was ours. To our astonishment, it nestled perfectly in the Sundance's trunk, a mechanical puzzle piece fitting into place. With the back seats surrendered to our ambition, we ferried our prize home, the engine's weight anchoring us to the road and each other.

My trusty S10's journey ended abruptly on the bustling Gardiner Expressway in the heart of Toronto. Amid the city's pulse, things worsened when an inattentive driver in a Honda Civic overlooked the halted sea of cars ahead. He slid under my truck's rear axle with no time to react. The impact was catastrophic—his vehicle was accordioned right up to the windshield, airbags bursting like sudden clouds. Amid the chaos, my coffee betrayed me, splashing a bitter brown across my clothes.

Frustration boiled within me as I surveyed the

damage: my S10's transmission and engine were shoved unceremoniously into the radiator, its lifeblood spilling onto the asphalt. The engine, barely broken in, now lay in a pool of its fluids—a disappointing dance with the insurance company ensued. Yet, fortune smiled upon me with a generous settlement and the silver lining. I kept the truck.

With a twist of fate, I resurrected the engine, giving it a new home in a 1989 Pontiac Formula Firebird—a machine that echoed the tremendous nostalgia of the iconic Knight Rider. The 350 engine under the hood wasn't just any motor; it shared its lineage with the Corvettes of the seventies—renowned for their formidable torque and horsepower. It was a hobby that kept my hands busy and my mind sharp, especially while Margret was immersed in her studies. It was my form of meditation, a way to channel my energy positively and avoid mischief.

The summer sun had set for the last time, and Margret was on the brink of a new chapter—university. As I stood in the driveway, the grey Ford pickup truck under the weight of her bed and the countless belongings she deemed essential for her first year in residence. My heart pounded with panic and fear, tears dripping silently down my cheeks as Margret prepared to leave. She tried to soothe my anxiety with promises of school breaks and Christmas visits, but her words felt like whispers.

Her parents, standing nearby, chuckled at my distress. It was as if they believed that once Margret was at university, she would find someone more fitting —someone with a future as bright as the sun, unlike me. Their reassurances to not worry and that I would see her again felt hollow, echoing insincerity. I accompanied Margret to the university, helping unload her life into a small dorm room. She proudly showed us around the campus, her brown Sundance car parked nearby, ready to bring her back to the farm during exams and holidays.

Occasionally, I would drive down to visit Margret, sneaking into her room despite her having a roommate and the co-ed nature of the dorms. Margret thrived there, donning a school jacket emblazoned with the Golden Hawks and Laurier. She immersed herself in sports, cheering at football and basketball games, and took up a job as a lifeguard at the pool to support herself. Margret had made some close friends with whom she spent her time on campus. Some of the girls were not Christian, which started to bother me as she went to the campus bar called the Turret for drinks, dancing, and social events. She told me she did not drink and was only being social with her friends, and I felt that might make us drift apart.

The distance between us grew as the days turned into months. Her time at university and my solitude seemed an unfortunate match for our future. Uncertainty loomed over us—would we last a year, or could we endure four? I clung to the need to feel loved by someone, even if it was fleeting, as the shadows of doubt crept in.

TRYING TO FIND MY PLACE IN THIS WORLD

Dating Margret for four years was a rollercoaster, especially for her. Despite my constant moving from city to city, her love for me remained unwavering and robust. From 1992 to 1996, I was a bit of a nomad, but I made sure to live in Kitchener on River Road to be closer to Margret and spend more time with her. During this time, I landed a job at the Williams Coffee Pub on King Street, near Waterloo University, where we often had our youth conventions. It was a stroke of luck that the district manager there was the same person who had trained me back in Stratford.

As the night supervisor, I mastered the art of crafting specialty drinks and serving food to a lively crowd of students who would hang out at all hours, sipping coffee and smoking. Every night, my eyes burned, and my clothes reared of smoke. Despite the vibrant atmosphere, the job took a toll on me, and after a few months, my depression set in, leading me to walk away.

During my summer in London, Ontario, I stayed at the Lambda Chi Alpha fraternity house at the University of Western Ontario. One evening, I met some frat boys at a local bar called 'The Ridout.' Over a few drinks, I shared my story about coming up from California for the summer and searching for a place to stay. As luck would have it, one of the guys mentioned that a room was available since one of their brothers had gone home for the summer. They offered me the front room, and just like that, I had a place to call home for the season. GT's was our central water hole where we would spend the weekends drinking and meeting girls.

One of the Alpha Omicron Pi girls, who looked like Heather Locklear from Melrose Place, took me back to their frat house, thinking I was a brother from California. After a shower, I walked shamefully into the kitchen the following day, where a dozen girls were having breakfast. They smiled and giggled, inviting me to join them. I politely declined and quickly exited before they could ask any fraternity-related questions I had no clue how to answer.

That moment didn't last long. One weekend in Toronto, I lounged on the grassy hill in downtown

College Park, enjoying people-watching. Suddenly, a few police officers approached me, accompanied by a Chinese man. The officers asked him if I was the person, and he confirmed with a nod. Before I knew it, I was arrested for theft and taken to the station. It all came rushing back to me then. I had forgotten about the time when a gay Chinese man had tried to solicit me for sex. He had taken me to his place, and while he was in the shower, I impulsively grabbed some of his expensive clothes and a necklace and ran away before he finished.

The police asked me where the items were, and I told them they were in London, where I was staying. They drove me there to collect the evidence against me, and foolishly, I went along, adding another mark to my criminal record. While gathering my things at the frat house, the boys got aggressive and demanded rent money. They saw the police outside, and I told them I was leaving with the officers. That was the end of that chapter, but at least I got a taste of university life.

After Margret's first year of school, she moved out of her dorm and rented a house with four other girls. Talk about six degrees of separation—one of her new housemates was Blake Burke, from my six years in foster care. What were the odds? Out of all the universities and programs, she ended up in the same one as my girlfriend. Blake knew all my secrets from ages ten to sixteen and had seen me naked more times than I could count. I was convinced she'd spill everything to Margret, ending our relationship.

Toronto became my sanctuary during our four years of dating, a city that seemed to pull me back into the depths of my past. Encouraged by countless comments about my looks and my six-foot frame, I decided to try my hand at modelling. I joined an agency in Toronto and competed for Top Model at the Regal Constellation Hotel near Pearson International Airport. The event was a magnet for top agencies from Toronto, the United States, and Europe, all scouting for fresh talent.

Walking down the runway in a pair of swimming trunks, shirtless, in front of hundreds of strangers was nerve-wracking. Despite my insecurities, I managed to complete all the categories. Judie Walsh and Elmer Olson stood out among the top model agencies in Toronto. I was fortunate enough to get a callback from Judie, a woman in her fifties with shaggy hair, oversized glasses, and a heavyset frame.

Judie lived in a Victorian brick house just off Yonge Street, north of Summerhill on Roxborough St. When I arrived, I was ushered into a room to wait for her, and hours seemed to pass before she finally attended to me. The house was teeming with cats, and the scent of alcohol lingered in the air as she spoke to me, adding to the surreal atmosphere of the encounter.

Judie sent me to one of the top photographers in Toronto, who spent an entire day capturing me in black and white. We worked on creating a versatile portfolio featuring me in various outfits and headshots that I could use for casting calls and meetings with international agencies. My efforts paid off as I landed features in store catalogues for Sears and Eaton and strutted down the runway in fashion shows across Toronto.

During this whirlwind of new experiences, I met a tall and stunningly beautiful Korean girl at the agency. Her elegance and charm were captivating, and for the first time, I found myself developing feelings for someone of Asian descent. It was an unexpected but exciting turn in my journey, adding another layer of complexity to my life in the modelling world.

We developed a physical connection, but it was short-lived. Financial constraints made it difficult to take her to hotels, and her father was adamantly opposed to her dating anyone who wasn't Korean. It was surprising to encounter such close-mindedness from someone who had lived in Canada for so long. In hindsight, he probably made the right choice. My interest in her was primarily superficial, driven by her stunning looks rather than any desire for a lasting relationship. My heart and future were already set on

Margret, and I looked forward to building a long-term relationship with her.

I decided to embark on an adventure to California, so I told Margret I was heading to Los Angeles to meet with some agencies. I booked a ticket on Greyhound bus lines, marking my first trip to the United States alone. The journey to California would take three days of continuous driving, and I was thrilled at the prospect of travelling through so many states.

My trip was planned with four connecting tickets, allowing me the flexibility to explore other cities along the way before catching the next bus. However, my excitement to reach Los Angeles kept me focused on my final destination. The anticipation of what awaited me in LA made every mile of the journey feel like a step closer to a new chapter in my life.

I had a black leather and wool jacket that I had customized with the bright yellow logo of Models Inc., a spinoff of Beverly Hills 90210, embroidered on the front. With my hair styled up and long sideburns reminiscent of Luke Perry, I transformed into a character straight out of the show. My go-to line when chatting with girls on the bus was that I was heading to Hollywood to join the cast for the upcoming season. Surprisingly, it worked like a charm. I was surrounded by girls, making out with strangers who were all too eager to believe my fabricated story. The journey was a whirlwind of excitement and adventure, fueled by the thrill of the unknown and the allure of my Hollywood fantasy.

The story took an unexpected turn once I reached Las Vegas. The money I had brought, including what I had set aside for my return trip to Toronto, was nearly all gone, squandered on slot machines and generous tips. I was left with only a few hundred dollars. When the bus finally arrived in downtown Los Angeles on 7th Street around 2 am, I felt like I had entered a different world. The area resembled East L.A. I stood out like a sore thumb in my red blazer and tie from LA Chateau.

The streets were eerily quiet, with no cars in sight. Burning garbage bins cast flickering shadows, and homeless people huddled under cardboard shelters. Overhead, the sound of an LAPD helicopter added to the tense atmosphere. I had never walked so fast, eager to find a safer place and escape the unsettling scene.

My journey took an unexpected turn when I found myself at Cherry Beach, a Spanish convent providing shelter for undocumented Mexicans who needed to improve their English. One of the girls there took a liking to me and kindly offered to show me around the LA bus system. With her guidance, I navigated the city and headed to the Metro station in Hollywood.

From there, I walked down the iconic Hollywood Blvd and Highland Ave, marvelling at the Chinese

Theater and the Hollywood Walk of Fame. The stars embedded in the sidewalk and the historic theatre brought the glitz and glamour of Hollywood to life. My adventure continued as I visited the vibrant Santa Monica Pier, the eclectic Venice Beach, and the luxurious Rodeo Drive. Each location offered a unique slice of LA's diverse culture and charm, making my trip an unforgettable experience.

Desperate to return to Canada, I was in a dire situation. I was kicked off the train for not having a valid ticket and had no money left for food. In a moment of panic, I called Margret and concocted a story about being in the hospital with a concussion after being robbed of all my money. I told her I had no way to get home and needed help. Ever the caring and supportive girlfriend,

Margret likely asked her father for assistance and sent me a few hundred dollars through Western Union. I was immensely relieved and grateful that she came through for me, but a wave of guilt washed over me for fabricating such a sad story to get the money. The weight of my deception lingered even as I boarded the bus back home, knowing I had taken advantage of her kindness.

During our time together, I embarked on a whirlwind journey to Europe and South America, chasing my dreams of becoming a model. These travels were more than just career moves; they were my lifeline, a way to combat my depression and hold onto hope for Margret and me. Despite my troubled past and the confessions I made to her—like admitting I had been with other girls while we were together—Margret stood by me, defying what anyone might have warned her about me.

Feeling stifled by Toronto's modelling scene, I set my sights on the electrifying fashion capitals of Paris and Milan. Ultimately, I chose Milan, immersing myself in this iconic city. Here, I discovered a world brimming with opportunities, a renewed sense of purpose, and an exhilarating energy that fueled my passion.

When I told Margret I was heading to Italy for a modelling gig with a top agency, I painted a picture of success and glamour. But the truth was, I needed this adventure to find happiness and stave off the creeping shadows of depression. This journey wasn't just about work but about rediscovering myself in the heart of fashion's most thrilling playground.

My journey began with a delightful flight on KLM to Amsterdam, Netherlands. The service was exceptional, and complimentary food and beverages, including alcohol, were provided. This was my first visit to Holland, the birthplace of Margret's family, and I was thrilled to experience everything I had heard about finally. The anticipation of exploring Amsterdam, with fond memories of Margret and my encounter with the Dutch acquaintance in our church, made my layover something to look forward to.

Imagine experiencing first-class treatment while seated in economy! My flight attendant, assigned to my section, struck up a conversation with me. I mentioned that it was my first time visiting Holland and that I had no idea where to go for the day. Surprisingly, she revealed that this was her last flight and offered to pick me up after I cleared customs. She suggested meeting in the parking area in front of the terminal.

I blinked in disbelief and shook my head to ensure I had heard her correctly. She was stunning, with bleach-blond hair, crystal blue eyes, and an utterly captivating accent. Her offer left me momentarily speechless, but I responded with a big smile: "Okay, see you after landing!" The car honked as she pulled up beside me. I swung the door open and leaped inside, feeling a rush of excitement. No need to stress about baggage claim—my luggage was already on its way to Milan!

She lived just outside Amsterdam, in the charming city of Haarlem, known for its picturesque cobblestone streets and medieval architecture. After a lovely day together, she drove me back to her flat. Once she changed her clothes in the living room, she kissed me tenderly, and we embraced each other tightly. I didn't want to rush things; she was too kind. Later,

She took me on a scenic drive through the breath-taking tulip fields and iconic windmills, a scene straight out of a postcard. Eventually, we headed back to the airport. I knew I would have a layover in Amsterdam on my return to Toronto, so I planned to explore downtown Amsterdam on my way back.

Upon arriving in Milan, Italy, I hopped on a train from the airport to the bustling Milano Centrale Railway Station. Stepping out into the streets, I was immediately struck by the stunning architecture and the flurry of pigeons darting through the air. It felt like I had walked straight into a scene from a movie.

Eager to explore, I jumped on the metro and visited the iconic Duomo. Climbing the stairs and emerging into the main square, I was greeted by the breathtaking sight of the Cathedral of Santa Maria, also known as the Milan Cathedral. To my right stood the Galleria Vittorio Emanuele II, Italy's oldest shopping gallery, with its magnificent glass dome and elegant arcades. The blend of history and modernity was mesmerizing.

Life in Milan was far less glamorous than I had envisioned for my modelling career. However, one night at Club Hollywood in downtown Milan's bustling Corso Como district changed everything. As I approached the club, my appearance granted me instant access, bypassing the long line of hopefuls waiting to get in. With a nod, the doorman spotted me and beckoned me over, leading me straight to the exclusive VIP area where luxury knew no bounds.

Drinks flowed freely, and the atmosphere buzzed with the presence of the top supermodels of the 90s, whose faces graced countless magazine covers. I mingled with renowned designers, dancing and celebrating until the early morning. It was a surreal experience, a fleeting taste of the 'plastic dream' I had always imagined.

A powerful woman in the industry once approached me; her name is now a distant memory. She was a talent scout with a keen eye, and she took me under her wing. But her intentions were far from noble. She sought to manipulate and control me, desiring me as her plaything. Her after-parties were a haze of excess, with tables laden with cocaine to keep me trapped while she exploited me. Male models, desperate for extra cash, often found themselves in secret bars, "Dancing For Dollars," a strip club for affluent women.

She whisked me away to one of Milan's top agencies, Eye for Me, and even paid them to take me under their wing. Despite the glamour, I was just a regular Canadian boy, uninterested in playing the game. Night after night at the club, the who's who of the fashion world slipped their phone numbers into my hand and made advances. But I wasn't gay, nor was I willing to advance my career based on who I hooked up with. I wanted to succeed on my terms, relying on my height and looks, not on compromising my values.

Imagine being whisked away to a hidden gem in Lake Como, where the majestic Alps guard a quaint village of cobblestone streets and charming little cafes. Each morning, after nights filled with revelry and the demands of pleasing the enigmatic madam, I would find solace in a cozy restaurant. By the window, I savoured the simple pleasure of a cappuccino paired with a crisp biscotti, watching the world wake up.

With her mysterious allure, the madam often reminded me I was merely her plaything, a fleeting amusement in her world. Yet, she promised to take care of me, a bittersweet assurance that lingered in my thoughts. As my days in Italy dwindled, my impending departure to Holland and Canada loomed ever closer, casting a shadow over my idyllic mornings in that enchanting village.

When I woke that morning, I knew it was time to return to Canada. She insisted I change my ticket to stay longer, wanting to control me until she no longer needed me. But I had a plan. I packed a small backpack, leaving my luggage in her room so she wouldn't suspect a thing. I told her it would cost 365,000 Lira, about two hundred US dollars, to change my ticket and that it had to be done at the airport.

As she got ready to drive me to Milan's Central

Station, I discreetly went through her room, slipping Versace leather pants, a hat, dress shirts, and some jewelry into my small backpack. We got into the car before she noticed anything was missing. When she dropped me off, I kissed her and promised to meet her back in the square around noon.

My flight was at 4 pm, and I was anxious she might catch up with me before I could leave. But she never did. As I boarded the plane, I felt relief and sadness. I was leaving Italy and my modelling dreams behind forever.

I couldn't wait to share my excitement with Margret as I walked through the door. "The trip was amazing!" I exclaimed, showing her the stunning photoshoots. "I got to work live runway shows for some of the top designers during Milan Fashion Week!" Margret's eyes lit up as she flipped through the photos. "Wow, these are incredible!"

I nodded, feeling a mix of pride and anxiety. "They said they'd pay me later, but… the money never came." I hesitated, then added, "I think they might have ripped me off." The truth was, things hadn't gone as smoothly as I'd let on. I just wanted to hold on to those moments in Milan and what could have been.

While in Toronto, I lived with an antique dealer whose family resided in Colombia, South America. One day, he invited me to join him on a week-long vacation to visit his relatives, generously offering to cover all the expenses. It sounded like an incredible opportunity, but I had a Rottweiler, a gift from my sister, who required a lot of attention and care.

Leaving my dog alone in the apartment wasn't an option, so I turned to a neighbour in my building who also had a dog. She agreed to look after my Rottweiler for the week. Our relationship was more complicated than just neighbours, as we were also romantically involved. I knew she would help me, even though I had taken advantage of her kindness. This trip was just one of my many adventures during that period, filled with complex relationships and unexpected journeys.

We touched down in the vibrant city of Cartagena, Colombia, nestled along the stunning Caribbean coast. Our home base was the charming house of my room-mate Miguel's cousin, a perfect starting point for our adventures. Miguel, ever the gracious host, took me on a captivating tour of Old Town, a historic gem dating back to the 16th century. As the sun set, we dined at quaint restaurants overlooking the picturesque harbour and cobblestone squares, the air filled with laughter and music.

The next day, we found ourselves at a cozy little café, savouring the local flavours. To my surprise, the waitress recognized Miguel and warmly introduced herself. Her presence was magnetic, a captivating blend of Shakira's fiery spirit and Penelope Cruz's elegance. Later, when I found myself alone, I couldn't resist the pull of her charm. We spent the night together at a nearby hotel, a whirlwind of passion and connection.

This enchanting encounter reignited my fascination with Spanish women. This flame had first sparked during a memorable trip to the Dominican Republic with my friend Richard a few years earlier. Cartagena, with its rich history and vibrant culture, had gifted me an unforgettable experience.

Miguel's offer of a free vacation with all expenses paid came with a catch. He wanted me to bring working girls back to the hotel at night. His thrill was watching me, a straight guy, with these girls. It was his money funding these encounters, after all. That was his thing, and it got him excited. So, when I casually mentioned that I had a fling with his friend at the café and missed out on the whole scene, he completely lost it.

We took a bus an hour away from Old Town to another city and got a hotel near the beach. Miguel and I walked along the boardwalk, and I noticed women dressed up standing near the light posts as it was getting dark. He told me they were working girls, and as we passed three women, Miguel started talking to them. He then looked at me and told me to pick one. Three generations stood together: a woman in her thirties, her mother in her fifties, and her daughter, who seemed to be around sixteen or seventeen.

The girl was slim, with long black curly hair, a tanned complexion, and dark brown eyes. She wore a one-piece Mandarin fitted dress. She looked so innocent that I couldn't believe she was there with her mother and grandmother. I told Miguel I wanted the girl who didn't speak any English. Miguel communicated this to the mother in Spanish and handed her some Pesos. The girl then returned to the hotel room with us.

I told Miguel I wanted to be alone with the girl, and he agreed to wait. I undressed the girl, and she lay there, just looking into my eyes as if she was lost. I felt a pang of guilt, which made me finish quickly. I gave her some extra money and told her to hide it from her mother. I think she understood me. Miguel was upset because I didn't let him participate.

The next day, we picked up another girl. This time, Miguel and I took turns with her. She seemed experienced and showed no emotions, which turned me off. She kept urging Miguel to finish so she could leave. It felt like being with a plastic doll, so I let Miguel finish and get dressed. I lost respect for myself and for Miguel. I was looking forward to returning to Canada, where I planned to end my association with him. I haven't heard from Miguel since.

When we returned from South America, I was greeted by a furious message from Margret demanding I pick up my dog immediately. The poor thing had been wreaking havoc in her room, leaving messes everywhere.

I was baffled. I thought I had left my dog with the girl from the park I'd been seeing. How did it end up at Margret's place? The park girl somehow got Margret's number and told her she couldn't take care of the dog anymore. Now, I'm dying to know what they talked about. Did the park girl spill the beans about us to Margret, knowing she was my girlfriend? The whole situation is a mystery!

Miguel and I shared a home for about a year while Margret was wrapping up her studies. We embarked on several adventures, including an unforgettable trip to Margarita Island in Venezuela. Having Miguel as my personal tour guide was a huge plus! I knew the cost of travelling with him, but the experience of exploring a beautiful Spanish-speaking country and the chance to share moments with a stunning Spanish woman made it all worthwhile. How could I possibly say no to such an adventure?

After leaving Miguel's apartment, I moved in with Roger, a friend from my club and bar days who had helped me get off the streets. We had kept in touch over the years, even after I started dating Margret. Living with Roger was an adventure. We travelled to Florida several times and flew to Las Vegas, where he, a die-hard Star Trek fan, took me to conventions. We would rent a convertible Mustang and cruise across California, making unforgettable memories.

Roger, being a property manager for several buildings, had me moving around the city quite a bit. Eventually, he settled into a house not far from his old apartment off Dufferin Street near Lawrence. This new place was perfect for me. It became my sanctuary where I could work on my Camaro and Firebird, adding performance parts and dressing up the engines with chrome and colourful wires. It was my other escape from depression, a passion that rivalled my love for travelling.

Dating Margret during her school years was a real challenge, as I couldn't be there for her as often as I wanted. This doesn't excuse my actions—my infidelity, lies, and relentless pursuit of money the wrong way. Returning to the spa felt like being shackled to a past I couldn't escape, and I unfairly used Margret as my way to try and break free from those chains.

It felt like Margret and I were drifting further apart, no matter how many times she forgave me. I couldn't find it myself to ignore my mistakes or seek her forgiveness. My heart hardened, and my soul darkened, even though I had given my life to Jesus. It was as if demons possessed me I couldn't cast out, the stronghold too overwhelming to bear. So, I pretended everything was fine, acting as if our relationship was on track to move to the next level, even though I knew it wasn't.

As I tried to distance myself from my past and grow closer to Margret, another wave of bad news hit me. It sent me spiralling back into a more profound depression, pushing Margret aside. Despite everything, I couldn't bring myself to leave her. With so much chaos, I felt utterly lost, unsure which direction to take.

13

PATRICK JOSEPH BROMLEY

One seemingly ordinary morning, I received an unexpected call from my sister, Janet. Her words hit me like a slap, forcing me to question everything I thought I knew about myself and my family. Who was I? And who was my father? Suddenly, the honesty of everyone in my family was in doubt. Why hadn't my mother been the one to break this news to me? It felt like it should have come from her lips.

The revelation was a bombshell, a smoking gun that pieced together the fragments of my family tree, revealing that one branch didn't belong. That branch was me. It had never occurred to me for twenty years to question my lineage. Despite the glaring clues, I had accepted what I was told: I was the only one among seven siblings with bleach-blond hair and blue eyes, while everyone else had hazel eyes and brown hair.

The phone call was direct: " Your father is sick in the hospital, and you need to see him." The tone of my sister's voice was not a revelation to her, as I would have assumed I was the only one in my family who was still in the dark about the truth. She told me to take down a phone number for a lady in St. John's, Newfoundland, who was my half-sister trying to contact me.

After hanging up with Janet, I immediately called my mother, eager to understand what was happening. She kept in close touch with all our relatives in St. John's, Newfoundland. When I asked her why my father was sick, I was under the impression she was referring to the father whose last name I bore, which left me bewildered. I hadn't heard from Bob Ryley since my teenage years. The only snippets of his life I knew were that he had remarried a stocky, outspoken, and controlling woman, and they lived on a farmhouse with horses. That was the extent of my knowledge about his current life.

This is when the bombshell hit me: " No, Jason Bob is not your father." Your birth father is Patrick Bromley from St. John's. You also have three sisters and two other brothers around the same age. I paused momentarily and then blurted out, " What the hell are you talking about?" I grew up all these years being passed from foster home to foster home, being tossed about as if I was disposable garbage, thinking my mother or father did not want me.

Who was Patrick Joseph Bromley? I did not know anything about him or that he even existed. Still, my mother kept this secret from me without being honest with me when I was nine years old, standing in the witness box at the family courthouse. The judge questioning both my mother and Mr. Ryley as to why I could no longer live with them would have been the appropriate time to stand up and come clean and say that there was another option for me to live with and get to know my birth father.

A whirlwind of emotions swirled in my mind when I thought about my mother, and resentment was undoubtedly among them. For nearly twenty-four years, she had kept a monumental secret from me. Yet, the blame wasn't hers alone. My biological father, Patrick, also played a part. He knew about my existence and received updates from my mother during my early years. However, he was married and had his own family, and they likely wanted to avoid the upheaval that my revelation would bring. They feared the backlash from his children, who would see their father not just as a parent but as a cheater who had fathered another child. This tangled web of secrecy and fear of judgment kept me hidden in the shadows of their lives.

When my father fell ill, I realized how little I knew about him. It wasn't until my mother sat me down and shared his story that I began to piece together his life. She handed me a couple of photographs: one of his wedding days, when he stood proudly beside his wife, and another of him laughing with friends. As I studied the images, I noticed the striking resemblance between us—the same chiselled jawline, cleft chin, and low eyebrows.

My mother then recounted how she met my father. They both worked at the same hospital in Ontario, and their story unfolded like an episode of "Three's Company." My mother and her husband, Bob Ryley, became close friends with my father, Patrick, through their work. Adding to the mix was my eccentric stepfather, Shane Bradley, who was searching for a place to stay and ended up renting a room from my mother and Bob. Their lives intertwined unexpectedly, creating a tapestry of relationships that shaped my understanding of family.

Patrick returned to his family in Newfoundland, leaving my mother pregnant and eventually giving birth to me. With my blue eyes, her husband must have had doubts about my paternity, which affected how he treated me until I was placed in foster care in 1979.

When I turned two, my mother divorced Bob and married Shane, with whom she had also been having an affair. I often wonder if my life would have changed if she had told Patrick I was his son. Perhaps my entire outlook on life and the following events would have changed.

With a mix of anxiety and urgency, I picked up the phone and dialled the number scribbled on the paper. A woman's voice answered, and I introduced myself as Patrick's son from Ontario. She paused, then revealed she was Bella, Patrick's eldest daughter. She had been trying to reach me about our father, who was gravely ill and admitted to Grace Hospital. Her voice trembled as she urged me to come quickly, fearing he might not have much time left. Bella, my newly discovered sister, shared that she was married, had a son, and lived in St. John's, where she worked as a teacher. She provided all her contact details, ensuring I could reach her once I arrived in Newfoundland.

After Margret's school classes, we finally had a heart-to-heart that night. I shared how my life had unravelled, feeling shocked and excited. My past trauma and stepfather had buried memories of that station wagon ride and the ferry to the island deep within me. I was so young then. Would those memories resurface once I was back on the ferry? I was about to revisit a significant part of my past and meet people who should have been in my life all along. Now, in the present, all paths converged, and we would finally come face to face.

With my bags packed and a mix of excitement and uncertainty, I boarded the VIA Rail train at Union Station in downtown Toronto. Saying goodbye to Margret was tough, especially since I didn't know when I'd be back. I promised to keep her updated about my father's situation. Settling into my cozy cabin seat, I couldn't help but feel a thrill of adventure. This was my first time taking a train journey across the East Coast to Halifax. From there, I'd catch a bus to Sydney, Nova Scotia, and finally board the ferry to Newfoundland. The journey ahead was long, but the promise of new experiences kept my spirits high.

I decided to stretch my legs and explore the train. The snack bar and lounge were bustling with activity, the aroma of freshly brewed coffee and baked goods wafting through the air. I grabbed a cup of coffee and went up to the Skyline dome. The panoramic view was breathtaking, with rolling hills and distant city land-scapes bathed in the golden hues of the setting sun. I sipped my drink, feeling the tension of the day melt away.

Returning to my seat, I noticed an older woman sitting alone across from me, perhaps in her 50s. Her eyes held a mix of anticipation and nostalgia. I started a conversation, and she said she would visit her children, whom she hadn't seen in years. Her face lit up as she spoke about them, and we exchanged stories over a couple of drinks. The evening grew darker, and the train's gentle rocking added a soothing rhythm to our conversation.

As the night deepened, I prepared my sleeping cabin, leaving the door slightly ajar. From my bed, I could see into her room opposite mine. She was reading a book, a soft smile playing on her lips. The sense of connection and shared humanity made the journey feel less lonely. The woman's persistent glances on the train were impossible to ignore. Eventually, she invited me to her cabin for a nightcap. It was clear where this was heading, and she brought back memories of Ingrid when I was sixteen—an older woman who knew exactly what she was doing.

After our nightcap and one-night stand, I wished her a good night and returned to my cabin, ensuring it was a comfortable farewell. As the cabins were dismantled and stored away the following day, we found ourselves seated apart, our conversations fading into silence. I enjoyed a quiet breakfast, reflecting on the journey ahead. Soon, the train pulled into Halifax, and I caught a bus to Nova Scotia. The scenic ride took about six to eight hours, and I arrived just in time to board the overnight ferry. As the ferry set sail, I looked forward to waking up in Newfoundland, ready for the bus adventure twelve hours to St. John's.

As the ferry glided into the quaint town of Channel-Port Aux Basques, nestled at the southwestern tip of Newfoundland, I stepped off the vessel into a landscape dotted with rugged rocks and lush grass. The small town, with its charming wooden houses scattered about, felt like Deja Vu from my past. I was here to catch the solitary morning bus that would take me across the island to the capital. There, I would finally meet my father face to face for the first time since my birth. Before his death, we would see eye to eye and unite our bloodlines.

After a long and tiring bus ride, I finally arrived in the bustling city and went to the hospital. This visit was special because I was about to meet my new sister for the first time. I hadn't told her I was in the province yet, so I wasn't sure if she was even at the hospital. I decided to call her after seeing my father. With the help of some incredibly friendly nurses, I found the floor and room where my father was staying.

As I approached the door, my heart began to race. I didn't know how I would react—would I cry or feel anything for this man I was about to see? The uncertainty of my emotions made each step heavier, but I knew this moment was critical.

I cautiously peeked through the small glass window

in the door, my heart pounding. Inside, a woman sat in a chair, her eyes fixed on the frail man lying on the bed, surrounded by a tangle of tubes and wires that monitored his every breath. The blonde-haired lady suddenly turned towards the door, her gaze on mine. My breath caught as she stood and walked towards me, her steps deliberate and measured.

She opened the door and stepped out, her eyes never leaving mine. "Hello," she said softly, a hint of a smile on her lips. "I'm Bella." My mind raced. Bella? The name echoed in my head. It was my sister, whom I had spoken to on the phone. As she stood before me, I was struck by our uncanny resemblance. It was like looking into a mirror but seeing a female version of myself.

"I've been trying to find you," she continued, her voice tinged with emotion. "I knew about you, but I didn't have any way to contact you until my mother reached out to your aunt. They were friends, and your aunt called your mother."

Her words hung in the air, the weight of our shared history pressing down on us. I felt a mix of emotions—relief, curiosity, and a deep sense of connection. This sister I had never known was standing before me, and our lives were about to change forever.

"Are you ready?" she whispered, her voice barely audible. She wanted me to meet our father. "He has been waiting for you," she added, her eyes filled with anticipation. With a deep breath, I opened the door and stepped into the room. The thin man on the bed turned his head towards me, his sunken eyes suddenly widening with recognition. A smile spread across his face, and a warm glow emanated from him.

His bony hand trembled as he lifted it towards me, reaching to hold my hand. I could see the effort it took for him to move, and my heart ached for him. As I grasped his hand, he tried to speak, his voice weak and raspy. I leaned in closer, lowering my ear to his mouth. "My son," he whispered, his voice filled with pride and emotion. "You are my son."

He couldn't speak much, the respirator's rhythmic hum filling the room. I sat in the chair beside him, holding his frail hand while Bella and I talked. His eyes followed our conversation intently as if he had been waiting almost twenty-four years to hear my voice.

Bella glanced at me, concern in her eyes. "Are you hungry?" she asked softly. "Father needs to rest, and the nurses will care for him." Reluctantly, I agreed. We left the room, and Mary drove me to her house; as we pulled up, a mix of nerves and excitement washed over me. I was about to meet her husband and son, extending the family I had only just begun to know.

After a delightful lunch with her family, Mary and I set out to meet my other two sisters. First, we met Mary, a few years younger but already following in her father's footsteps. She was tall and thin, with bright orange hair that seemed to glow in the sunlight and a strong Newfie accent that added a musical lilt to her words. She looked like a damsel straight out of the cobbled streets of Belfast, Ireland.

Bella suggested we stay at Mary's apartment overnight to bond and get to know each other better. The idea made me nervous—staying alone with two attractive women who were essentially strangers. But Bella insisted; for some reason, she didn't want to stay with her son and husband. It seemed she wanted to make up for lost time with me. With excitement and apprehension, we drove to the other side of St. John's, to Mount Pearl, to meet their youngest sister, Lily. As we approached, I couldn't help but wonder what she would be like.

She was the complete opposite of her sisters—short, chubby, with jet-black hair. She had a wild side to her, and her mischievous grin hinted at a rebellious spirit. Despite her differences, we all had an undeniable connection, a bond waiting to be discovered. Bella also told me I had two brothers living in Halifax, Luke and Jackson, who were also my age but were not close and did not know about me.

After all the family gatherings, we headed back to the hospital. I spoke with the doctors about my father's condition, but I didn't delve too deeply into the medical details. My father had been a long-time drinker, and I just wanted to focus on spending quality time with him. Leukemia had taken its toll on him, and his organs were failing with no chance to survive.

He could speak a little, and in those precious moments, he told me he had always talked about me. His ex-wife knew about me, too. Despite the years apart, his words had a sense of connection.

He had been living with his girlfriend for some years in a little house, and they graciously allowed me to stay there instead of getting a hotel room while I was in Newfoundland. It felt like a small piece of home in a place that was still so new to me.

So that night, we drove back to Mary's apartment, and Bella suggested we have a pyjama party where the three of us would sleep in the same bed. I remembered doing that as a child with my other sisters, but I was five then, not twenty-four, and I knew my other sisters well. These were strangers to me and only step-sisters at that, which made the situation more uncomfortable as I found myself sexually attracted to them.

The three of us clambered into the queen-sized bed, with Bella inside. I hadn't brought any sleeping clothes, so Mary kindly lent me a pair of her boyfriend's shorts and a shirt. In her thin, one-piece pyjama, Bella looked both comfortable and vulnerable. As we lay there, we reminisced about our childhoods, sharing stories of growing up in different provinces. The room was filled with laughter and nostalgia until we finally drifted off to sleep.

Bella, initially facing away from me, gradually shifted closer, her body pressing against mine. Instinctively, I wrapped my arm around her, holding her gently as she fell asleep. Sensing the intimacy and uneasiness, Mary left the room and slept on the couch. Bella's demeanour towards me had changed; she no longer saw me as her brother but as someone she might have met at Sam Shades, one of the popular bars on George Street.

The next day, I had a heartfelt conversation with my father about his family and my life. He expressed his happiness that I had spent time with Bella and urged me to care for her. It felt like he could finally find peace, having reunited with his Prodigal Son. As I pondered the whereabouts of his other two sons and why they lived so far away, I couldn't help but wonder if their upbringing had been similar to mine. Perhaps my father had been like Shane, as they were all friends. The mysteries of their past lingered in my mind, leaving me with more questions than answers.

Bella brought me to our father's girlfriend's charming little wooden house in Newfoundland, where I could stay while my father was in the hospital. The house was just a short stroll away from Signal Hill, a renowned landmark featuring Cabot Tower and scenic hiking trails that offer breathtaking views of the harbour and city. In the spring, you can even glimpse majestic whales in the harbour.

I decided to hike the trail, feeling the crisp air invigorate my senses. As I reached the top of the hill, I noticed a girl sitting alone, intently sketching the breathtaking landscape before her. Intrigued, I approached and sat nearby. She appeared to be around seventeen, her eyes focused and mysterious.

Curiosity got the better of me, and I asked her what she was drawing. Without a word, she stood up, walked over, and sat beside me, her sketchbook clutched tightly. The air seemed to thicken with an unspoken story waiting to be unveiled. Maybe I have some force field that says I'm damaged or sexually available, but as soon as she sat down, she misbehaved in public, committing an act while nobody else was around.

She recounted the day her mother decided to send her away to Newfoundland. Barrie, Ontario, had become a labyrinth of bad influences, and her mother hoped the distance would provide a fresh start. The streets of Barrie, once familiar and comforting, had turned into a web of dangerous connections that trapped her.

She was supposed to find solace and a chance to rebuild in Newfoundland. But as she spoke, it became clear that she wasn't just a victim of her circumstances. There was a spark in her eyes, a hint of rebellion that suggested she had played a role in her downfall. Her interactions with me were no different. She was bold, almost daring, as if testing the boundaries of her newfound freedom.

I wasn't a predator, but I wasn't innocent either. I saw an opportunity in her vulnerability and seized it. Her past became a tool for me to manipulate to get what I wanted. I invited her back to the house I had all to myself, where I could control the narrative. It was a decision that would blur the lines between right and wrong, leaving us both questioning our choices.

After spending time together on the couch, she wanted to ensure she wouldn't get pregnant, but I didn't tell her everything. As we got up, my father's girlfriend entered the house and almost caught us. I quickly told her the girl was my cousin and we were visiting each other. We then left the house, and after that day, I never saw the girl from Signal Hill again.

Days in the hospital seemed to stretch endlessly, each moment blending into the next. My father spent most of his time in a deep sleep, surrounded by the constant hum of medical equipment and the diligent care of nurses. My precious moments with Patrick were fleeting as I tried to share Jesus' message. As his condition deteriorated, we prayed the sinner's prayer together, and he embraced his faith.

One poignant memory stands out: the doctors had just shaved him, and I leaned over the hospital bed, wrapping my arm around my father, with Bella on the other side. We captured a few selfies, trying to hold onto the fleeting moments. My father, in a rare moment of clarity, removed his respirator and smiled broadly, gripping my hand with surprising strength.

What was meant to be a brief stay turned into an agonizingly long week. As his pain medication took effect, he drifted into a sedated state, leaving me with more time to converse with Bella. I watched over him, this once-vibrant man now reduced to a fragile figure in a blue hospital gown. His eyes were sunken, cheekbones protruding, and ribs painfully visible. He was fading away before my eyes, a haunting reminder of the relentless passage of time.

Holding my hand, he leaned in close and whispered, "I love you." I whispered back, "I love you too, more than words can say. I'm so grateful for every moment we've shared, for getting to know you." His eyes widened as he took his final breath, and I saw the acceptance in his gaze. In that instant, his heart ceased to beat, and his eyes became empty, like a shell. He was gone.

The three sisters and Patrick's ex-wife came

together to prepare for the funeral and wake. Two days later, friends and family gathered to pay their respects. On the third day, we held the funeral service, following the procession of vehicles to the cemetery to lay my father to rest. I never learned the name of the cemetery and will never visit it, as I believe his spirit resides in Heaven. I travelled to Newfoundland, saw him, said my peace, and met my siblings.

It was time for me to return to Toronto and make sense of everything that had happened in Newfoundland with my father and sisters. Whatever transpired between Bella and me—the tension and disagreements—would be left behind in Newfoundland, buried with my father and forgotten. When I left, I never saw or heard from them again.

Margret had just finished school and returned to the farm, eagerly waiting for me. She was brimming with ideas about her dream wedding. But I had to sit her down and confess something weighing heavily on my heart. I had been unfaithful to her multiple times throughout our relationship, starting from our youth group days and continuing through all four years of her university life.

I tried to explain my troubled upbringing and the abuse I had endured, attempting to rationalize my actions. I admitted that my behaviour was not just sinful but a condition that required forgiveness and divine intervention. I needed God's help to change my mindset and see women not as objects but with the same respect and love I had for my mother.

Margret cried the entire night, but her love for me remained steadfast. Despite my recent infidelities and the chaos of my father's death, she still wanted to marry me. Her willingness to forgive and overlook my adultery showed me just how much bigger her heart was compared to mine. Everything was confusing, but her love gave me hope.

14

THE WEDDING PLANNER

Fresh from her university graduation, Margret stood at the crossroads of life. She dreamed of becoming a high school teacher, and her final year at the University of Toronto's Teachers College awaited her. But love had other plans.

As lilac trees burst into fragrant bloom that spring, Margret was torn between academia and romance. The delicate purple and white hues mirrored her conflicting emotions. She agreed to marry before embarking on her teaching program, and together, we chose a date: Saturday, May 11, 1996. The church's pastor nodded approvingly, granting us time to organize and plan the wedding for that memorable day.

Margret and her best friend Kate took the reins of wedding planning, orchestrating a day that would forever intertwine love and commitment. Meanwhile, I turned to my outspoken friend Jay, inviting him to be our Master of Ceremonies. Margret's circle of friends formed her bridesmaids, and my niece, a vision in white petals, became the flower girl. Margret's youngest brother carried the precious rings while I asked Margret's eldest brother to stand by my side as my best man. A trip to Toronto reunited me with my seldom-seen brother Charles, completing our wedding party. But one absence was my younger step-brother, Stan, Laura's brother and spawn of my wicked stepfather, a reminder of a past I sought to leave behind.

As I embarked on a journey back to my childhood roots, it felt like I was descending into a chilling night-mare. Our family home was not nestled on Elm Street, yet the eerie anticipation of that haunting melody filled the air around me, whispering, "One, Two, he's coming for you."

My car's engine fell silent, its hum replaced by my heart pounding as I parked opposite the house with many memories. It was where the chapters of my life had begun to unfold.

A flicker of movement caught my eye - a curtain twitched and then hastily retreated as if the house itself was startled by my presence. It had been a decade since I last saw Stan and my stepfather. The passage of time had done little to quell the uncertainty that gnawed at me.

Standing there, on the precipice of the past, I was unsure of the reception that awaited me on the other side of that door. Yet, I knew I had to knock, to face whatever lay beyond. The past was calling, and I had to answer.

The door swung open to reveal a woman of Hungarian descent, Shane's partner, her figure full and commanding. Her eyes bore into mine, a silent question hanging in the air. I found my voice, introducing myself as Stan's brother. I asked after him, expressing my wish to have a word if he was around.

No sooner had the words left my mouth than a chillingly familiar voice echoed from upstairs. It was a spectral reminder of times long past, instantly transporting me back to the genesis of this narrative. It was a narrative that began with Charles and me making our way home, unaware of the intricate plot that life was weaving around us. The past, it seemed, was not content with being a mere memory; it was alive, breathing, and beckoning me to step back into its fold.

The door creaked open to reveal an elderly Hungarian man, small and withered, his grey hair a testament to the passage of time. He stood there, trembling like a frightened Chihuahua, his frailty invoking a wave of pity within me. The full extent of his abusive past was something I was yet to comprehend, for I had buried deep within me the memories of my childhood. All I could recall were the instances of physical and sexual abuse that had once been my reality.

Despite his timidity, a broad grin spread across his face, starkly contrasting the fear that seemed to grip him. It was as if he was welcoming me into his lair, a strange sense of motivation emanating from him.

Suddenly, my brother Stan appeared in the living room upstairs. He was no longer the boy I remembered; he was now a twenty-four-year-old man. He had grown into a robust version of his father, his physique husky and imposing. More than just his physical resemblance, he inherited the same mentality and beliefs as our father. It was a chilling reminder of the past and a stark revelation of how deeply our upbringing can shape us.

As we sat on the couch, nestled in the soft glow of nostalgia, we journeyed back to the past. But our conversation was a carefully curated collection of pleasant memories, a conscious effort to steer clear of the shadows lurking in our shared history's corners.

I shared with them the story of my life, of how I continued to live in the same area where I had spent my years in foster care. I spoke of the rides he gave me back home, the faith I found in Christianity and the girl from my church who had become my beacon of love.

We were on the cusp of a new beginning, about to embark on the journey of marriage.

His eyes welled up with pride as he heard of my transformation, of the maturity that life had instilled in me. Tears trickled down his cheeks as he repeatedly implored me to forgive him for his past transgressions. In my mind, I associated his plea with the physical abuse I had endured, oblivious to any more profound implications. And so, with a heart free of malice, I assured him that I had indeed forgiven him. Forgiveness, after all, is the first step towards healing.

With a heart full of anticipation, I shared with them the news that would forever change our lives. I was about to embark on the beautiful journey of matrimony, and I wanted nothing more than to have Stan stand by my side as a groomsman. The bond we shared as brothers was unbreakable, and having him there would make the day even more special.

I also mentioned that Charles, our other pillar of strength, was already at the wedding party. This moment symbolizes our unity as three brothers, a grand reunion that will forever be etched in our hearts.

Stan, with his obedience, turned to his father, seeking his silent approval upon receiving a reassuring nod, a radiant smile spread across his face. It was a smile that spoke volumes and reflected the joy of brotherhood and the excitement of the upcoming celebration. I know deep down he missed his brothers and sisters but was controlled and brainwashed by his father.

And thus, we embarked on reminiscing about the last ten years. Each memory, each moment, brought us closer, strengthening the bond we shared as brothers. This was not just a wedding but a celebration of our brotherhood, a testament to our love, and a promise of the many joyful moments ahead.

Stan was always looking up to me as his older brother, his enthusiasm infectious. His excitement about joining the wedding party was noticeable. On the other hand, Shane, the puppet master, sat quietly, his face a mask of anticipation as he awaited a personal invitation to the wedding.

Shane had a passion for photography that dates back to our childhood. He had a peculiar habit of arranging us naked in the bathtub and capturing those moments of innocence. As we grew older, I understood his photography's twisted perspective. However, some might argue that such material could be considered inappropriate today.

When the wedding photography topic came up, I informed Shane that we had engaged a professional photographer from Exeter. Additionally, a lady from our church was kind enough to offer her services for video recording. Ever the enthusiast, Shane proposed that he could also contribute by taking pictures at the wedding free of charge. He insisted it would be his pleasure. However, I couldn't help but sense an ulterior motive. I suspected that his offer was driven more by the desire to capture additional moments of his son rather than focusing on the bridal party. And so it was settled that Stan was part of my wedding party and Shane was going to be an additional photographer at the wedding.

The day I finally arrived when I had to gather Stan and Charles for our tuxedo fittings in the heart of downtown Toronto. We had decided to rent our tuxedos and shoes to ensure uniformity, and as the groom, I took on the responsibility of covering the rental costs for all my groomsmen. Margret's brothers had their fitting on a separate day, and it was up to me to collect all the tuxedos and transport them to the church. I also had the task of renting a tuxedo for Jay, who was to be my master of ceremonies.

Our destination was Sid Silvers, a renowned men's suit store and rental shop located at the bustling inter-section of Yonge and College Street. The tuxedos were explicitly rented for the wedding and were due to be returned the day after. We each took turns trying on our tuxedos and shoes, with matching red bow ties, vests, and cummerbunds to complement the brides-maid's dresses. My tuxedo, however, was distinct from the rest; it featured a coattail and black vest, setting me apart as the groom. After the fitting, I dropped my brothers off and embarked on returning home to Exeter.

Margret embarked on a shopping expedition in London, accompanied by her mother and Kate, in search of the perfect wedding dress. After trying many dresses, she finally found the one that captured her heart. The dress, which cost around eight hundred dollars then, was carefully brought home, protected by a plastic cover, and accompanied by a delicate veil.

The dress was a vision of beauty, crafted from fine silk and adorned with intricate lace and pearl beads, creating a captivating design. I was eager to see Margret in the dress. To complement her dress, I purchased a matching pearl necklace and earrings with a vintage appeal from the Hudson's Bay store in London. The ensemble promised to be nothing short of stunning.

Amid our financial constraints, with our savings dwindling and Margret's student loans casting a long shadow, we were determined to orchestrate a wedding that would not exceed $5,000. It was a challenge, but we embraced it with open hearts and creative minds.

Our primary expenditures were earmarked for two key elements that we believed would make our day unique: the flowers and the photographer. We embarked on a journey to find the perfect balance between cost and quality, setting up appointments with various professionals in both fields.

After meeting with several photographers, we finally found one who understood our vision. We chose a wedding package that fit our budget and promised to capture our love story in a photo album we could cherish forever.

Next, we turned our attention to the florist. The scent of fresh flowers filled the air as we walked into the shop, instantly lifting our spirits. We spent an hour poring over different arrangements, finally selecting four stunning displays that would grace the front of the church. Each arrangement was a symphony of colour and fragrance, promising to add a touch of elegance and beauty to our ceremony.

And then, there were the bouquets. The brides-maids' bouquets were charming, but the bride's bouquet was a masterpiece. Handpicked by Margret, it was a stunning collection of her favourite flowers, a reflection of her personality and taste—every decision we made and every dollar we spent was a testament to our love and commitment. Despite the financial constraints, we created a day that would be as beautiful and memorable as our journey together.

Margret and Kate, our dynamic duo, took the reins of the decoration department, transforming the church and the reception hall into a dreamy wonderland. They brought home boxes brimming with Kleenex tissues, which they meticulously crafted into round carnation flowers. We spent countless hours pulling them apart, each flower blooming under our careful touch. These handmade blossoms were destined to adorn the church pews, creating a floral pathway for our vows. They also found their way around the church and onto the cars, adding a touch of whimsy and charm to our surroundings.

But their creativity didn't stop there. They poured their hearts into crafting ornaments that would take center stage on the tables at the reception. Each ornament was a testament to their dedication and love for us. They also put together delightful little gift bags, a token of our appreciation for our guests.

The hours they invested in preparing for our big day were countless. Their hands were always busy, their minds always brimming with ideas. And amidst all this, I couldn't help but feel a bit overwhelmed. It felt like they were doing everything; all I had to do was show up on the day. But in reality, their efforts were a gift, a labour of love that made our wedding day all the more special.

15

BACHELORHOOD TO MARRIAGE

After weeks of anticipation, the day I had been waiting for had finally dawned—the day I would transition from a carefree bachelor to a committed husband. My past was filled with a myriad of experiences, most of which included being sexually active. But now, I was on the cusp of a decision that would change my life forever. Was I ready to forsake all others for the love of one woman?

At twenty-five, with no formal education or stable job, I questioned what I could bring to Margret's table. She had a university degree and was soon becoming a high school teacher. My resume, filled with stints at gas stations and retail stores, paled in comparison. Yet, she saw something in me that I struggled to see in myself.

Margret had always been transparent about her

intentions. She once told me she would marry the first man she kissed. We had long since crossed that milestone, and there was no turning back. That weekend in Toronto, I grappled with the reality of our financial situation. I had dreamt of renting a BMW for our wedding, but my empty pockets echoed the harsh truth. How could I tell her that we couldn't afford a car?

But Margret, ever the pragmatist, had a solution. Her parents had gifted her the Dodge Sundance as a graduation present, and she suggested we use that for our wedding. She didn't see the need for an expensive rental. With a heavy heart, I boarded the bus back to Exeter while my brothers hitched a ride with our stepfather.

The groomsmen, including Margret's three brothers, convened at the church on the wedding day. Jay and I arrived with the tuxedos, ready to step into our roles. Meanwhile, Margret, Kate, and the bridesmaids were at Margret's house, a flurry of activity as they finished their hair and makeup. The air was filled with excitement and a touch of nervous anticipation. The wedding photographer was there too, capturing these precious pre-wedding moments. It was the beginning of our new journey together, and despite the uncertainties, I knew I was ready to face whatever came our way as long as I had Margret by my side.

With my hair permed into tight curls and trimmed

short on the sides, I stood in the men's washroom, adjusting my bowtie. A wave of nervousness washed over me, making my stomach churn. Seeing the church pews filled to the brim was overwhelming as I stepped out. On one side were friends of the Vandyke family, their faces a sea of familiar smiles. On the other side were my own family and friends. My sisters, aunt, and stepfather were seated in the front rows, their eyes filled with pride and joy.

Yet, amidst the happiness, there was a pang of sadness. My mother was conspicuously absent, leaving a void that couldn't be filled. I wasn't sure why she hadn't come. Standing on the cusp of a new chapter in my life, I couldn't help but wish she was there to share this moment with me. But life is a mix of joy and sorrow, and today, I chose to focus on the pleasure of marrying the woman I loved.

The grand organ began its musical symphony as the wedding procession started, filling the church with a harmonious blend of notes. Margret and I had meticulously chosen songs that resonated with her heart, creating a personal and inviting atmosphere. A lady with a voice as smooth as silk graced us with an opening song, her melody intertwining beautifully with the organ's music.

As the song unfolded, the groomsmen, dressed in their finest, accompanied me to the front of the church.

We ascended the steps, our footsteps echoing softly in the hallowed hall. The pastor, a beacon of calm and serenity, joined us, standing shoulder to shoulder in unity.

Then, the first notes of "Pachelbel's Canon in D" filled the air, a timeless piece that added a touch of elegance to the occasion. The four bridesmaids began their graceful journey down the aisle as the music flowed like a gentle river. Their steps were in perfect harmony with the rhythm of the music, a dance as old as time itself. They lined up on the opposite side of the stairs, their smiles radiant under the soft glow of the church lights.

The moment everyone had been waiting for arrived. My niece, looking like a miniature princess, and Margret's youngest brother, the proud ring bearer, made their entrance. Their innocence and joy added a touch of magic to the occasion, a reminder of the purity and promise of the love we were all there to celebrate. Their presence was the perfect prelude to the bride's arrival, setting the stage for the beautiful journey that was about to begin.

The grand double doors swung open, revealing Margret, a vision of beauty in her pristine white wedding gown and veil. She began her graceful procession towards the front of the church, her father by her side, their steps measured and in sync with the enchanting music. As they moved, every person in the church rose to their feet, their eyes filled with admiration and joy.

Upon reaching the front, Margret's father performed the time-honoured tradition of handing his daughter off to me. It was a poignant moment, filled with love and a hint of bittersweet farewell. We then turned to face the crowd of familiar faces standing together on the stage at the front of the church.

We exchanged vows before our loved ones, each word a promise to love, honour, and cherish each other. The exchange of wedding rings was a tangible symbol of these promises, a circle of love and commitment that was now ours to keep.

Then came the moment that sealed our union. We both said, "I do," which echoed in the hallowed hall, binding us together in matrimony. The veil was gently lifted, revealing Margret's radiant face. I leaned in and kissed the bride, my wife, marking the beginning of our journey together as husband and wife. It was a moment of pure joy, a testament to our love, and a promise of the beautiful journey ahead of us.

As we stood on stage, the pastor delivered a personal Bible sermon tailored to our journey into marriage. Margret and I exchanged glances, silently hoping his chosen verses and topics would resonate with our unique situation.

However, as the pastor's speech stretched on, a wave of nausea washed over me. The excitement and emotions of the day had taken their toll. I needed to sit down on the stairs while Margret, the pillar of strength, continued to stand and attentively listen to the pastor.

For ten long minutes, I rested, trying to regain my composure. The world around me seemed to slow down, the pastor's words becoming a distant echo. Gradually, the nausea subsided, and I found the strength to stand again.

Just as I rose, the pastor concluded his sermon. His final words hung in the air, a blessing for our future together. He then turned to us, a warm smile on his face, and congratulated us. At that moment, we were no longer just Margret and I. We were now Mr. and Mrs. McGrath, embarking on a beautiful journey of love and togetherness. It was a moment we would cherish forever.

Hand in hand, we descended from the stage, the crowd's applause echoing in our ears. We made our way to the back of the church, where the bridal party was arranging themselves for the receiving line. Our guests lined up individually, their faces beaming with joy and excitement. This was their chance to personally greet us, express their gratitude for the invitation, and bless us.

As the receiving line dwindled, the guests began to

mingle, their laughter and chatter filling the church. The atmosphere was electric with joy and celebration, a perfect backdrop for the next chapter of our special day.

Margret and I then slipped away from the festivities to capture our wedding day in photographs. We chose a picturesque park as our backdrop, its natural beauty reflecting our love and happiness. Margret had been hoping for the lilac blossoms to be in full bloom, their vibrant colours adding a touch of magic to our photos. However, nature had other plans, and the lilacs were not fully blooming. But even without the lilacs, the park was beautiful, and our photos captured the essence of our love and the joy of our special day. It was a moment frozen in time, a memory we would cherish forever.

After spending a few delightful hours capturing our joy in photographs around the park and the church, it was time to transition to the much-anticipated reception. In the cozy basement of the church, Jay had his booth all setup, ready to entertain and engage our guests with his unique flair.

The meticulously arranged tables, adorned with elegant chinaware, sparkled under the soft lighting. The church ladies had poured their hearts into preparing and catering for our special day. Their dedication and hard work resulted in a feast fit for a king. They helped us significantly cut costs that would have otherwise gone to a professional catering company.

The bridal table was strategically placed along the side of the wall, facing all the other tables. This arrangement ensured we were at the heart of the celebration, front and center for all the fun and games. Margret and Kate had put their creative minds together to develop a series of entertaining games designed to engage our guests and add more fun to the festivities.

As we settled into our seats and looked at the smiling faces, we couldn't help but feel a sense of profound gratitude. On our special day, it turned out to be more beautiful than we could have imagined, thanks to the love and support of our dear ones. It celebrated love, unity, and the beginning of our new journey as Mr. and Mrs. McGrath. The guests had a question-and-answer sheet on each table to see how well they knew Margret and me when we started dating. The correct answers led to us kissing.

As the reception continued, a video projector cast a warm glow on the wall, displaying a slideshow of pictures; these mages traced Margret and my journey, from our innocent childhood days to the cherished moments of our dating life. The room was filled with soft murmurs and nostalgic smiles as our guests relived these memories with us.

One particular image stood out - a tender moment

captured between Margret and her father when she was just a baby. Seeing his little girl, now a beautiful bride, being given away in marriage was perhaps a bittersweet moment for him. The joy of seeing her embark on a new journey was tinged with the sadness of letting go. Margret's mother, too, was overcome with emotion, her tears a testament to the love and pride she felt for her daughter.

Amidst the emotional moments, the reception was filled with laughter and lively conversation. Everyone savoured the delicious dinner, their spirits high and hearts full. Margret and Kate thoughtfully planned the games, adding fun and camaraderie to the evening.

Although I don't recall all the details, one game that stood out involved other couples demonstrating a kiss, which Margret and I had to imitate. It was a light-hearted and amusing activity that brought much laughter and cheer to the room. Somehow, I had to flip myself upside down and kiss Margret while she was bent over. As the evening unfolded, it was clear that our wedding was not just a celebration of our love but also a testament to the love and support of our family and friends. It was a day we would never forget, filled with moments that would forever be etched in our hearts.

As the evening drew close, marking the end of a day filled with love, laughter, and family, we began our farewell rituals. We collected the generous gifts and money envelopes from the back table, each a token of love and well wishes from our dear ones. Carefully, we loaded them into the car, a tangible reminder of the love and support surrounding us on our special day.

We then changed out of our wedding attire, the beautiful clothes that had borne witness to our vows and the celebration of our union. I gathered all the tuxedos, their fabric still holding the warmth and joy of the day. These were handed over to Margret's brother, who graciously agreed to return them for us. His help was invaluable, allowing us to leave for our honeymoon in Niagara Falls without any worries.

Finally, it was time to say goodbye. We bid farewell to Margret's parents, their eyes filled with tears of joy and a hint of sadness. We hugged our friends, their warm wishes echoing in our ears. And then, hand in hand, we stepped into our car and drove away from the church.

As we left the church, we were no longer just Margret and me. We were Mr. and Mrs. McGrath, embarking on our first journey as a married couple. The church, now a speck in the rearview mirror, held the memories of our beautiful wedding, a day that marked the beginning of our forever. As we drove into the night, our hearts were full of love and anticipation for the beautiful journey ahead.

We resumed our journey with a quick stop at Tim

Horton's for a comforting cup of coffee and a pit stop to fill up the gas. Back in the car, we set our sights on Niagara Falls, leaving the familiar landscapes of Exeter behind. The road ahead was not just a path to our honeymoon destination but a metaphor for the new journey we had embarked upon.

As we drove, we stole glances at each other, our hands intertwined, a silent testament to our bond. It felt surreal, this new reality of ours. We were married. The words echoed in our minds, their weight and significance slowly sinking in. After five long years of togetherness, from our innocent teenage years to the threshold of adulthood, we were now a married couple. We had grown together and evolved together, and now, we were embarking on a new journey together— building a family and creating a life that reflected our love. As we drove on, the reality of our marriage, the joy of our union, and the excitement of what lay ahead filled us with contentment and anticipation.

As we entered the vibrant city of Niagara Falls, we began the search for a hotel. We hadn't made any bookings, preferring to keep our options open. Our search led us to a charming hotel nestled off Clifton Hill, right in the heart of all the amusement attractions. Its location was perfect, just a stroll away from the majestic American and Horseshoe Falls.

The room we booked was a delightful surprise. It

boasted a heart-shaped jacuzzi, its romantic appeal further enhanced by the surrounding mirrors. The decor was a nostalgic throwback to the seventies, giving the room a unique charm. Despite showing signs of being well-used, it had a cozy and welcoming ambiance.

Now, all that was missing was that we went and got bath bubbles filling the jacuzzi and a glass of champagne in our hands. As we imagined this, a sense of contentment washed over us. We were here, in Niagara Falls, as a married couple, ready to start the first day of the rest of our lives together. It was the perfect end to a perfect day and the beginning of our forever.

16

NEW TOWNS, NEW JOBS

Our journey together began in the quaint town of Mitchell, not far from Staffa, where Margret's parents' comforting presence was a mere twenty-minute drive away. We found our first shared sanctuary in a one-bedroom apartment tucked away in a serene St. Andrew Street house. Our home was behind the town's post office and cradled by a gentle backyard river. It was a large two-story building with a few units other than ours.

As I embarked on a quest for employment, I stumbled upon a restaurant on the main street, a bustling diner, a beacon of culinary delight renowned for its delectable breakfast. Stepping inside, the Manager, the original owner's son, greeted me. He was a towering figure, his large frame and high blood pressure painting a picture of a man teetering on the edge of a health crisis. Despite his imposing presence, he was steering the diner's course solo, his family having stepped away from the business.

With a hopeful heart, I expressed my desire to join their team. Recognizing my eagerness, he welcomed me aboard as a morning waiter, entrusted with the breakfast and lunch shifts. My responsibilities span setting the tables, serving our patrons their meals, clearing the tables, and ensuring the dishes were safely tucked into the dishwasher. Each day, they brought new challenges and the joy of being part of a community hub where food and fellowship intertwine.

Our humble home was graced with a housewarming gift from Margret's father: a sleek 27" RCA TV, a welcome addition to our sparse living space. As we had yet to acquire furniture, we invested in a versatile futon and bed frame, serving as our daily couch and a cozy bed by night.

The summer unfolded beautifully, but a storm was brewing at the diner. The manager, notorious for his fiery temper, shadowed the workplace. His voice, often raised in anger, echoed through the restaurant as he chastised his staff for not meeting his exacting standards. He would berate them publicly and put their embarrassment on display for all the customers to witness.

I bore the brunt of his wrath for as long as I could, but the constant barrage took its toll. A cloud of depression began to loom, and in a moment of self-preservation, I walked away from the job. I left without a safety net or backup plan but a newfound resolve to find a healthier work environment. In the blink of an eye,

I embarked on a new professional journey at Ford Dickison, a poultry equipment manufacturer near our home. The factory specialized in crafting chicken cages, a field I was entirely unfamiliar with. My knowledge of CNC machines and programming was virtually non-existent, which did not deter my new employers.

They saw my potential and were willing to invest their time and resources to equip me with the necessary skills. They offered me a lifeline, a chance to learn, grow, and secure a better position with a higher wage. It was a testament to their belief in nurturing talent and fostering growth, a philosophy that resonated deeply with me. This opportunity marked a new chapter in my life, one filled with promise and endless possibilities.

I found myself at the helm of the punch press machine, a world of coordinates and die tools unfolding before me. My hands are over the controls, programming the y and x axes precisely. I felt a sense of accomplishment with each long sheet of galvanized steel I slid into the machines. The press hummed to life, cutting out the materials with mechanical precision before dispatching them to the assembly line in the heart of the building.

This responsibility weighed heavily on my shoulders, especially considering my educational background extended only to grade nine. However, the road to learning is often paved with mistakes, and I was no exception. In an unfortunate turn of events, I loaded mismatched cutting tools into the machine. The result was a catastrophic clash when the machine closed, leading to broken dies and a complete shutdown of the machines.

This incident served as a stark reminder of the complexities of my new role and the importance of meticulous attention to detail. It was a learning curve, a stepping stone on my journey towards mastering the intricacies of CNC machines and programming. Despite the setbacks, I remained undeterred, ready to face the challenges ahead.

One fateful weekend in our apartment, we were assailed by an overpowering stench that permeated the walls. It was a disgusting, putrid smell that evoked images of decay and death. The odour was so intense that it induced a visceral reaction in both Margret and me, making us feel physically ill.

Unfortunately, our apartment, nestled by the river, was near a growing mound of garbage from the other apartments. I initially attributed the foul smell to the rotting waste, a bustling hub for sewer rats. However, our ordeal was far from over. We soon noticed an issue with our stove - some elements malfunctioned. As I pulled the stove away from the wall, the smell intensified, and to our horror, we saw maggots cascading from the back of the stove.

Driven by dread and curiosity, we decided to investigate further. Removing the stove's back cover revealed a sight that stunned us both. A sewer rat had infiltrated the stove wiring, chewed through the cables, and met its untimely end by electrocution. This grim discovery explained the source of the unbearable stench plaguing our home. It was a stark reminder of the challenges of our living situation and the urgent need for a more sanitary environment.

I immediately contacted our landlord after discovering the grim reality behind the unbearable stench. I detailed the horrifying situation, emphasizing the unlivable conditions we were subjected to. He acknowledged the severity of the issue, deeming it unacceptable but warranting no immediate action. He told us that we should remove and dispose of the rat correctly and that our stove would be repaired or replaced.

However, the ordeal had taken its toll on us. The living conditions had been far from ideal, and we felt it was only fair to seek compensation for our hardships. So, we decided to take legal action. We engaged in a legal battle with the landlord for a month at the housing tribunal. We aimed to sue him for the substandard living conditions and to recover our rent.

This transformative experience sparked a profound shift in our lives. It dawned on us that our quest for a sanctuary, a haven where we could breathe easy and feel the warmth of security, had become an urgent necessity. Our challenges were formidable, yet they failed to dampen our spirits. Instead, they fueled our resolve, filling us with resilient hope.

Our hearts were drawn to the charming city of Stratford, known for its vibrant culture and welcoming community. We embarked on a diligent search, exploring every nook and cranny of the town, seeking a place we could call home. Our perseverance paid off when we discovered a gem close to the bustling main street and the lively mall - the apartments at 25 Kappele Circle.

Our new abode was unique. Our bedroom was tucked away in the basement, down the stairs, and the first door on the right. The street-level windows served as our lens to the sidewalk, allowing us to observe the rhythm of those coming and going out of the apartment. We moved the futon, TV, and other things into our new place and called it home.

Margret was thrilled when she landed a long-term occasional teaching position at Stratford Collegiate Institute, nestled in the heart of downtown Stratford. As a physical education instructor, she led gym classes and took on the challenge of teaching history and other secondary subjects. What started as a temporary role soon blossomed into a full-time position, providing her with ample hours and the convenience of being close to home.

Downtown Stratford, renowned for its iconic Shakespeare Theater, is a picturesque area by the river. The river winds gracefully through a downtown section, creating a serene backdrop for the town. We enjoyed watching the lively dragon boat races and observing the elegant swans and playful ducks gliding along the water while others rented paddleboats to get closer to the wildlife.

While Margret was at work, I often took Dylan for long, leisurely walks in his stroller, enjoying the fresh air and exercise. Our favourite spot was the playground, where Dylan's laughter and playfulness added a unique charm to my days.

We embarked on a journey of church hopping, searching for a place that felt like home. The Pentecostal church in Exeter was a bit too far for regular visits, so we only attended when visiting Margret's family on Sundays. However, the Pentecostal church in

Stratford had too many ties to Exeter and Margret's parents, making it feel less like our own space.

After exploring several churches, we stumbled upon a quaint little church called The Word of Life Church on a corner street. Despite its small size and lack of Sunday school classes for children, we decided to try it. I was accustomed to vibrant worship bands with live drums and guitars, but here, they only had a tape deck playing music while someone sang into a microphone, with the lyrics projected onto a screen.

I had grown weary of the large seeker churches that seemed more focused on expanding their congregations through the offering plate than building genuine connections. So, despite the sleepy music, I thought a smaller church might offer the community we were looking for. The pastor and his wife were around our age and had a couple of children, just like us. They lived near the gas station where I worked, making connecting with them easy.

We quickly became friends with the pastor's family, often visiting their home and camping together. However, after some time, the pastor received a job offer in another city and decided to move, taking his family with him. Though their departure was bittersweet, our friendships and experiences left a lasting impression of a good pastor, and Margret kept in touch with Lisa, the pastor's wife.

Recognizing the imminent demise of our trusty Dodge Sundance and the aging green Chrysler K-car with a blown engine, we decided to begin a new chapter of vehicle hunting. We set our sights on the Chrysler dealership in Mitchell, a place teeming with possibilities and the promise of a new car.

In a gesture of familial love and generosity, Margret returned her car to her parents, providing her brothers with a means of transportation. This act of giving was not just about a car; it symbolized Margret's values and the bond that held her family together.

Our journey led us to a delightful discovery - a charming 1995 Dodge Neon, resplendent in an eye-catching shade of electric blue, sitting on the corner of the lot facing the town's main intersection. It was more than just a vehicle; it symbolized our journey and hopes for the future. With hearts filled with anticipation, we completed the necessary paperwork, the ink on the finance papers serving as a testament to our commitment.

As we drove away in our first family car, we couldn't help but feel a sense of accomplishment. This was not just about owning a car; it was about the journey we had embarked on and the memories we had yet to complete. This Dodge Neon was not just a means of transportation but a part of our family's story.

While looking for a new job, I discovered a

charming little restaurant—Williams Coffee Pub—on the corner of Ontario Street. This quaint, family-run coffee house, which first opened its doors in 1993, was more than just a café. It was a home away from home for many, including myself. This location had Chinese ownership, and a Scottish trainer from the head office imparted wisdom to the recruits.

Unlike your average Tim Hortons, Williams Coffee Pub exuded a unique style that drew in a crowd of students seeking a cozy corner to delve into their studies. It was akin to Starbucks, offering specialty coffees and delectable desserts, but it provided more. The menu was a delightful mix of comfort food - all-day breakfast, savoury quiches, and a variety of toasted and grilled sandwiches paired perfectly with the soup.

Mastering the art of crafting those specialty coffees was a journey in itself, but one that I thoroughly enjoyed. The camaraderie among the staff, the joy of serving customers, and the lively chatter that filled the air made each day a pleasure. It was a stark contrast to my previous job at the Diner in Mitchell, not to mention the pay was significantly better.

Over time, I climbed the ranks, earning the supervisor role. The responsibility of opening and closing the store was entrusted to me, a testament to the owner's faith in me. However, every rose has its thorns; it was the lingering cigarette smoke for me. It stung my eyes, seeped into my clothes, and left a harsh nicotine scent on my skin after work. My lungs bore the brunt of the chemicals, a constant reminder of the job's limitations. Yet, the experience was enriching, shaping me in ways I hadn't imagined.

During our stay in Stratford, I dabbled in a few fleeting jobs that added to my repertoire of experiences. One such stint was at a Shell station, a compact kiosk, where I found myself donning the hat of a gas station attendant. In those days, gas stations were all full-serve, a concept that seems almost alien now. I would fill up the gas, check the oil and fluids, and even clean the customer's windshield while they comfortably waited in their vehicle. It was a dance of service that I had mastered over time.

Then there were the nocturnal shifts at Seven Eleven, a job that was as diverse as it was demanding. Not only did it have a gas bar, but it also involved serving customers and maintaining the cleanliness of the convenience store throughout the night. Despite the challenges, it was an experience that broadened my horizons. However, this job was short-lived, lasting only a few weeks. Yet, no matter how brief, each job left an indelible mark.

A factory stood in the heart of Milverton, Ontario, a quaint town just north of Stratford. This wasn't just any factory, but one deeply rooted in the farming communities of the Amish-Mennonite. As one of the few employees who arrived by car, I immersed myself in a world that felt like a step back. Most of my colleagues came in traditional black horses and buggies, a charming and unique sight.

The factory grounds were equipped with stables, where these majestic horses were tied up and nourished with water and grain. This was my first real encounter with the Amish, a community I had only previously seen in the Harrison Ford movie "Witness." Their attire was distinctive and uniform - black and blue shirts held up by suspenders, straw hats shielding their faces, and long beards that conspicuously lacked mustaches.

Driving on the roads was an experience in itself. Signs warning of horses and buggies were a common sight, and trailing behind these large, powerful creatures was like straddling two different eras. Upon arriving at the factory, I was assigned to a large German punch press, creating and assembling wheelbarrows. The factory was a hive of activity, with almost all the men puffing away on cigarettes or cigars.

The air was thick, with the stench of smoke permeating every corner of the workspace. One fateful day, as I fed sheet metal into the press, the sharp edge sliced through my knuckle, cutting right to the bone at the joint. The pain was immediate and intense, necessitating medical attention.

The incident resulted in six stitches and a prescription for painkillers to manage the nerve damage to my finger. The injury rendered me unable to bend my finger, marking the end of my tenure at the factory. The combination of the smoke-filled environment and the stark cultural differences with the Amish community had taken its toll. It was time for a new chapter.

No matter the job, no matter the effort I put in, a sense of frustration would inevitably creep in over time. It was as if a shadow of depression loomed over me, casting a pall of panic whenever I stayed too long at one job. It felt like I was unwittingly sabotaging my success, a silent battle within me.

The stress of monotony, of being rooted in one place for too long, would become unbearable. It would push me to step away, to seek solace in the unfamiliar quietly. The allure of something new, something different from the norm, was a siren call I found hard to resist. It was a cycle, a pattern of seeking change, that became a part of my journey.

My jobs mirror my past experiences, a reflection of the foster homes and the myriad encounters I had with people. It was like I had constructed an invisible fortress around myself, a protective barrier against the world. Each time someone managed to breach this wall, I would retreat, only to rebuild it elsewhere. This wall was my shield, my armour against the world, a means of self-preservation.

After an eternity of anticipation, Margret's patience finally bore fruit. She was offered a teaching position in Phys ed at a Peel Region high school in Brampton, Ontario, close to Shoppers World Mall. Every day, she would embark on her commute, leaving behind the familiar sights of home to embrace the challenges of shaping young minds. Meanwhile, I found myself in the role of primary caregiver for our little Dylan, a responsibility I cherished. Our home was filled with laughter and learning, a testament to our love.

Amid this new routine, Margret searched for a new place to call home. Her quest led her to the quaint town of Acton, a place known far and wide for its historic Old Hyde House leather store. With its famous commercial catchphrase, "It's Worth the Drive to Acton," this store had become a local legend. But was it worth the drive? The allure of a ten-thousand-dollar couch set or a thousand-dollar leather coat might be tempting for some. But for us, it was about more than just material possessions. It was about finding a place where we could build memories, a place that felt like home. And so, our search continued…

Our new abode—the Ransom Street apartment—was just off Highway 25 North, fifteen minutes from Milton, adjacent to a serene cemetery. We resided in unit 203, a cozy space that offered an eerie yet intriguing view of the graveyard. The thought of sleeping just a stone's throw away from dozens of resting souls added an uncanny charm to our dwelling.

The apartment, though modest, was a canvas for our creativity. I breathed life into the walls with a rich brown glaze and a hint of gold, lending them a vintage aura. The trim, too, received a fresh coat of paint, enhancing the overall aesthetics. Our humble futon found its place against the wall while the TV perched on a table stand, ready to entertain us during our downtime. Our family grew with the addition of a captivating Siamese cat. Her brown and grey coat complemented her bright blue eyes, making her an irresistible addition to our home.

Despite our financial constraints, we found joy in life's simple pleasures. I am a movie enthusiast, and to cater to this passion, I invested in a US Direct TV satellite. It came with a box and a card to be programmed to access all the US channels and premium movies. I took it upon myself to learn the programming, turning our living room into a mini cinema. When the channels went down, I found a way to turn this skill into a small business, charging friends twenty dollars to program their cards. Life, as they say, always finds a way.

I embarked on my first job adventure at Pizzaville, hiding in the cozy corner of the plaza at the edge of town. Picture it: the scent of freshly baked pizza dough wafting through the air, mingling with the tantalizing aroma of Kentucky Fried Chicken. And right next door, Jumbo Video beckoned with its colourful movie posters, promising cinematic sleepovers.

Once a bustling hub for crispy chicken lovers, the KFC eventually transformed into a Giant Tiger, its shelves stocked with everything from discount clothing to quirky home goods. The change rippled through the plaza, rearranging the familiar landscape like a game of Tetris.

My stint at Pizzaville was a whirlwind of cheesy pizzas, pepperoni toppings, and late-night shifts. I perfected the art of tossing dough, ensuring each slice emerged from the oven with that perfect blend of crispy crust, cornmeal, and gooey cheese. Customers became regulars, sharing stories over pizza and coffee. When the clock struck closing time, I'd grab a VHS tape from Jumbo Video—action and new releases from the top ten wall—and settle in for a movie night.

But life had more surprises in store. The gas pumps at Petro Canada beckoned, and I found myself back in the world of fuel nozzles and windshield wipes. The owner, Mario—an affable Italian with his red 280Z Datsun—entrusted me with the gas bar and car wash. Suddenly, I was the gatekeeper of fuel efficiency, the maestro of squeegees. Mario had other locations and relied on me to manage his Georgetown location when he was not there.

Georgetown also had a Shell station humming with activity. Here, a Russian manager named Sergei taught me the delicate art of fuel pricing and inventory management. He told me stories about distant lands, his accent weaving tales of global experiences under the USSR during Soviet rule. As I wiped down windshields, I wondered about the lives of the drivers passing through—where they were headed and what dreams fueled their journeys.

Brampton marked the final chapter of my gas station saga: another Petro Canada, another adventure. The familiar hum of engines and the rhythmic clink of coins in the cash register felt like home. I'd become a connoisseur of fuel grades, a whisperer to engines needing a little TLC. As I stood under the fluorescent lights, I realized that these gas stations held more than gasoline—they were the building blocks for my survival and building in me the patience to stick it out and not give up.

So, there you have it—the winding path from pizza ovens to gas pumps, from KFC to Giant Tiger. Each stop left its imprint, memories etched into my past of that unassuming plaza. Looking back, I realize that those seemingly ordinary jobs were my passport to a world beyond the counter where stories unfolded, one slice of pizza or a litre of gas at a time.

Ransom Street—whispered through the rustling leaves about a year later. One day, the landlord's footsteps echoed down the hallway. Notices appeared stark against the peeling paint. The building, he informed us, would transform into sleek condominiums. Yet, we held a peculiar privilege: first dibs on ownership—a chance to be part of history in these aging floorboards.

The ground floor buzzed with activity—the scent of fresh paint and the rhythmic tap of hammers. Units emptied, their echoes replaced by promises of open-concept kitchens and glossy tiles. New sliding windows and balcony doors were installed. We wandered through the renovations, skepticism gnawing at our curiosity.

The kitchen, once a cramped alcove, now sprawls open-armed. Walls vanish, revealing a stage for culinary theatrics. But beneath the veneer, the old pipes clung stubbornly to their rustic echoes. The wiring is patched and frayed, and the price tag is a cruel joke.

We convened in the dimly lit hallway, our voices hushed. Was this our chance to etch our names into the building's chronicle? Or a trap, baited with aesthetics? The decision loomed—a delicate balance between sentiment and sanity.

As the days passed, we faced our truth, casting

shadows across Ransom Street. The illusion shimmered, but authenticity lay elsewhere—in the worn floorboards and the flickering light above the stairwell. We chose to step away, leaving behind the chance to own our condominium. Our memories, etched in the grain of wood, would linger long after the last coat of paint dried.

And so, Ransom Street whispered its final chapter—a memoir to Acton of choosing roots over facades. We moved on, leaving behind the illusionists and the glittering tiles. Our hearts, forever entwined with the old building, carried its story into another part of Acton on the other side of the tracks.

Before bidding farewell to the apartment and relocating to the other side of Acton, I endured a harrowing experience with my brother Charles. This incident felt like a piece of my soul, and cherished childhood memories were ripped away, profoundly altering my life and leaving an indelible mark on my current and future relationships.

17

REST IN PEACE, CHARLES RYLEY

In the spring of 1998, life took an unexpected turn. Frank Gabriel, my criminal lawyer, who represented me in a couple of cases I'd been charged with, reached out to me. Frank was no ordinary attorney; he was my brother Charles's confidant, and their bond ran more profound than mere legal matters. Frank never billed me for those cases, perhaps because he saw a reflection of Charles in me. It was as if our shared bloodline extended to the courtroom.

One day, Frank asked me to meet him urgently. His tone was grave, and I sensed something was amiss. We met with his partner at a dimly lit restaurant, where they treated me to a fine dining dinner. Frank's eyes held a mix of concern and sadness. He leaned in, his breath carrying the weight of the news he was about to deliver. "Charles is sick," he said, his voice barely above a whisper.

Charles—my enigmatic brother, had slipped through the cracks of my life like sand through my fingers. We hadn't spoken in years, our paths diverging after that chaotic Christmas party at my sister Janet's house in Scarborough. Charles had been there, laughing and cracking Newfie jokes, nursing a solitary beer. But then it happened—the tremors, the vacant stare, the collapse. He fell, and crimson stained the floor as his head met the unforgiving edge of a table.

The hospital visit that followed revealed the truth: Charles had alcohol-induced epilepsy. His body had become a battleground, alcohol waging war against his nervous system. I remembered those nights when Charles haunted the bars, a spectral figure swaying to the rhythm of liquid courage. He'd skip meals, forsaking sustenance for the intoxicating embrace of spirits. For him, alcohol wasn't just a drink; it was his lifeline, the fuel that kept him going.

And so, as spring blossomed outside, I grappled with the complexities of brotherhood, illness, and the fragile threads that bound us together. Frank's words echoed in my mind: "Charles is sick." It was a refrain that would shape the chapters of my life, tragedy, and resilience into the memories of our shared history. See, nobody had the bond that Charles and I had and the secrets and horrors we faced together with our stepfather and living on the streets, so we knew each other better than anyone else. In those two years, Charles's body waged a silent rebellion—a quiet mutiny against its existence. Hepatitis C and Cirrhosis, like unwelcome guests, took residence within him. Our shared history unfolded against Frank's presence, not the lawyer but Charles's partner, a steadfast companion.

After my release from jail at seventeen, fate led me back to Charles. The bars—their dimly lit refuge—reunited us. Frank became our anchor with his Queen Street East restaurant and Logan Avenue house. Breakfasts at that grungy pub-style place were more than meals; they were moments suspended in time. Frank, the culinary maestro, conjured sustenance from humble ingredients. Men in the corner gambled on machines as we ate, their hopes and losses echoing through the smoky air. And so, within those walls, we navigated brotherhood, illness, and the fragile threads that bound us. Charles, Frank, and I were our own messed up family, and Frank was the stepfather abusing us for his sexual gratification in exchange for alcohol and money.

My sister Janet was fascinated with this guy, convinced he was the best thing that ever happened to Charles. She'd invite him over for dinner or suggest visits to Frank's restaurant. But Janet was oblivious to the darkness lurking behind his dark brown eyes and sinister smile. What she didn't know was that both Charles and I had endured unspeakable trauma under our stepfather's roof. The sexual abuse had begun during our childhood and persisted into our adult lives. We were like wounded prey, marked by predators who sensed our vulnerability.

In this twisted tale, it was Frank who took Charles under his wing, perpetuating the cycle of abuse. Charles wasn't gay; he loved Heather and countless other girls. Yet, survival meant enduring the torment Frank inflicted upon him—just as I had learned to do. Janet turned her back on me when I was just sixteen. She believed Shane and Laura's accusations, painting me as the predator. From that moment on, she never forgave me or looked at me the same way again. Our family remained oblivious to the unique bond Charles and I shared—the unbreakable connection forged through living together and enduring hell.

Meeting Mr. Gabriel at the restaurant marked a turning point. Charles and I headed to his downtown Toronto office for a crucial discussion. Acting on Charles's behalf, Frank requested that I become his power of attorney. When the time arrives and Charles can no longer make health-related decisions, that responsibility will fall to me. Amidst the weighty discussion, I asked Charles, 'Are you sure about this?'

His eyes held mine, unwavering. 'We're brothers,' he said, voice steady. 'When the time comes, I want you by my side, making those tough calls if I can't."

As evening came and I made my way home to Acton, I sat down with Margret and shared the truth about my brother's prolonged illness. I asked if she recalled that Christmas dinner at my sister's house when Charles stumbled and fell. It was then that I revealed the reason behind his sickness. I explained that I might need weekly trips to Toronto to check on him and offer companionship. Memories of our shared childhood flooded back—the laughter, the struggles, and the unbreakable bond. Charles had always been proud of my journey—from the streets to meeting Margret and building a life together.

The urgency of the call pulled me back to Toronto, where St. Joseph's Hospital stood—a place of healing and heartache. Frank, Charles's partner, delivered the news: Charles had been admitted. We met in the hospital, and memories resurfaced as we sat over coffee. Frank hadn't changed much since my departure to Exeter, where I found love with Margret. Despite my inner conflict, I acknowledged that Frank had become Charles's family, watching over him. Yet, it was Frank who had led Charles down this dangerous path, allowing him to drown his sorrows in alcohol—a slow descent toward the hospital bed where he now lay, fading away.

I settled into the worn armchair beside Charles, the leather creaking in protest. The hospital room smelled of disinfectant. Charles leaned in closer with his fragile body and large intruding midsection. His eyes held a lifetime of sorrows. His voice, husky and weathered, carried the weight of those years. "Vancouver," he said, his gaze distant. Rain-soaked streets, mist clinging to your skin and clothes. I lived there once, chasing dreams."

I nodded, eager for more. Charles had always been a wanderer, a restless soul seeking solace in far-off places. "And you?" Charles asked, his eyes piercing. "Tell me about your son." I hesitated, then spilled my heart. "Dylan," I said. "Bright-eyed, curious—a miniature version of me. We play hide-and-seek in the backyard, and he insists on being the seeker every time. And now," I paused, my hand resting on my belly, "another little one is on the way." A secret whispered between him and me.

The door swung open, and two nurses bustled in. Their footsteps echoed like soldiers. Charles winced as they adjusted his pillows, their gloved hands gentle yet efficient. His abdomen, once lean and taut, now bulged like a watermelon. The fluid—the toxins from a failing liver—had swelled him from within. "Charles," I said softly, "are you scared?" He chuckled, a brittle sound. "Scared? No. I've danced with death too many times to be scared. But this time…" His eyes flickered toward the window, where raindrops raced down the glass. "This time, I'm tired. Tired of running, tired of pretending."

The nurse performed a procedure called paracentesis or abdominal tap to drain the excess fluid from Charles's abdominal cavity by using a long catheter, alleviating discomfort and making Charles more comfortable lying in the bed. This procedure they performed a few times a day, and Charles would hold the side railing of the bed and try to turn himself sideways while grunting in pain. The doctors had spoken to me earlier. Charles, they said, wasn't eligible for the transplant waiting list. His past—a dance with alcohol, plus the hepatitis C—had left its mark—a scarlet letter etched into his medical records. "He won't make it," they whispered, their voices heavy with regret. "Not this time."

I glanced at Charles, his face etched with lines of pain and defiance. He'd fought battles—against the bottle, against himself. But now, as the rain tapped against the window, he was losing the war. "Charles," I said, trembling, "what if there's a way? A loophole, a hidden path?" He raised an eyebrow. "And what would that be?" I leaned in, my breath mingling with his.

"What if," I whispered, "I share my liver? You and I. We'll share it, piece by piece. Maybe then, the doctors won't say no."

His laughter was a fragile thing, like wings beating against a storm. "You're a dreamer," he said. "But I like that about you." And so, in that dim hospital room, we made a pact. Two souls, bound by stories and scars, ready to defy fate. Charles, the wanderer, and me—the dreamer. We'd rewrite the ending together, even if it meant dancing on the edge of impossibility.

On that poignant Friday evening, the hospital corridors echoed with hushed conversations and the antiseptic scent. I grappled with the uncertainty—had I already dialled my mother and sisters, or was Frank the one who'd made that call? Charles, frail yet resolute, lay in his sterile room, his life hanging in the balance. The next day, I returned, determined to bring a spark of joy. With Dylan and Margaret by my side, we entered Charles's room. His eyes crinkled with delight as he beheld his nephew—a mirror image of me, missing tooth and all. Charles enveloped Dylan in a warm hug, whispering, "You're just like your dad." In that fleeting moment, family bonds transcended illness.

Life's twists and turns often lead us to unexpected crossroads, where family dynamics, like weddings or funerals, play out intricately. Charles's final days became a blend of love, tension, and shedding tears for the unknown. Frank and I stood side by side, our shared history etched in the lines of our faces. Charles weakened but resolute, held no doubt: I was his brother, and that bond transcended all else. Yet, our upbringing cast shadows—had we been nurtured in a different context, perhaps our roles would have shifted. Janet and my mother sought direction from Frank. He, however, carried Charles's silent wishes—to let me make the medical decisions, while Janet's insistence mirrored a legal common-law partnership. In that fragile balance, we grappled with love, control, and the uncharted territory of family ties.

As Charles's health waned, my siblings took turns at his bedside. The weight of responsibility settled on my shoulders when Mr. Gabriel handed me the legal documents, granting me power of attorney. Now, discussions between our family and the doctors flowed through me. Ever resilient, Charles cracked jokes with his siblings, bringing laughter into our bittersweet farewell. Some sisters were absent, bound by work, while Nicole—the steadfast police constable—parked her cruiser in the emergency area and came upstairs wearing her uniform. I spoke to her, conveying the truth: Charles's organs were faltering. In that room, duty and family blurred, and mortality hung heavy in the air.

The following day, I enjoyed breakfast at Frank's

restaurant before going to the hospital. My brother's health was deteriorating rapidly, and his partner seemed intent on filling the void left by my brother's impending departure, offering me a hundred dollars. It was a delicate situation, complicated by memories from our shared past when I was seventeen. His attempt to rekindle that connection was misguided, as I was now married with children and not inclined toward the same gender. His motivations seemed shallow, driven by physical desire rather than genuine emotion. It was a stark reminder that some people view others as objects, easily discarded when their purpose is fulfilled.

That morning, I sat down with the doctor and nurses, eager for any news about Charles. The room felt sterile, the air heavy with anticipation. The doctor's voice was measured as they delivered the verdict: Charles's kidneys were shutting down, his body poisoned from within. His organs, once resilient, now faltered like a symphony losing its rhythm. Life support and kidney dialysis were our last options, but even those couldn't promise salvation. As I absorbed this grim reality, I knew I had to gather my family—the final decision rested with me. The weight of it all settled on my shoulders, a burden I couldn't shake.

Outside, Janet and my mother huddled with Frank, their voices hushed. The topic? Arranging for a priest to administer the Last Rites to Charles—a solemn ritual to prepare him for the journey beyond. But here's the twist: Charles wasn't religious. Our upbringing had been staunchly Baptist, and I couldn't recall ever stepping into a Catholic mass. My faith leaned toward born-again Christianity, and I grappled with the idea of Charles losing his salvation due to practices that felt foreign to me. It was a delicate balance—respecting tradition while staying true to my beliefs.

The priest's words echoed outside Charle's room—a rehearsed litany devoid of the fire I'd expected. Holy water dripped from Charles's forehead, and the ancient verses looped like a broken record. But the Spirit? Absent. When the ritual concluded, they retreated to the waiting room. Besides Charles, I felt the weight of his curiosity. His eyes searched mine, seeking answers. How had I escaped the streets? Why was my joy so palpable? I leaned in, whispering my truth: "Jesus found me. He lifted my burdens and filled me with purpose. Salvation isn't a distant promise—it's here, now, in this room." Charles listened, perhaps finding solace in my unwavering faith.

In that sacred moment, with tears tracing paths down Charles's cheeks, we stood on the precipice of eternity. The sinner's prayer hung in the air—a plea for redemption, a bridge between brokenness and grace. I shared the story of the two thieves crucified alongside Jesus—their lives diverging in those final breaths. One mocked, the other repented. Charles, too, faced that choice: to cling to despair or reach for salvation. His voice trembled as he echoed my words, inviting Jesus into his heart and seeking forgiveness. The room seemed to hold its breath, suspended between earthly pain and heavenly hope. And there, in the quiet, Charles surrendered. The weight of guilt lifted, replaced by a promise—a homecoming beyond this world.

In that poignant moment, I held Charles tightly, our connection transcending the fragile boundary between life and death. As his breath wavered, uncertainty and hope flickered in his eyes. His grip on my hand intensified as if anchoring him to this world. And then, with a final exhale, he slipped away. His eyes, once vibrant, turned black as his spirit departed, leaving behind an empty vessel—the warmth drained from his skin, replaced by an eerie gray pallor. I had never witnessed a human passing so intimately, especially not a beloved family member. Yet, amidst the shock, a strange peace settled within me. I whispered to Charles; promising paradise awaited him. Perhaps it was my desperate hope, but I believed it. The knowledge that he was saved, that we would reunite someday, eased the ache of loss. I didn't mourn a brother; instead, I clung to the solace of having saved one.

I turned to my mother as she entered the room from

talking to my sisters. "He's gone," I whispered. She collapsed beside him, repeating the same anguished question: "Why, Charles? Why?" The nurses arrived, confirming what we already knew. Charles had left us. His wishes were clear—no earthly plot for him. Instead, he longed for the vastness of the ocean, the place where he began. So, we would honour him by sending his ashes back to Newfoundland, to St. John's. The waves would carry him away there, and I found solace in knowing he was saved, awaiting our reunion. In that moment, grief and hope intertwined, and I held onto the belief that Charles had found his paradise. In the days that followed, Frank meticulously orchestrated Charles's final farewell.

The weight of exhaustion clung to me like a heavy shroud—I had spent countless hours at Charles's bedside in the hospital, witnessing the frailty of life. Each beep of the monitor echoed the rhythm of our shared heartbeats, and I longed for the solace that only time could bring.

The call came—an invitation to say our last good-byes. We returned to Toronto, dressed in sombre Sunday attire, the fabric clinging to our grief. The funeral home stood just down the street from Frank's bustling restaurant. As we stepped inside, the air grew thick with sorrow, and I felt the weight of Charles's absence settle upon my chest. There he lay, Charles, in a rented casket—a vessel transformed. His black suit and tie were impeccably arranged, eyes and mouth closed as if in peaceful slumber. The room buzzed with whispered conversations, memories shared, and tears shed. But Charles remained still, untouched by the world's tumult. His departure left a void—an ache that defied words.

I stood there, torn between grief and gratitude. Charles was more than flesh and bone; he was laughter, late-night conversations, and shared secrets. Now, reduced to this silent form, he seemed distant and close. I wondered about his journey beyond—whether heaven awaited him, its gates open wide. In my heart, I whispered prayers, hoping that his intentions for salvation were sincere and that his heart had found its way home.

And so, we gathered—the living and the departed—in that solemn room, bound by love and loss. The wake began a fragile bridge connecting this world to the next. As I touched Charles's cold hand, I realized that our stories, woven together over the years, now unravelled into memory.

Charles was taken to the crematorium, where he was gently removed from his rental casket and placed into a rigid cardboard container. As he was transferred into the incinerator furnace, I stood behind a glass window, watching in sorrow as his body was consumed by flames reaching 1000 degrees Celsius. It was a profound moment, witnessing my brother's transformation from flesh and bone to ashes, a poignant reminder of the biblical phrase, "From dust, you came, and to dust, you shall return."

Once the cremation was complete, his ashes were carefully collected, placed into a bag, and then transferred into a small wooden box with a lid. This box was handed to Frank, who was entrusted with fulfilling Charles's final wish: to have his ashes scattered over the ocean in Newfoundland. However, this wish was thwarted when Bob's wife, Charles's stepmother, took possession of the ashes. She insisted on bringing them back home, effectively imprisoning Charles's remains in a wooden box within their home, never to be released and set free as he had desired. This selfishness prevented Charles from finding the peace he longed for, leaving his spirit confined and his final wish unfulfilled.

He was gone, but his essence lingered—a whisper in the hush of grief, a testament to our shared humanity. He was my friend and brother, but he was now gone. Goodbye, Charles.

18

BLUE HOUSE ACROSS THE TRACKS

Fate nudged us across town, away from the clamour of apartment buildings and into the quieter embrace of a different neighbourhood. The air shifted—less exhaust, more possibility. We found it: a blue bungalow, modest but promising. Two bedrooms, snug within 1,200 square feet on Peel Street.

Our basement, a relic of ancient times, was a makeshift bedroom, its door hanging askew, refusing to close with a satisfying click. With each step, the stairs, a symphony of creaks and groans led down to the entrance of our room, inside a carpet, a shaggy relic from the seventies. It held a musty scent, a cocktail of dampness and mould, a silent testament to the moisture that seeped in uninvited. A tiny window, more an ornament than a functional feature, was nailed shut, its view obscured by a tapestry of cobwebs.

Outside our room, against the wall, the washer and dryer hummed their mechanical lullabies, keeping company with the water heater. Another room was tucked under the stairs, a treasure trove of forgotten items - metal scraps, rusty nails, and half-empty paint cans.

We couldn't bear the thought of our little Dylan growing up in this damp environment, the mould a silent threat to his health. We feared the spectre of asthma that might haunt his childhood. So, we nestled him in the room upstairs, a cocoon of safety where we could hear his every stir and murmur.

The kitchen was a quaint picture of the past, with its ceramic white stove and fridge, the stove still boasting fuses. Just beyond the kitchen's back door was a mudroom, a sanctuary for coats and shoes. It was a room untouched by the warmth of the living, its insulation lacking, its windows bearing the scars of time. Yet, with a touch of creativity and a handful of large sticker tiles, I transformed the floor, infusing a semblance of homeliness into the space.

Our landlord, Andrew, was a mere two houses away. A solitary figure, his size was only matched by his fortune - a collection of properties bequeathed to him upon his parents' passing. His obesity, coupled with a relentless smoking habit, left him gasping for breath with every step.

Not long after we had settled into our new home, I received a call from Margret. She said Andrew was in our backyard, shears in hand, tending to the trees and shrubs. A sense of unease washed over me. We had barely unpacked our lives into this house, and it seemed we were already on the brink of a problem.

It appeared that Andrew considered the house his domain, a place he could enter without a courtesy call. His presence reminded me of the invisible strings attached to our new home, which he held firmly. I brought it to his attention that though it was his house, he needed to give us 24-hour notice to enter the property.

In a spirited quest to combat the creeping menace of mould in our basement, I armed myself with a can of waterproof grey paint, a symbol of resilience against the damp. The worn and weary steps bore the brunt of time, their paint flaking off like autumn leaves. With a painter's precision, I breathed new life into them, extending the rejuvenation to the wall that stretched up to the kitchen, a silent sentinel dividing spaces.

Once a rustic charm, the wood panels, now marred by water stains and mould, clung to the cement walls. Their removal was a necessity, revealing the raw bricks beneath. Each brick, a bulwark against the mould, received a coat of my trusty grey paint, sealing in the mould and halting its relentless march.

But the battle was far from over. A relic from the 1980s lurked above—the wiring in the ceiling, swathed in asbestos cloth. A silent threat, it held the potential to expose our family to the risk of mesothelioma. This discovery underscored the importance of our mission, reminding us that sometimes, the most significant threats are hidden from view.

With her green thumb, Margret added a splash of color to our home's facade by planting a vibrant array of flowers. Meanwhile, I embarked on a mission in our backyard, uprooting patches of grass to make way for a promising vegetable garden. This act, however, stirred a ripple in our neighbourly relations. Andrew was surprised, questioning why his permission wasn't sought for our horticultural endeavour.

On a brighter note, Margret's parents graced us with their presence, their hands bearing a house-warming gift—a barbeque set still nestled in its box, waiting for me to piece it together. They also brought Kate, Margret's friend, into our midst for the weekend.

While Margret was indoors and engaged in warm conversations with her parents, Kate became my ally in the barbeque assembly project. She was there, handing me screws and bolts, her gaze often meeting mine as she lay under my working space. There was an unspoken tension, a hint of unsaid feelings. It seemed she harboured a soft spot for me, yet she remained silent, perhaps because her loyalty lay with her best friend, Margret.

Just across the street, a spectacle unfolded that never piqued our interest. The neighbourhood was a colourful tapestry of characters, each with their intriguing narratives. One such character was Steve, a single father navigating the tumultuous waters of divorce while raising his energetic daughter, Anna. Anna was a bundle of energy with her red hair and freckles, her zest for life undiminished by her slightly overweight frame.

Their next-door neighbours presented a stark contrast. A household of two adult women and their mother, they seemed to thrive on conflict. Their favourite pastime appeared to be calling the police on Steve and Andrew, spinning tales of Steve littering their yard or Andrew casting inappropriate glances at their daughter during her lawn mowing sessions.

This constant drama added excitement to the otherwise peaceful Peel Street. The house of the three women, always shrouded in mystery with its perpetually covered windows, earned the moniker of 'the creepy house.' It was a source of endless fascination and speculation for the residents, making our neighbourhood far from mundane.

Our neighbour Steve had a Scottish girlfriend known for loving lively discussions and social drinking. Their visits to our place during the evenings for casual beers were memorable. The girlfriend was noticeably friendly towards me, which didn't go unnoticed even in Margret's presence. I often wondered if she was intuitively picking up on my inner turmoil or unfulfilled desires.

One evening, Steve invited me for a card game while Margret stayed home with Dylan. The evening, she turned unexpectedly when Steve's girlfriend returned from her room and sat beside me. She was dressed in a far too revealing manner for a casual gathering—no shirt, no bra, just her underwear and breasts. She seemed unfazed by her attire, even going as far as to ask if it bothered me. On the other hand, Steve wore an insincere smile, seemingly indifferent to the situation.

Faced with an escalating situation, I decided to excuse myself. Citing the late hour and Dylan's bedtime, I swiftly exited. The following day, Steve extended an apology for his girlfriend's behaviour. Like many others, this incident added to the tapestry of our neighbourhood interactions.

On May 2, 2000, a momentous event graced our lives—the birth of our daughter, Gwen. My heart swelled with joy as I held my little girl in my arms for the first time. Dylan, our son, was my pride and joy, but the arrival of Gwen added a new dimension to our family. There's a unique bond between a father and his daughter, a bond that is as delicate and beautiful as a princess in a fairy tale.

Gwen arrived in our world with hair as dark as a raven's feather and eyes a mesmerizing slate colour, reflecting the mysteries of the universe. But as time passed, her hair lightened, taking on the hue of golden sunshine, and her eyes transformed into a captivating blue, mirroring the clear skies. They were the same mesmerizing blue as her mother's and Dylan's, creating a beautiful symmetry in our family.

The names Gwen and Dylan were not chosen lightly. They were carefully selected from a list of Irish names, a nod to our heritage. Their middle names, however, were borrowed from our family tree, a tribute to the generations that came before us. This blend of tradition and individuality in their names is a testament to our family's journey and the legacy we hope to pass on to them.

We settled in our community in Acton, which welcomed us with open arms. Friendships blossomed, and I found my second home in Tim Horton's warm, inviting atmosphere. I became a familiar face among the regular parents. After dropping off our children at school, we would all meet and have coffee, and the moms would gossip while I hung out with Jeff, a single dad who was big on programming Direct TV cards, so we got along great.

Our son, Dylan, embarked on his educational journey, attending kindergarten at the public school just a stone's throw away from our house. Meanwhile, Gwen, our little bundle of energy, was exploring the world uniquely. She was a whirlwind of activity, running around, playing, and causing the delightful chaos that only a toddler can.

We observed Margret's relationship with her brothers, noticing the chasm a significant age gap can create. They had little in common, their interests diverged, and their circles of friends rarely overlapped. We wanted a different experience for our children. We wanted them to grow up together, sharing friends, hobbies, laughter, and occasional disputes.

So, we made a decision. We decided to welcome one more child into our family, bringing the count to three. This felt like the perfect number for us, a complete set. With this decision, we closed the chapter on expanding our family, content with the joyous chaos and boundless love that filled our home. So, on September 14th, 2002, we welcomed our second daughter, Megan, to our family. Her eyes and hair matched her siblings, making them all blond and blue eyes except me, who had lost most of my hair by this age.

In our quest to make our backyard a haven of fun and laughter, we introduced an above-ground pool to our family. This circular oasis, twelve feet in diameter and four feet deep, became a summer staple. Equipped with a pump, it was our private retreat during the warm months, and in the winters, it was carefully packed away.

However, this addition still needs to be met with universal approval. Andrew, ever the guardian of our green spaces, was less than thrilled. The pool, while a source of joy and refreshment, had an unintended consequence. It left its mark on our lawn, quite literally. The grass under the tarp didn't survive, leaving behind a large patch of dirt that stood out in stark contrast to the surrounding greenery.

Undeterred by this minor setback, I added another fun element to our backyard - a wooden fort playground. Complete with a slide and swings; it was a miniature adventure park for our little ones. But I didn't stop there. I added an extra section on top of the slide, a lookout point. From there, they could stand tall and peer over the fence, their curious eyes taking in the sights of the school playground. Our backyard was transformed into a realm of endless possibilities, a testament to the joy of childhood. I wanted them to have all the fun things I missed out on growing up, as any parent wants the best for their children.

After a series of jobs in gas stations and coffee shops, I found myself at a crossroads despite my earnest attempts to return to school to earn my high school diploma. I needed to secure a more stable and lucrative career. After all, I had a family to support. Even though Margret was the primary breadwinner, I keenly felt the weight of my responsibilities.

One fateful night, Margret handed me a newspaper clipping. A job advertisement that immediately piqued my interest. The bold, captivating title read, "Private Investigator Wanted." It was as if destiny was calling, offering me a chance to embark on a new, exciting journey. Little did I know, this was the beginning of a new chapter in our lives.

My knowledge of Private Investigating was, admittedly, quite limited. It was gleaned from the thrilling adventures of Magnum P.I. on television, where crime-solving seemed as exciting as it was effortless. Like the legendary Sherlock Holmes and the intrepid Hardy Boys, unravelling mysteries had a certain allure. The thought of stepping into their shoes, navigating the intricate web of clues, and emerging victorious was daunting and exhilarating. Little did I know, this was the start of a journey that would redefine my life.

With a mix of anticipation and curiosity, I made a call and scheduled an appointment. The destination was Mississauga, on a street named Millcreek Drive.

Nestled in a quaint plaza, I found my destination - a door bearing the sign 'Riscon Services.'

To my surprise, a high school education was optional for the position. They offered comprehensive training, both in their office and in the field. Moreover, they even covered the cost of the private investigator license upon completion of the training. It seemed like a golden opportunity, a door opening to a new path.

However, reality often differs from our expectations. Yes, the role required one to act in character, much like the detectives I admired on television. But the job itself was different from what I had envisioned. It was a stark reminder that real life seldom mirrors the glossy sheen of TV shows. Yet, it was a step, a beginning, and I was ready to embark on this unexpected journey.

I stepped into the role of Loss Prevention. My journey began at a Sobeys store not far from the office. There, I met my trainer, Kofi, a company supervisor who would guide me through the intricacies of the job.

My task was an intriguing blend of the mundane and the extraordinary. On the surface, I was just another customer, strolling through the aisles, seemingly engrossed in shopping. But beneath this ordinary facade, I was on a mission. My eyes were trained on the other customers, watching their every move with hawk-like vigilance. My goal? To spot shoplifters in the act of stealing groceries.

When I identified a shoplifter, it was my responsibility to apprehend them. In those moments, I felt an adrenaline rush akin to what a police officer might feel. I had the power to arrest people, which was daunting and exhilarating. It was a far cry from the world of gas stations and coffee shops, yet it felt strangely fitting. It was not the path I had envisioned, but it was a path that I was ready to tread.

"Imagine a world where it takes a thief to catch a thief. That's the world I thrived in, honing my skills to an art form, thanks to my survival upbringing that gifted me an uncanny ability to spot shoplifters. Picture this: a bustling Winners store, where I first crossed paths with Stephen, my soon-to-be best friend. Fresh from the battlefields of Israel, Stephen was a soldier with a treasure trove of tales. As I took him under my wing, training him for the company in my new role as a field training officer, we found common ground and soon became inseparable, even off duty. Together, we were an unstoppable force, racking up more monthly arrests than any other investigators. This not only lined our pockets with higher pay but also propelled us to better positions within the company. Our story is a testament to friendship, teamwork, and the thrill of the chase."

A more prominent security company called Garda eventually overtook the company out of Quebec. The owner, Bill, left the company, but his daughter, Michelle, became my new boss. While she was taking me to some of the stores, we stopped at a park, and she took advantage of me and seduced me inside the car, doing an indecent act on me while I was sitting in the seat. I felt used, but she gave me a raise and gave herself to me in her apartment in front of the windows.

Amid my life's journey, I was entangled in a web of contradictions. My marriage, once a sacred bond, had become a mere facade, a hollow shell devoid of the love and commitment it once held. Yet, the thought of my innocent children, their eyes filled with untainted joy and curiosity, anchored me to this semblance of stability. Their youth and vulnerability demanded my presence, my protection.

Simultaneously, another life beckoned me, a life of unattached freedom reminiscent of a carefree bachelorhood. This life was a whirlwind of fleeting encounters, a pursuit of physical connections as numerous as they were hollow. It was a life where emotions were foreign, where the cold thrill of the chase replaced the warmth of genuine affection.

The strain of straddling these two worlds was beginning to wear me down. The constant juggling act, the relentless oscillation between the responsible family man and the reckless bachelor, became increasingly unsustainable. I yearned for a more spartan existence, where I couldn't hide or pretend and be true to myself and those around me.

Margret gently persuaded me to undergo a vasectomy following the birth of our third and final child. Our family was complete, and the thought of an unexpected pregnancy was something she wished to avoid. The surgical procedure and recovery time for a tubal ligation, a procedure she would have to undergo, was significantly more extensive than a vasectomy.

I embarked on a research journey, seeking to understand the implications of the procedure. It was a strange realization, knowing that my body would continue to produce sperm, but it would be treated as an unwelcome intruder, fought off and expelled by my own body. This knowledge was unsettling, a reminder of the alien nature of the procedure.

Yet, amidst the discomfort, there was a silver lining. The vasectomy ensured that I could not inadvertently cause a pregnancy. This fact brought relief and freedom from the fear of unintended consequences. It was a small consolation, a positive aspect in an otherwise challenging situation.

19

SEPARATION AND RECONCILIATION

My career in the security industry has been a journey of constant growth and exploration. Having worked with half a dozen security companies, I've had the opportunity to expand my knowledge across various sectors. Each role has added a new dimension to my expertise, from supervising security operations to conducting internal and external investigations, from sales to managing entire security divisions.

However, after gaining experience in third-party security companies, I felt the need for a change. An opportunity presented itself in the form of an in-house security position at The Hudson Bay Company. They had an opening for a loss prevention role at their

Zellers store in the Milton Mall, just fifteen minutes from Acton.

Taking up this role meant I was the sole employee running the loss prevention department, a challenge I was ready to embrace. Reporting directly to the store manager, I was entrusted with the responsibility of ensuring the safety and security of the store. This new chapter in my career promised to be as enriching and exciting as before.

The transition to The Hudson Bay Company brought a welcome change in my daily routine. Gone were the days of driving across Ontario, navigating through traffic, and spending precious time and gas visiting different stores. Now, my work was concentrated in one location - the Zellers store in Milton Mall.

This position was perfect in terms of logistics and financially rewarding. The pay was a significant step from what I earned at the previous security company. Moreover, being part of the HBC family was a boon for my family.

Not long after I joined, the store embarked on a transformation journey. It underwent a comprehensive renovation, changing its layout and expanding its size in preparation for Target's upcoming takeover. As I watched the store evolve and grow, I felt a sense of anticipation and excitement for the new challenges and opportunities ahead.

Before the store's transformation, my office was tucked away behind the receiving department. However, recognizing the need for a more strategic location, I persuaded the manager to construct a dedicated security office for me. The new office was ideally situated on the main floor, adjacent to the bustling entertainment department.

The store was grappling with a high theft rate, and cases were piling up at an alarming rate. From students pilfering DVD games and movies to girls shoplifting swimsuits and bras, the variety of cases was as diverse as challenging. The sheer volume of incidents kept me on my toes, constantly vigilant and ready to act.

To tackle this issue, we initiated loss prevention meetings involving other stores and the local police. These meetings served as a platform to discuss suspects and share case details, fostering a collaborative approach to loss prevention. This collective effort was instrumental in our fight against theft, helping us protect the store's assets while ensuring a safe shopping environment for our customers.

During the renovation phase, my role expanded beyond the confines of the store. The manager entrusted me with transporting merchandise from our sister stores in Kitchener and Guelph. This involved renting a truck trailer and meticulously organizing the items for transport. The process demanded a high level of organization and careful paperwork tracking to ensure that every item was accounted for from the moment it left the other stores until it was safely locked up and scanned into our inventory. The problem was that it did not exist and usually followed months later and never matched what was in inventory.

However, this period also brought with it a growing sense of disillusionment. Over the years, I have witnessed countless instances of theft, with criminals often escaping justice and reaping substantial profits from their illicit activities. This exposure began to cloud my perception of right and wrong.

I found myself questioning the corporate world's ethics. These companies, raking millions of dollars, seemed to undervalue their most loyal employees. It struck me as unjust that managers who had dedicated over a decade to the company were earning less than me and the part-time employees even less. This disparity between the company's profits and its treatment of employees began to weigh heavily on my conscience.

In my role at The Hudson Bay Company, I found myself in a unique position where I could discreetly remove high-value items like brand-new Acer laptops and PS3 consoles without detection. This was due to the chaotic environment created by the store's renovation and the influx of merchandise from other stores.

Simultaneously, I was conducting an internal investigation into an employee from the entertainment department. This individual was colluding with students, smuggling DVD box sets and headphones out of the store in their backpacks after shifts. Upon discovery, the employee was terminated and required to reimburse the store for the stolen items. This incident conveniently covered any other missing items from the lockup that the terminated employee assumed had been stolen.

During my tenure at Zellers, I found myself drawn to a colleague from the jewelry department. Her name was Brandy, a name as unique and captivating as her French surname. She held a supervisory role and was a key-holder, having been a part of the team long before I joined.

Our camaraderie grew over time, evolving into a close friendship that didn't go unnoticed. The other supervisors and store management were aware of our growing bond. Despite this, the manager remained indifferent, though he was aware of my marital status and my children. His only advice was a word of caution, a gentle reminder to tread carefully given my circumstances.

I can't quite pinpoint what led me to develop feelings for Brandy. It was an inexplicable attraction that seemed to have blossomed out of nowhere. Our relationship took a significant turn one day at the back of the store. Brandy was disposing of some cardboard when I stopped her at the doorway.

There was a moment of silence as she turned to look at me, her eyes reflecting myriad emotions. Drawn by an irresistible force, I moved closer, gently cradling her head. As our lips met in a tender kiss, time seemed to stand still. She reciprocated with a passionate French kiss, a moment that lingered even as she returned to the hustle and bustle of the store. This began a new chapter in our relationship that was as unexpected as profound.

Behind the scenes, Brandy and I embarked on a new journey together. We were searching for a place we could call our own in Milton. While her previous living situation details are hazy, she shared her space with a roommate.

Our search led us to a charming apartment on Main Street in Milton. Nestled above a furniture store, it promised a fresh start. Together, we transformed this empty apartment into a cozy home. We furnished it with essentials—a comfortable bed, a plush couch, and a television—creating a warm and inviting space.

We added our personal touch to the place by painting the walls, infusing them with colors that reflected our personalities. The apartment boasted windows that offered diverse views - some faced the serene back of the building, others opened up to the lively scenes of the front, and one even provided a unique vantage point onto the roof. This window was accompanied by a door, offering easy access to the roof, where one could sit and soak in the surroundings. This apartment, with its unique features and our personal touches, marked the beginning of our shared journey.

During this period, my days were a blur of long hours at the store and quiet evenings with Brandy, both serving as distractions from thoughts of Margret and the kids. Steve, the ever-inquisitive neighbor across the street, had quickly caught wind of my move. He took it upon himself to keep his daughter playing with my children, using it as an excuse to spend time with Margret in the backyard. Despite the comfort I found in Brandy's company, it wasn't long before the guilt of being away from my family began to gnaw at me, making our brief time together feel even shorter.

I continued visiting the house to see the children, and during those visits, Margret and I often talked about the possibility of reconciling. She loved and forgave me, but I struggled with forgiving myself, convinced it was too late to repair the damage. I knew how hard it was for her to juggle work and care for our three young children. My time with Brandy, though comforting, never felt like a severe or long-term solution. The longing for my children grew more robust, and I realized I needed to try to mend our relationship and end my affair with Brandy.

Margret's parents were well aware of my departure and had been supporting her through the tough times. When I decided to move back in, they welcomed me as if nothing had happened. Margret's mother even pulled me aside to express her relief and happiness, especially for the sake of the young children. Steve, on the other hand, seemed taken aback by my return. I could sense that Margret was relieved, too, as his visits became less frequent, mainly when I was around.

Margret chose to keep our separation hidden from her grandmother, fearing it might cast me in a negative light. She also refrained from sharing the situation with her uncle. Upon my return to the house, her brothers remained silent, offering no words to me. However, the children, particularly Megan, were overjoyed to have me back home.

I decided to leave the security industry and resign from my position at HBC. My departure was driven by ethical concerns and a growing sense that the internal investigators were becoming suspicious about the missing inventory. Adding to the complexity, our manager had recently left to join Giant Tiger, and his replacement, a strict and uncompromising female manager, and I often clashed over store operations. On a personal note, I realized that if I wanted to salvage my marriage, I couldn't continue working there with Brandy despite our affair being over. The environment had become too toxic and untenable for me to stay.

A bustling plaza with a Canadian Tire store was just five minutes away, down the same street and over the tracks. Intrigued by the possibility of a new career path, I approached the automotive department to inquire about becoming an apprentice. With my extensive experience with cars and engines, I was thrilled when they accepted me into their class-A mechanic program after a quick application process. The program spanned four years, requiring hands-on shop hours and class-room learning. It felt like the perfect opportunity to turn my passion for automobiles into a professional skill set.

To get started, I needed to provide all my tools. So, I headed inside Canadian Tire and invested in a heavy-duty Mastercraft tool cabinet with various-sized drawers and a locking cover to keep my tools safe from potential theft by other employees. It was a significant expense, costing around eight hundred dollars. The essential tools included an impact gun with heavy-duty sockets for removing wheel lug nuts, wrenches, screw-drivers, gloves, an air pressure gauge, and other items.

Once a week, a Snap-On dealer would visit with a truck filled with every tool a mechanic could dream of, though they came with a hefty price tag. We could purchase these tools on credit, deducted from our paychecks, but I couldn't afford to take on that financial burden. Plus, I was still uncertain about how this apprenticeship program would pan out for me.

Everything was going smoothly as I settled into my new role. My tasks included changing over winter to spring tires, removing the rubber from the rims, fitting them onto new rims, performing oil changes, checking fluids, and replacing windshield wiper blades. These were the typical jobs assigned to students, while the licensed mechanics handled the more complex tasks that occupied most of the shift.

I developed a good rapport with Frank, the main mechanic, who occasionally let me assist with more intricate jobs like changing head gaskets and radiators. However, not all students were as fortunate. Some frequently got into trouble for forgetting to replace the oil plug in customers' cars, neglecting to add oil to the engine, or scratching customers' rims. Despite these challenges, I found the experience rewarding and educational.

The job extended through the summer and winter, providing me with experience. I earned certification in the Ministry Emissions Test Program, which involved loading vehicles onto a machine, inserting a sensor into the exhaust pipe, and accelerating the car to sixty kilometers per hour until the computer completed the test.

Diesel and Volkswagen cars were exempt from this process, as they didn't need to go on the dyno machine. It was crucial to position the vehicle correctly, depending on whether it was front or rear-wheel drive, as all-wheel-drive cars couldn't be tested on the dyno machine.

This added layer of complexity kept the job exciting and challenging. Sometimes, we got exotic cars from nearby dealerships, such as Ferrari and Lamborghini, and I refused to test those cars or drive them into the bay on the machine in case any damage occurred. I was not going to take the blame; during the winter months, it got frustrating as the doors always had to be down, and my fingers were permanently frozen while changing the oil and having dirty salty slush dropping on my head and clothes.

I quickly began to understand the shop's intricate pecking order. When new orders arrived at the front desk, they were placed in a tray. However, two main mechanics would swoop in, grabbing all the orders and putting them on their desks. This left no jobs for the other employees, creating a clear divide. This favoritism between the service manager and these mechanics meant we were stuck with the less desirable tasks. This bred resentment and stifled our opportunities to learn the essential skills needed to advance a Class A mechanic. It was a frustrating cycle, making it nearly impossible to climb the professional ladder.

We ended abruptly at the rental house as Andrew's incessant intrusions became unbearable. His unannounced visits not only violated our privacy but also skirted the boundaries of the Landlord Protection Act. Andrew gave us notice that he wanted us to move out. We were determined to find our place, so Margret and I embarked on a house-hunting adventure around Acton. We explored different properties each day, imagining our future in each one.

Our evening walks around the neighborhood became a cherished routine, offering us a glimpse into the community we hoped to join. One day, we stumbled upon a charming house that piqued our interest. Curiously, there was no "For Sale" sign out front. We later discovered that the owners were discreetly selling, not wanting to alert their neighbors. This added an air of mystery and excitement to our search, making us even more eager to learn about this property.

The house was ideally situated just two doors from the Pentecostal church we attended and close to the Christian Reformed Dutch Church. Its location directly across from the children's school was a dream come true, making morning drop-offs a breeze. We could stand on our front porch and watch as they eagerly ran to their lineups each morning.

Remarkably, it was just two houses away from our current rental, making the transition even more seamless. It felt like divine intervention, an answer to our prayers. However, we faced a significant hurdle: we didn't have a down payment ready on such short notice. The thought of losing this perfect home to another buyer was daunting. We knew we needed help to seize this opportunity before it slipped through our fingers.

We knocked on the door and were greeted by the owner, who seemed taken aback by our request to see the house. She hesitated, explaining that the place needed to be neater and more prepared for a showing. However, we assured her we were more interested in the property's potential than its current state. Reluctantly, she agreed to let us take a look around.

Its spaciousness immediately struck us as we walked through the house. The upstairs boasted four generous bedrooms, perfect for our growing family. There was a bathroom on each floor, including one in the basement, which added a layer of convenience we hadn't expected. The main floor featured a large kitchen that seemed ideal for family gatherings, a dining room that could host many memorable meals, and a cozy living room with a charming stone fireplace that instantly felt like home. The house, spanning around 2,000 square feet, had all the space we needed and more.

As we descended the stairs, we noticed a door that initially led to the garage but had been cleverly converted into a spare room or office. At the bottom of the stairs, we were greeted by an unexpected sight: a Jacuzzi hot tub in the corner beside the furnace room. Next to it was a custom sauna, spacious enough to accommodate a dozen people and a small washroom.

The washer and dryer were conveniently located beside the furnace. We were both astonished by the array of features this house offered, especially considering it was priced around the two hundred-thousand-dollar range. It felt like we had stumbled upon a hidden treasure packed with amenities that seemed too good to be true.

Then came the backyard. As we slid open the kitchen door, we stepped onto a half-finished deck with a stunning view of an eighteen-foot-long pool complete with a diving board. The pool deck was beautifully paved with interlocked bricks, and a custom cabana pool bar stood ready for summer gatherings. This was the icing on the cake, the final touch that made us fall in love with the house. Despite the absence of a complete garage, we were both convinced that this property was meant to be ours. It had everything we could have hoped for and more, and we decided to make it our home.

Thanks to Margret's parents' generous offer to help

with the down payment, we eagerly met with the real estate agent, signed the offer, and anxiously awaited a response. We only needed five thousand dollars to make the offer, conduct a home inspection, and secure mortgage approval. The anticipation was palpable as we waited for the bank's decision.

When the call finally came, the bank congratulated us on purchasing our house and invited us to sign the papers. The down payment wouldn't be needed until closing day, which would go to the lawyer and the bank cheque. We were overjoyed, knowing our dream of owning a home had finally come true. The sense of accomplishment and happiness we felt was indescribable.

20

NEW HOMES SAME STRUGGLES

We finally took possession of our new house on closing day, and with a few days left at Andrew's home, we began the big move. Margret's brothers and father were a tremendous help, loading the larger boxes into their farm pickup truck. We walked them to the new place for the smaller items, enjoying the short journey. One of my first tasks was to disassemble the kids' fort and reassemble it in our new backyard, which offered a charming view of the neighbor's fence. It felt like a fresh start for the whole family.

Moving my Pontiac Fiero was another adventure. Since it wasn't running, Margret's brother and I had to push it while Margret steered. I had ambitiously cut off the roof to transform it into a Ferrari replica. Unfortunately, the garage was packed with my work tools and boxes, leaving no room for the car. It was a chaotic but memorable start to our new chapter.

It was early spring, and we first saw the house in winter. The pool was winterized and covered, so we had yet to learn about its condition or whether the pump and lines worked. As the snow and ice began to melt, I found myself in the backyard with Steve, our old next-door neighbor, giving him a tour of the property.

Megan was just a few years old and was playing near the pool's edge when she suddenly fell into the shallow end, slipping through the tarp that covered it. Panic surged through me as I reached down to grab her arm. But before I could react, Steve leaped into the pool, scooping her up and bringing her to safety. I quickly wrapped her in a blanket to warm her up, grateful for Steve's quick thinking despite his overreaction.

Finally, we could change the property without worrying about a landlord's approval. This was our house, and we could shape it exactly how we wanted. I eagerly dove into renovations, starting with the kitchen and dining room.

In the kitchen, I lowered the island's top to make it more functional and added a stylish tiled backsplash, complete with an extra outlet for convenience. The dining room received a modern makeover with box squares and crown molding, transforming into a classy space with white beams and rich chocolate centers. Seeing our vision come to life in our own home felt incredibly satisfying.

The deck outside needed attention, with no railing and incomplete steps. Determined to transform it, I headed to Home Depot and ordered pressure-treated wood and sleek black poles to create a sturdy and stylish railing. To add a touch of charm, I installed elegant black solar lights that beautifully accented the deck, along with a convenient sit-up shelf perfect for drinks during pool parties.

Around the deck, I built two steps to the brick patio near the pool's edge, leaving just enough space to walk by and reach the diving board. The improvements enhanced the deck's safety and functionality, making it a welcoming space for gatherings and relaxation.

To ensure the children's safety, I installed a self-closing gate on the deck, preventing them from accessing the pool unsupervised. This added peace of mind allowed us to enjoy our outdoor space without constant worry, knowing the kids were safe while playing on the deck.

As spring unfolded, Margret's green thumb brought life to our new home. She lovingly planted bulbs in front of the house, and soon, vibrant tulips and peonies burst into bloom, painting our yard with a riot of colors. Our weekends were spent exploring local nurseries, where we carefully selected more plants, mulch, and a graceful weeping Mulberry tree.

I meticulously landscaped the front yard, placing the Mulberry tree along the driveway, bordered by a line of rustic quarry stones. To give our home a fresh, modern look, I added black shutters to the windows and painted the garage and main doors sleek black. The transformation was remarkable, and our house felt like a true reflection of us.

I eagerly removed the cover from our new inground pool, opening all the jets and priming the pump as the water level rose to the top of the liner. This was my first experience with an inground pool, but thankfully, Margret's expertise as a former lifeguard proved invaluable. With her guidance, we installed the diving board, and soon, the water was crystal clear, inviting us to dive in.

The pool party kicked off with the kids splashing in the shallow end, their laughter echoing through the yard. As the days passed, they grew more confident, eventually mastering the deep end. Watching them transform from hesitant beginners to enthusiastic swimmers was a joy.

As time went by, our house underwent a series of small yet significant transformations. One of the biggest projects was dismantling the old kabana, a challenging task due to its heavy wood beams. Armed with a chainsaw, I carefully cut it apart, and we repurposed the wood by burning it in a fireplace I constructed using extra bricks we had lying around.

The backyard saw the addition of a giant trampoline, which quickly became the centerpiece, occupying most of the space. On the other side of the house, we built vegetable gardens, adding a touch of greenery and a source of fresh produce to our home. Each change brought us closer to making the house truly our own.

The jacuzzi in the basement was a disappointment, broken and non-functional, a detail the previous owners conveniently omitted. However, I envisioned transforming the basement into a mini spa. I began by removing the wall between the cramped washroom and the sauna. By reducing the sauna's size by half,

I created space for a standard washroom, replacing the tiny 24" shower and the barely usable toilet. I constructed an entirely new bathroom with proper ventilation and elegant pot lights. The new toilet, sink, and corner shower were all adorned with beautiful travertine stone tiles, adding a touch of luxury.

Despite the reduction in size, the sauna remained spacious enough for eight people and, to my delight, heated up faster after the renovation. To complete the transformation, I enclosed the hot tub, washroom, and sauna with a wall made of glass blocks, giving the entire area an authentic spa-like ambiance. The basement had become a serene retreat, a perfect escape within our home.

The basement evolved into a man cave where Dylan and I spent countless hours playing Xbox games like Halo and Splinter Cell. Dylan's love for video games inspired me to upgrade our console to a limited-edition Crystal-Clear version, complete with matching controllers, which he adored. I also installed shelves to display our growing collection of movies and games, many of which I found at the local flea market.

I set up a custom-built computer in the converted garage, with neon lights and heavy-duty fans. It looked like a futuristic spaceship, glowing lime green with a transparent side panel that showcased all the moving components.

With my illegal Direct TV box satellite and some software, I began burning movies onto CDs, packaging them in full-sleeve cases reminiscent of Blockbuster and Jumbo Video. Selling them for ten dollars each became my little side hustle, adding an entrepreneurial twist to our basement adventures.

I cherished the countless hours spent lounging on the couch with my son and daughters, immersing ourselves in various movies. The animated films, in particular, brought endless joy and laughter to our living room.

Meanwhile, Margret was often tucked away in her office, diligently preparing for school lessons or meticulously grading papers. With my late shifts at Canadian Tire, our paths rarely crossed, and the precious moments of quality time together became few and far between.

Perceiving four exhausting years at Canadian Tire, I realized that my efforts to move beyond changing oil and tires were in vain. Despite my attempts to impress the service manager, it became clear that advancing to other roles was outside the cards for me. Burned and disheartened, I abandoned my dream of becoming an auto mechanic. The only other job I felt confident in was security, which became my new focus.

I decided to sell all my tools and my Mastercraft rolling storage cabinet online, and they were snapped up quickly. However, the proceeds weren't enough to cover the cost of the pricey Snap-On sets and power sockets I needed. So, I reapplied for my Private Investigator and Security Guard license. With the high demand for skilled investigators, I soon joined a reputable company in Woodbridge, stepping into the role of a real private investigator.

By this stage, I had become a master at presenting myself in the best light to secure the positions I desired.

With a robust portfolio of security experience, I could confidently navigate any interview, even in a new area of security that I had yet to learn. My ability to adapt and talk my way through any situation became my greatest asset.

In my new job, I investigated injury claims for insurance companies. This role demanded a reliable, inconspicuous vehicle and the ability to capture clear video footage with a Sony video recorder. I then had to upload the videos into a Word document with a comprehensive report and accompanying pictures to close each file and receive payment. The meticulous nature of this work kept me on my toes and sharpened my investigative skills.

Over the years, Margret and I had gone through many vehicles since we married, but our Dodge Minivan proved perfect for undercover work. I ingeniously blacked out the windows with curtains and set up a tripod in the back, allowing the camera lens to peer through the tinted window discreetly. This setup ensured that nobody could see me. However, a recurring issue was that when I parked outside someone's house in a subdivision or near a school, concerned neighbors would often call the police. Their arrival would inevitably blow my cover, causing me to lose the case.

After grueling months of working long hours, losing

suspects at red lights, and dealing with investigations that didn't go as planned, I became increasingly frustrated. The constant stress was compounded by the owner of the investigation company, whose high blood pressure and perpetually red face were matched only by his constant yelling. Realizing that this chaotic environment and style of investigation were not what I wanted, I decided to quit the job and seek a path better suited to my skills and aspirations.

As my relationship with Margret declined, I found solace in my morning coffee sessions with the ladies at Tim Horton's. One woman, whose child was the same age as ours and who had another baby in a stroller, began to show interest in me. Her smiles and attention became a source of comfort.

Before I knew it, we found ourselves in the back of her van, parked somewhere in Acton, engaging in actions I knew were wrong. Yet, it was the only way I knew to stave off the creeping depression. We had one more encounter at her house, on her husband's bed, before we decided to stop seeing each other. After that, she stopped coming to Tim Horton's, and our brief affair ended.

By this point, my relationship with Margret had devolved into a mere act of convenience, driven by the paralyzing fear of losing my children at such a tender age. Our failed attempts at marriage counseling with our pastor in Acton only deepened the chasm between us. My past traumas and experiences of sexual abuse had left indelible scars, hardening my heart to any genuine understanding of love. This emotional numbness extended to Margret and everyone else. Despite my profound love for my children, I could not shed tears in real life. Ironically, the movie's sorrowful scenes brought me to tears, allowing me to cry for strangers while remaining emotionally detached from my blood relatives.

I continued my routine of having morning coffee with the parent's group, carefully avoiding the one lady with whom I had an affair. During these mornings, I formed a connection with Teresa, a local regular at the coffee shop. Teresa was the go-to person for town gossip, always in the know about everyone and everything. We got along splendidly, finding solace in our shared experiences. Teresa lived with her son just outside of town in her own house. Like me, she was divorced and had endured the heavy burdens of depression and abuse. Our mutual understanding and similar struggles created a bond that made our conversations both comforting and meaningful.

One day, Teresa invited another friend from another town to join us for coffee. With her unmistakable British accent, this woman quickly became a fascinating addition to our group. She lived with her boyfriend and their son. Her boyfriend, a mechanic with a shop specializing in Mustang parts and service, and I found common ground despite my lack of enthusiasm for Ford. Our initial camaraderie, however, took an unexpected turn. I chose not to reveal their names as our relationship evolved into something unusual, dark, and twisted, so I'll call her Clair and her boyfriend Jack.

During one of our conversations, Clair mentioned she had an English mastiff, a gentle giant about a year old. She asked if I liked dogs and had a family and then offered me the opportunity to adopt her dog for free. The Mastiff had become too much for her to handle, and she didn't have the time to invest in his care. Having previously owned Rottweilers and a Husky, I had a deep affection for large breed dogs. Knowing that Mastiffs are among the most giant breeds in the world, I eagerly agreed. I was sure my children would be thrilled to welcome a new pet into our home.

One weekend, Jack and Clair drove the dog to our house, marking my first encounter with Jack. He was aware of my friendship with Teresa and Clair. As a couple, they seemed mismatched; with her classy attire and Lincoln Town Car, Clair contrasted sharply with Jack's long, messy hair and his resemblance to a guitarist from an 80s band. When the dog leaped out of the car, my eyes widened in astonishment at his size. Weighing around 170 pounds, his head reached up to my waist. The kids were ecstatic, jumping up and down as the dog enthusiastically licked them, his tail wagging so violently that it smacked everyone in its path.

Clair introduced him as Strider, a name that instantly resonated with us and spared us the task of brainstorming one ourselves. Clair generously handed over dog dishes, a sturdy leash, and essentials we hadn't yet acquired. Determined to make Strider feel at home,

I headed to the pet store and picked up a hefty bag of the premium dog food Clair had recommended for large breeds. To ensure we had better control during our walks, I also bought a body harness and, for a touch of flair, a black studded collar that gave Strider a bold, confident look. While Jack remained silent, Clair knelt and gave Strider a heartfelt hug and goodbye. But Strider, already brimming with energy, was off in a flash, joyfully playing with the kids. It was clear he was going to fit right into our family.

We eagerly signed Dylan and Gwen up for soccer, a sport they enthusiastically played across the street at the school fields during evenings and weekends. In Acton, it seemed like every helicopter parent had their children enrolled in soccer and hockey, the go-to sports for kids. After work, I would join them, bringing Strider to frolic with the other dogs. It was always amusing to hear the other children and parents marvel at Strider's size, comparing him to a horse and joking that Megan could ride on his back. Their admiration for Strider added a delightful touch to our family outings, making those moments even more special.

During the winter, we would embark on a road trip to Florida, near Disneyland, either during Christmas break or March Break. Our goal was to give the children the joy of experiencing the ocean and the thrill of travel and to escape the daily grind while spending quality time together. One winter, we followed my sister, her family, and my mother to Florida. They were seasoned travelers to the Sunshine State, and it was also a nostalgic journey for me. The familiar sights and sounds brought back cherished memories of past trips, making the experience even more special. It was a beautiful blend of creating new memories with my children while reminiscing about the old ones.

One leisurely morning, as I sipped my coffee on a day off, Clair suggested we visit her town to see her house and check out Jack's shop. They lived in a charming new subdivision, and their house was lovely. Jack fired up the BBQ in the backyard, inviting a few friends over, and we enjoyed some beers he had stocked in the kitchen. It was a relaxed and enjoyable afternoon. However, I couldn't help but wonder why Clair hadn't invited Teresa, especially since they were friends. Later, in a candid conversation, Clair confided in me that Teresa had a habit of judging others and rarely had anything positive to say about Jack or her other friends. This revelation shed light on the dynamics of their friendship and made me appreciate Clair's honesty.

Instead of meeting for coffee at Tim's in Acton, I began visiting Clair at her home before heading to work. We would chat and enjoy each other's company. Jack knew our time together and didn't mind having another man around his partner. One evening, after her son had gone to bed, we were in the living room. The conversation took an unexpected turn, reminiscent of a scene from a provocative movie. I sat beside Clair on the couch while Jack faced us in a chair. Suddenly, Clair called out to Jack, expressing her desire for me to give it to her on the sofa while he watched.

What was happening? I couldn't believe my eyes. Jack smirked at me and said, "Go ahead, give it to her however you want." It was just another tally in my book, another face and memory devoid of emotion. What was wrong with me? Was I broken or sick, or was this some addiction rooted in my childhood? Regardless, my relationship was deteriorating. From the moment I started dating Margret in 1991, through her years at university and teachers' college, to our marriage and fifteen years together with three children, my infidelity count had already surpassed 200 women. My relationship wasn't just stagnant; it was in a freefall, and I pushed it over the edge.

After years of honing my private investigations and in-house security skills for HBC and Loblaws, I returned to my true calling—loss prevention. This time, I joined a security company where I could put my expertise to good use. However, I quickly realized that working for security companies came with its own set of challenges. The politics and hierarchy meant that I often had to take orders from supervisors with less experience than me. Determined to make a real impact, I decided to join a specialized company in Toronto that focused on loss prevention for retail and grocery chains. Here, I could leverage my extensive background and excel in my field.

I spent countless hours away from Margret and the children, as my job had me driving all over Ontario. The company expected me to cover the cost of gas and time to work at remote stores until closing. Most nights, I wouldn't get home until after 11 p.m. One particular Shopper's Drug Mart inside a bustling mall in Brampton became a frequent stop for me. I worked there several times a week, and one evening, I caught a glimpse of a young girl from Thailand, around nineteen years old, attempting to steal. Her name was Julie.

It was late in the evening, and we had to wait for the police, who were taking their sweet time to arrive. As we waited, I struck up a conversation with her. She candidly shared that she thought I was watching her because I found her attractive, not because I was security-keeping an eye on her. I couldn't help but tell her she was excellent, but I watched her steal.

The police finally arrived after 11 p.m., long after all the stores had closed and the buses had stopped running. She looked at me with those captivating eyes as if she had some fantasy about law enforcement. Despite my position and my struggles with addiction, I knew the correct answer should have been no. But her little pout, the curve of her lips, dark skin, and long brown hair and eyes made it impossible to resist. She asked me for a ride home, not wanting to call her parents, and I agreed—not because she was stranded, but because she was into me.

I was driving my green Chevy Impala with tinted windows, and she lived in a new subdivision that had just been built in Castlemore, north of Brampton. She asked me to park down the street, away from her house. Before long, we found ourselves in the back seat, sharing a moment of intimacy. Her allure was irresistible; she was an aphrodisiac, and the age gap only heightened my attraction. We continued seeing each other for a few months until she began questioning why I never brought her to my house and always chose hotels. She eventually did a marriage search and discovered I was married. We decided to part ways after one last trip to Windsor to look at a car I was interested in.

I transitioned into sales, securing security contracts for my current employer. This role was fantastic because it connected me with all the major retail stores and District Loss Prevention Managers of the big box stores, which would be invaluable when I eventually started my own company. Regardless of my company or store, I often formed close relationships with managers, supervisors, clients, or customers in the bedroom.

While doing sales in Brampton, I passed Shopper's World Mall and noticed a grand opening for a new Chinese supermarket called Ocean's Fresh Food Supermarket. This was their third location, and I thought it would be a good idea to stop in and see if they required security services. Inside, I had the chance to meet the president and CEO. We discussed the possibility of a security contract, and he mentioned that he was dissatisfied with the service from his current provider. I seized the opportunity to convince him to hire our company full-time, seven days a week, with multiple security personnel at all three locations.

What did I get in commission for bringing in thousand-dollar contracts to the company? Nothing, not even a "well done." All they cared about was what my next contract would be. Frustrated, I approached the owner of Ocean's and suggested he cancel the contract with the security company and hire me personally as a security manager to oversee the stores. I assured him I would handle all the security needs in-house. The owner of the security company was furious and threatened to sue me for breach of contract. I calmly explained that she had no grounds, as I had quit and was hired by Ocean's only after their contract was canceled.

I worked at the store myself, often sitting upstairs with the owners while they chain-smoked in the office. My main task was to monitor the CCTV cameras and catch shoplifters. The pay was better than any other company I had worked for. The staff were mostly Chinese immigrants, many of whom had just arrived and spoke little to no English. The store manager, Andy, and I got along excellent. He gave me free rein to do whatever I needed and never questioned my actions. He even enjoyed getting involved in some of the altercations.

One day, while working, I took a break and went to the washroom inside the store. As I passed the Chinese buffet, I noticed two Chinese girls sitting at a table, enjoying their meal. One stood out, dressed in an Anime-inspired outfit like Sailor Moon. Her appearance was striking, with plastic surgery on her nose and eyes to resemble a doll, and even her figure had been enhanced. I had previously dated a Korean girl but never a Chinese girl, so I decided to sit at their table. We chatted for a while, and before I left, I had her phone number.

I decided to open my own security company, fill out all the necessary forms, attend an interview, and present my business plan. The owner of Ocean's, who became my partner, generously provided fifty thousand dollars to help me start the company and set up the office. He even offered me office space in the store's warehouse and provided an accountant to handle our books and payroll. After investing about twenty thousand dollars in office equipment, uniforms, and supplies, I felt uneasy about the accountant's bookkeeping. He never disclosed the balancing account and constantly asked me to sign checks without explaining them.

My office became a private place where I could spend time with the Chinese girl, who had a bit of a wild side. I told her about going to clubs every weekend with her friends and dressing in minimal clothes, but she brushed it off, and eventually, we decided to part ways. I often found myself forming connections with women in the mall, from a Filipina working in a breakfast food court who would make me complimentary breakfast and spend time with me in the back kitchen to the manager of the Rexall pharmacy, who was Portuguese and married with children.

One day, I noticed someone who looked familiar from my past, but I couldn't recall his name. It turned out to be Ricky from the spa in Toronto. Back when I had just gotten out of foster care and was living on the streets, he had been one of my clients. Ricky recognized me and started a conversation. I kept my distance; he was very striking, and I didn't want any employees to get the wrong impression. Ricky was a regular shopper at the store, living behind the mall with his mother.

As my list of contacts grew, so did the pressure from the business. I found myself spending more on my car and travel expenses. The owner was becoming increasingly unhappy with how I managed things and requested that I remove his name from the directorship and the banking. Surprisingly, he didn't ask me to repay his invested money. I feared he might cancel my contract, but instead, I could keep it. From that point on, it was me running the show.

My life felt like it was falling apart. My marriage was a mess, filled with unhappiness, lies, and deceit. I knew I had to do something, but trying to fix my marriage only made me feel suffocated and anxious. I felt trapped in a relationship with someone I no longer loved, only feeling guilt and the remnants of a teenage crush.

Ricky had invited me to join him on a vacation to Australia, offering to cover the costs if I accompanied him. Meanwhile, Margret planned to take the children East to Prince Edward Island. We both needed a break to determine if anything was worth salvaging in our marriage. So, I decided to take Ricky up on his offer and informed Oceans that I would be away for a few weeks on vacation.

21

EMBRACING THE UNKNOWN
DOWN UNDER

As I write this chapter from the far reaches of Australia, it is hard not to feel the weight of my decisions. A seventeen-hour flight from my loved ones feels like a selfish act, one that others and I would agree was a necessary step in my journey. Like the Israelites in the Bible, wandering for forty years before reaching the Promised Land, I have been on a journey of self-discovery and redemption for four decades.

Questions swirl in my mind as I reflect on my life's path. Why was I born in a cold country? Why did I choose the life I have led? These thoughts have plagued me, driving me to explore the world and seek answers to the deeper meaning of my existence. Leaving Margret and my children behind to travel across

Canada was a difficult choice but one I felt compelled to make to find clarity and purpose.

Australia was a revelation, a world away from the familiar landscapes of home. Travelling with Ricky, a Filipino companion, offered a new perspective and a sense of camaraderie. Despite our differences, Ricky's willingness to fund the trip and his companionship provided comfort in the unknown.

Our journey began in Sydney, where Ricky's cousin showed us around the city, including the iconic Opera House. The sheer magnitude of the structure left me in awe, and I captured its grandeur in photographs, each image a testament to the wonders I was experiencing. However, travelling with Ricky came with its challenges. His flamboyant nature often made others assume we were a couple, a misconception that bothered me. While Ricky struggled with his own identity and kept his sexuality hidden from his mother, I found myself navigating a new culture and environment, trying to blend in while remaining true to myself.

Heading north to Queensland, we arrived in Cairns, greeted by warmer temperatures and the scent of the sea. The palm trees and tropical surroundings starkly contrasted the cold city we had left behind, signalling a new chapter in my adventure. Australia was the beginning of my journey, a stepping stone toward self-discovery and acceptance. As I explored new landscapes and cultures, I began to unravel the mysteries of my past and embrace the unknown future ahead.

Leaving the airport, Ricky and I hailed a taxi to the heart of Cairns, near the ocean. We settled into a hostel, lugging our backpacks to the second floor. The hostel was bustling with noise and activity, a stark reminder of my age among the young crowd. Yet, amidst the youthful energy, I felt a sense of loss for the youth I never fully experienced, bypassing carefree days for early adulthood responsibilities. In the morning, I resolved to make the most of my time in this remarkable country. I marvelled at the fate that had brought me to Australia, a place many only dream of visiting. Setting out for breakfast, we strolled through streets reminiscent of a bygone era, with colonial-style buildings that charmed like New Orleans or Key West.

Arriving at the waterfront, I was captivated by the boats offering tours and fishing trips. I had always been intrigued by the idea of scuba diving, especially at the Great Barrier Reef, renowned for its stunning coral life. Ricky, however, was hesitant due to a fear of water and sharks, so I decided to embark on the adventure alone.

The following day, I headed to the docks, eager for the experience. Boarding the boat, I settled in for the journey, grateful for solitude amidst the bustling tour. As we navigated the choppy waters, motion sickness set in, a sensation I had not felt since my time in foster care. Despite the discomfort, I was determined to make the most of this opportunity.

After suiting up and familiarizing myself with the diving equipment, I descended into the ocean, a mixture of excitement and apprehension coursing through me. Adjusting to breathing underwater was a challenge, but my fears melted away as I explored the vibrant underwater world. I encountered a plethora of marine life, from clownfish to massive groupers, each moment a testament to the awe-inspiring beauty of the reef.

One encounter stood out: a giant grouper, its body dwarfing mine, swam past me. I reached out, tentatively stroking its side. To my surprise, the fish paused, enjoying the contact. As I continued my dive, touching velvet-like sea cucumbers and marvelling at the underwater landscape, I felt a profound connection to the ocean, a sense of peace and wonderment that transcended words. Australia opened my eyes to new experiences and perspectives, reminding me of the vastness of the world and the endless possibilities.

Descending again into the depths, I marvelled at the underwater world's beauty, but the motion sickness intensified. Suddenly, I vomited into my mask and regulator, the vomit dispersing into the ocean. Surrounded by a cloud of vomit, I watched as fish swarmed to feast on the unexpected meal. Back on the boat, I tried to compose myself, feeling queasy and weak.

Returning to shore, I found a quiet spot to rest under a tree, hoping to alleviate the motion sickness. The next day, Ricky suggested heading to Darwin, but I was growing weary of his company and longed to explore on my own. Despite his protests, I decided to part ways with Ricky when we arrived in Darwin. Gathering my backpack, I headed for the exit, leaving Ricky behind, his protests fading into the distance. As I made my way through the airport, the weight of my decision began to sink in. I was alone in a foreign land, but the sense of freedom was exhilarating. Darwin awaited, with its tropical allure and promise of adventure.

Ricky's unexpected appearance in Darwin caught me off guard. I noticed his pugnacious gaze from across the street, and he approached me within moments. His demeanour was like a stray dog, tail between his legs. He inquired about my accommodation, and I mentioned the hostel, hoping to dissuade him from following me. However, he persisted, and I reluctantly divulged that I was staying at Mitchell Street Backpackers. I hurried back, hoping to shake him off.

With a week remaining in Australia, I felt a pang of homesickness creeping in. I yearned to be back with my children. The expenses were mounting, especially with the high conversion rate of the Australian dollar. I relied heavily on ATM withdrawals and my credit card to cover costs. Ricky suggested I could still return with him on our scheduled flight, as he had not cancelled it. However, I had made up my mind to leave earlier. I visited a flight center travel agency to inquire about the cost of a new one-way ticket back to Canada, including a connecting flight from Darwin to Sydney.

As I wandered around Darwin, trying to soak in the last moments of my Australian adventure, I could not shake off the feeling of unease Ricky's presence brought. I spent my days exploring the city and visiting its museums and parks, but now and then, I would catch a glimpse of him in the distance, a constant reminder of the past I was trying to leave behind.

One evening, as I sat at a local restaurant, I felt a tap on my shoulder. It was Ricky, looking more dejected than ever. He asked if we could talk, and against my better judgment, I agreed. We sat down, and he began apologizing for his behaviour, admitting that he had been struggling with personal issues. He asked if I would consider giving our friendship another chance, promising to respect my boundaries and space.

I was torn. Part of me wanted to believe him, to give him the benefit of the doubt. But another part of me knew I needed to prioritize my well-being and happiness. After a lengthy conversation, I thanked him for his apology but told him I needed to move on. With a heavy heart, I bid farewell to Ricky and boarded my flight back to Canada, ready to start a new chapter in my life. The cost totalled about twelve hundred dollars, with two stopovers through LAX in Los Angeles and another in Chicago before reaching Toronto. Despite my efforts to avoid him, Ricky insisted on being friends and invited me to see a movie at a nearby theatre. After the movie, as we returned to the hostel, I informed Ricky of my plans to leave in a few days and spend the rest of my vacation in Fiji. Although he expressed a desire to join me, I explained that I had already purchased my ticket, failing to mention that it was only a connecting flight.

Unbeknownst to Ricky, my destination was the United States, where I had a connecting flight from Fiji to Los Angeles. However, Ricky needed to understand and switch his return ticket to Fiji instead of leaving Australia a week later because I had mentioned my departure date. This behaviour further reinforced my decision to distance myself from him, as I had been trying to remove negative influences from my life.

I boarded the plane back to Sydney and ensured I would keep my distance from Ricky, especially when I arrived in Fiji. As we landed and proceeded through customs and immigration, I seized the opportunity to make my escape while Ricky was next in line. I directed him to the correct line for arriving flights into Fiji, and I quickly made my way in the opposite direction when his back was to me for connecting flights without leaving the airport.

During my layover in Fiji, which lasted about four hours, I grabbed some food and a drink while waiting for my connecting flight. Boarding the plane, I noticed Ricky standing in line behind me, glaring. We flew to LAX in Los Angeles, where I attempted to lose him again but found him waiting for me outside the arrival entrance. When he asked where I was going, I mentioned spending the following week at Venice Beach and the Santa Monica pier.

After a day exploring Beverly Hills and Hollywood, we returned to the hotel room around five, as I needed to be at the airport three hours before my flight departure for check-in. This time, it was a connecting flight to Chicago, with a three-hour layover before heading straight to Toronto. Ricky had booked a hotel on Hollywood Blvd, where I had stayed many times, so I left my luggage in the room to avoid dragging it everywhere, but it was now time to leave Los Angeles and go back to LAX.

I picked up my luggage at the hotel and headed to the door. Ricky asked where I was going, and I explained that I had a plane to catch back to Toronto. He seemed surprised, thinking I was staying, but I clarified that the room was for him to stay in, not me. Despite this, he followed me back to the airport and attempted to change his ticket again. However, he was told he could not change his ticket and would have to wait until the next day to buy another one. I proceeded through customs and immigration, and that was the last time I saw Ricky, except for a chance encounter shopping for groceries. As the plane took off from the runway, I rested my head back, knowing I could now relax for a while. However, I also realized that I would soon return to deal with my situation at home.

A wave of relief washed over me as my plane touched down in Toronto. I was home. Yet, a pang of disappointment tugged at my heartstrings. I was no longer in Australia, immersed in the thrill of diving and the exotic taste of crocodile and kangaroo. I loaded my luggage into the car and embarked on the journey back to Acton, acutely aware of the impending storm in my marriage. The inevitable confrontation with Margret loomed over me.

Margret and the kids had returned from their Eastern escapade. I arrived home late, seeking refuge in the basement, choosing the couch over our shared bed. Margret's early morning departure for work relieved the inevitable conversation. My days were spent in Brampton, ensuring the security of a Chinese supermarket in Shopper's World Mall.

The year was 2009. Fifteen years of matrimony and three children later, I found myself teetering on the edge of marital dissolution. Despite our attempts at marriage counselling with the senior pastor at the Pentecostal church, the prospect of maintaining our union solely for the sake of our children, two of whom were still incredibly young, seemed untenable. The damage was irreparable. The counselling sessions echoed the harsh reality - if the love was gone, so should the marriage. The psychological toll of living a lie, of feigning happiness and love to the world and her family, was unbearable. My infidelity and distorted perception of love led me to the painful decision to end our marriage.

Margret was indeed deserving of more. She was an extraordinary, loyal wife who merited a husband of equal calibre. I was not that man. I was merely an eighteen-year-old city boy whom she had fallen for, and I manipulated her feelings for my own selfish needs. What did I understand about love? I was not in love with her, but rather with the concept of marriage and the family life that I never had. The fear of lifelong solitude was daunting, and I revelled that someone loved me.

I managed to sabotage my only perfect relationship, yet I was blind to the reality that was staring me in the face. Margret had the ideal life and family, something I lacked, and I yearned to be a part of that and gain acceptance. It was not that my love for Margret had faded, but rather that I was in love with the idea, not Margret herself. It was all guilt - guilt for stealing her innocence and the purity of that young girl. I felt a sense of loyalty to her and her family, especially what they had done for us, including helping us secure our house and the loans from her father. I repaid him ten thousand dollars from the money I received from my abuse case with the victim witnesses against my stepfather Shane, but I still felt indebted to her. It was something but just a drop in the bucket for what they deserved.

In the bustling Chinese supermarket where I worked, I was inexplicably drawn to a woman affectionately known as Beca. She was a vibrant presence in the deli department, her laughter and smiles infectious. Despite my attempts to engage her in conversation, she remained elusive, always finding a reason to retreat behind the counter whenever I approached. My interest in Beca grew as my marriage teetered on the brink of collapse. Beca was petite, standing at just four foot ten inches and weighing about eighty-five pounds. Her long black hair and deep brown eyes reminded me of a delicate Chinese doll.

A recent immigrant to Canada, she was a permanent resident and had just worked a few other jobs before her aunt suggested she work at the supermarket. One early morning, I arrived at work before the store opened. Beca was already there, waiting on a bench outside. I joined her, attempting to strike up a conversation. However, our dialogue could have been improved due to her fundamental understanding of English. She playfully accused me of being a player, having seen me with a Chinese international student from a nearby university.

Over time, we began talking more at work, but after a week, she told me she was returning to China for a month to visit her parents and sister, and I wanted to chat with her because I had missed seeing her around the store. While sitting on my couch in the basement, I decided to FaceTime with her on an app called QQ, a Chinese social media platform. The connection came through, and I saw her sitting with three other Chinese girls on the couch. She was laughing with them at me, and I was sitting on my couch with no shirt. We looked at each other for a few minutes, and then the connection was lost, or she disconnected the call. We then just texted each other. Each message was a paper plane, gliding across the ocean, carrying tales of mundane routines and shared dreams.

The anticipation of her return brewed a sweet concoction of hope and curiosity—what stories would she bring back? What new laughter would echo in the aisles of our store? The countdown had begun, and with each passing day, the narrative of our unique friendship continued to unfold, promising new chapters yet to be written. While Beca was in China, I always talked to her friend and told her how much I missed and cared about her. I knew she would be conversing with Beca and was getting her on my side to sweetly talk her into dating me.

The day came, and Beca was back in Toronto at the airport. I wanted to pick her up, but she told me her aunt would get her. It was her birthday, and she was supposed to be going on a date with a guy she had been talking to while conversing with me. I talked her out of that date and got together for coffee. We went to Second Cup inside the Chapters Book store, had a coffee and cake, and wished her happy birthday. I then drove her back home to her aunt's house.

Amidst the quiet hum of the car engine, we wove through the streets, our breaths mingling with the scent of freshly brewed coffee. The warmth of the paper cup seeped into my palms as we sat in her aunt's driveway, the night sky a canvas of secrets waiting to be shared. And share we did—our words dancing between laughter and vulnerability. I unravelled the threads of my life, the fraying edges of a marriage that had once held promise.

The confession hung in the air, heavy with the

weight of endings and beginnings. She bore her truth—a technical marriage, a bond forged in paperwork but never evaluated by shared walls. Our circumstances aligned, two souls navigating love's complexities. And then, like a whisper carried by the wind, an idea bloomed. China is the land of dragons, cherry blossoms, ancient temples, and bustling markets. I had always dreamed of stepping onto its soil, tracing the footsteps of emperors and poets. And so, with a heart that beat coordinated with hers, I proposed: "Would you like to return home for a month? Let us chase adventure together, our shared stories etched against the backdrop of a thousand years."

Her eyes held mine and, at that moment, as the coffee grew cold and the night deepened, we became co-authors of a chapter yet unwritten—a journey that would bridge continents and hearts, where coffee cups would yield to tea leaves, and our laughter would echo through the Great Wall.

This proposition forced me to confront the difficult decision to end my current marriage, knowing it would impact my relationship with my three children. Was this merely a crush, or was it the allure of the exotic? I had never been with a Chinese woman before. Beca filled the void as I grappled with loneliness and the fear of not finding love again.

22

FOREIGN AFFAIRS TO FOREIGN SOIL

In the dimly lit corners of my basement refuge, the walls seemed to close in on me as Beca's presence around me grew more assertive at work, casting a shadow over my once-solitary existence. Margret's patience frayed like worn fabric, her voice echoing a final ultimatum through the hollow space—no more roommates, only a husband to share her bed—the demand for separation cut through the air, a stark reminder of the chasm between us. I saw the truth in her eyes, and it filled me with discomfort that turned my stomach, the animosity between us, an unwelcome guest in our home.

The prospect of discarding fifteen years of woven memories to embrace the uncertainty of a new love left me reeling. My heart ached at the thought of my three treasures caught in the storm of our parting. Dylan, at twelve, seemed to lean into Margret's embrace, seeking solace where I could not give. Yet, Gwen's silent strength at nine and Megan's innocent eyes at five

held me captive. They were the heartbeat of my world, my little girls who knew me as their fortress.

As the reality of divorce loomed, Dylan and Gwen bore the weight of understanding with quiet resilience. But Megan, my tiny princess, felt the tremors most deeply. Adorned with the vibrant hues of Disney royalty with her princess castle canopy, the storm clouds of our separation now overshadowed her world. My heart mirrored hers, fracturing in silent solidarity with her pain while Dylan and Gwen's hurt remained veiled behind their brave faces.

In the heart of Mississauga, a dream emerged amidst the hustle of working at the Chinese super-market—my very own security company, Omega. Built within the warehouse, the office sprung to life, fueled by a partnership with trust and a generous investment of fifty thousand dollars. Each dollar was a brushstroke in the grand renovation, transforming the space with sleek desks and state-of-the-art computers. At the same time, the vigilant eyes of CCTV cameras stood guard at every door, a testament to my commitment to excellence as I awaited the Ministry's approval.

With her unwavering support, Beca bridged the gap between ambition and reality. Her hand penned the application for a Chinese visa while her parents' invitation letter sang of familial bonds and distant lands. The Toronto visa office became a gateway to adventure, processing my passport to the future. And then, the wait was over. Passport in hand, visa stamped with promise, I stood on the cusp of a journey to the land of dragons and legends, where Kung Fu epics dance across silver screens and National Geographic chronicles unfold in vivid detail. My pulse quickened, anticipation coursing through my veins as visions of China's storied landscapes beckoned me forth.

The first thing was to find a place to live so I would not have to put Margret through any more torture of me sleeping in the basement and silenced lips. So Beca and I decided to find a place together. I searched the local papers and walls in the grocery stores for an apartment. We found a basement apartment across the street from our work, just a five minute walk across a field to the mall.

The house owners were from India, and the smells from the cooking upstairs came through the vents into our bedroom in the basement. It was so unbearable that I had to shove a shirt into the vent to block the smell. Our first shared space could have been better. The closet needed shelves or poles to hang our clothes. Undeterred, I took matters into my own hands.

After a trip to Home Depot, a purchase of wire racks, and a bit of drilling later, we had makeshift closet shelves. However, the discomfort did not end there. Our apartment was a constant hub of activity, with men strolling down the stairs at all hours to access the shared laundry facilities. Despite our door being locked, my silver necklace mysteriously disappeared. Beca was understandably anxious, especially when alone in the basement. To alleviate her fears, I adjusted my schedule to match hers.

One day, Beca was browsing through my phone when she stumbled upon an old profile of a Chinese girl from the university across the street from our house. She accused me of infidelity. I tried to explain that it was an old message, but she was too upset to listen. Anger, she stormed out of the house, heading towards the mall. Beca's temper was fiery, and this was not the first time it had flared up. Thankfully, her best friend calmed her down and reassured her of my feelings for her. I realized then that we needed some time away from the city, away from all distractions, to bond indeed.

Beca made a bold decision. She informed her deli manager that she was quitting her job to return to

China with me. The news spread like wildfire around the store, and soon, everyone knew that Beca and I were an item.

With our airline tickets and itinerary, we made a hasty exit. We left without a word to our landlord, abandoning our apartment in our wake. As a final act of defiance, I ripped the shelving out of the wall, leaving about twenty holes in the drywall. It was late at night, and we packed our things into our vehicle. I locked the bedroom door so they would not see the room empty.

The journey began with our next destination, the vibrant city of Hong Kong. We were to embark on this journey aboard the renowned Cathay Pacific. The flight was projected to last approximately seventeen hours, a test of endurance for even the most seasoned travellers.

As I nestled into the window seat, I was pleasantly surprised by the amenities provided. Slippers, socks, a plush pillow, a warm blanket, and an eye covering were all handed to me. The level of service was astounding, akin to the luxury of first class. Sleep eluded me, combining the adrenaline rush and the disorienting time zone differences. To pass the time, I immersed myself in a marathon of movies, each a new adventure that temporarily transported me away from the confines of the airplane.

Finally, the moment arrived. We began our descent

into Hong Kong. The view from the window was breathtaking. At first, the landscape was dominated by mountains and the vast expanse of the ocean. Then, as we drew closer, the cityscape came into view—skyscrapers reaching for the sky, famous landmarks dotting the horizon - a remarkable sight. With a gentle touchdown, I was officially in China.

After navigating through customs, Beca took on the role of my personal tour guide. Our first stop was downtown Hong Kong, home to a massive shopping center called "The One." We strolled along the waterfront, our eyes drawn to the high-end fashion boutiques lined the streets, including the iconic Louis Vuitton.

Our adventure continued with a ferry ride across to Victoria Harbour, the bustling business hub of Hong Kong. The skyline was remarkable, dominated by the Bank of China Tower and The International Commerce Center. The cityscape was a testament to Hong Kong's architectural prowess, with over four thousand skyscrapers and nine thousand high-rise buildings. It was a breathtaking panorama that left us in awe.

However, the city had another side. We saw rows of women from Indonesia, Malaysia, and the Philippines near a McDonald's that spanned an entire block. They appeared to be in Hong Kong searching for employment, but their circumstances seemed dire. They looked like vagrants, living out of bags, their clothes unwashed and worn. It was a stark contrast to the glitz and glamour of the city, a sobering reminder of the harsh realities many face.

This duality was ever-present as we embarked on our journey to the Ngong Ping Cable Cars 360. Opting for the crystal cabin, boasting an impressive 80% visibility, we were enveloped in a near-complete panoramic experience. My fear of heights was palpable, the transparent floor beneath us turning my excitement into a thrilling trepidation as we ascended from downtown Tung Chung towards the serene Lantau Island.

As the cable car ascended, the Hong Kong International Airport became a miniature in the vast tapestry of the landscape, slowly disappearing into the horizon. The ride, a 25-minute voyage across six kilometres, claimed the title of the longest cable car journey in Asia. It was more than a mere transit; it celebrated engineering and natural beauty intertwined as we scaled the mountain's flank.

Reaching an elevation that pierced the clouds at over three thousand feet, the Tian Tan Buddha greeted us—a colossal bronze figure, thirty-four meters in height, with a benevolent hand raised in a silent blessing. The 260-step ascent to the Buddha promised a spiritual odyssey, but time was not our ally. With the

Buddha's sanctuary closing at 5:30 PM, we were resigned to explore the earthly delights at its base.

The museum, a treasure trove of relics, whispered tales of the past, while the surrounding shops offered a mosaic of cultural artifacts. As we leisurely strolled, the Ngong Ping Plateau unfurled before us, offering a 360-degree panorama that stretched out to the Pearl River, a majestic sight that etched itself into memory. This was more than a destination; it was a profound journey through culture, history, and self-discovery set against an ever-changing skyline.

A visa was only needed if our destination was Hong Kong. However, our adventure was to take us deeper into the heart of mainland China, necessitating a visa. My companion, Beca, was to reunite with her aunt and uncle in Shenzhen, a city sharing its border with Hong Kong. We boarded a train from the airport, heading straight for the border. The air was charged with anticipation as we waited to clear customs and immigration into mainland China, a thrilling step into the unknown.

Once inside Shenzhen, we navigated to a bus terminal and embarked on a bus journey to another part of the city. Here, Beca's relatives warmly welcomed us. We left our luggage at their condominium, a haven amid the bustling city and headed out for something to eat.

Lunch was an experience. We found ourselves in a

restaurant buzzing with activity, large round tables filling the room, the air thick with the scent of food and a hint of cigarette smoke. Beca and her aunt took the lead in ordering the food, and their fluency in the local language proved invaluable. I found myself in the company of people who did not speak English, but their warm smiles spoke volumes. I reciprocated with a smile and a nod, a universal language of goodwill.

Post lunch, we ventured into downtown Shenzhen. The buildings here were a treasure trove, housing every designer knockoff imaginable. It was a shopper's paradise, a testament to the city's reputation as a global shopping destination. My shopping spree in Shenzhen was far from over. I treated myself to a luxurious Prada leather side bag and stylish shirts from renowned brands like D&G and Armani. However, my eyes were drawn to something far more enticing.

The ultimate symbol of affluence, a Rolex or Breitling watch, was within my reach. These were not just any watches; they were super clones - exact replicas of the authentic ones. The price tag converted to three hundred Canadian dollars, but with a bit of haggling, Beca managed to bring them down to one hundred and fifty.

Each shop was a world of its own, staffed by charming Chinese girls. They held catalogues containing every watch manufacturer and fashion designer of whom you could think. From replica hand-bags to shoes, they had it all. It was a shopper's paradise, a testament to the city's reputation as a global shopping destination. After a day of navigating China's new and familiar streets, we retreated to Beca's aunt's home, only to venture out again as evening approached.

Our destination was a renowned outdoor seafood restaurant, a local favourite known for its lively atmosphere and exceptional fare. The restaurant was a hub of activity, yet we found ourselves seated promptly, a testament to Beca's aunt's familiarity with this culinary gem. The Menu was an ode to the sea, offering an array of dishes that promised to challenge and delight the palate.

I was introduced to a captivating variety of seafood, a world away from the familiar fish and lobster of the West. Each dish was a revelation, a journey through unique flavours and textures that were both foreign and exhilarating. As the night deepened, we returned to the comfort of their condominium, the day's experiences settling around us like a soft blanket. The jetlag and time difference took its toll. I surrendered to sleep, my mind still adrift, thinking about today's culinary adventure.

The day's journey through taste and tradition had etched into my senses—a vivid mosaic of flavours and emotions. As dawn painted the sky, I stirred from my slumber, momentarily disoriented. The realization washed over me: I was on the other side of the world, perched high above the bustling city of Shenzhen. The floor-to-ceiling windows framed a panorama that thrilled and unnerved me—the sprawling metropolis, a tapestry of steel and glass stretching out like a pulsating heartbeat.

The streets below buzzed with life—a symphony of honking horns, street vendors' calls, and the rhythmic shuffle of pedestrians. I pressed my palm against the cool glass, feeling the city's pulse against my skin. Fear of heights had always been my silent adversary, and here it was, taunting me from the safety of our hotel room. Vertigo tugged at my insides, a reminder that adventure often came with a price.

Beca's aunt, a spirited guide, led us through the labyrinthine alleys of the Luohu Commercial Building. The air hummed with commerce, and the scent of incense clung to our clothes. Her Aunt haggles over silk scarves, our laughter punctuating the negotiations. Each Purchase became a talisman—a memory to carry across borders and time zones. The friendly banter with the vendors, the excitement of getting a good deal, and the sense of accomplishment after each successful negotiation all added to the richness of the experience.

As twilight draped the city, we made our way to the airport—a gateway to another chapter of our adventure. The train whisked us across Shenzhen, its rhythmic clatter a lullaby of anticipation—our destination: Hainan, an island cradled by the South China Sea. The flight was a mere breath—an hour suspended between worlds. Through the oval window, I glimpsed the contours of Hainan—a serene jewel set against the azure expanse. Palm trees swayed in the breeze, their fronds whispering secrets of sun-kissed shores, starkly contrasting the hustle and bustle of the city we had left behind.

The plane touched down, and the midnight air enveloped us. Details blurred—the silhouettes of hills, the glimmer of moonlight on the water—but promise hung thick. Beca's voice, a bridge between languages, guided us. We claimed our luggage, stepping into the embrace of a tropical night. And there, waiting in the dimly lit parking lot, stood her father—a man of quiet strength. His smile etched lines of welcome, and his eyes crinkled with stories untold.

Beside him rested an old black Audi, its paint weathered by years under the relentless sun. It bore witness to countless journeys—each scratch a memory etched into its metal skin. Our worlds converged as he extended his hand—a handshake transcending language. His nod spoke volumes, a silent acknowledgment of shared purpose. He turned to Beca, their conversation a blend of Mandarin and friction. Meanwhile, Beca's mother awaited us at home, wrapped in the warmth of her bed.

And so, in that midnight tableau, we stepped into a new chapter—a family's embrace and a land showing promise. The night held its secrets close, and as we drove toward Haikou City, I wondered what stories the palm trees whispered to the stars and what Beca's father, a man of few words but a stern voice, was discussing with her. The journey had just begun, and I surrendered to it, eager to unravel the history of Hainan—a place where tradition danced with the sea and the ordinary shimmered with magic, or so I thought.

As we ventured from the airport, the road ahead was shrouded in darkness, illuminated only by sparse streetlights. Beca's father, who was at the wheel, asked Beca if a stop at McDonald's would be welcome. We consented, and soon, I found myself sipping coffee and savouring a Big Mac, the fatigue of travel momentarily forgotten amidst the comforting familiarity of the golden arches. The cool air carried a hint of the sea, a reminder of our proximity to the coast.

Communication promised an adventure; Beca's father spoke no English, leaving us to rely on her translations to bridge our worlds. The anticipation of how our vacation would unfold with this linguistic dance loomed in my mind. Our car meandered through an alley flanked by modest apartment buildings, their stature not exceeding seven stories. Relief washed over me as we halted at their second-floor residence—grateful for the absence of a lengthy climb since elevators were nowhere to be found. Heaving our luggage up the stairs proved to be its journey.

Beca's father bid us a brief farewell inside before disappearing into the night. We were then greeted by her mother—a delicate figure with strands of grey amidst her hair, her presence exuding a quiet strength that commanded respect. Our greetings were exchanged with nods; her world spun in the orbits of Mandarin and Cantonese.

Beca led me to our sanctuary during our stay—her childhood room. The air was thick with the scent of old wood and memories, a testament to the years this room had witnessed. Adjacent lay her mother's quarters, separated by a thin wall that held countless whispered stories. The room was simple yet intimate—a wooden frame bed adorned with bamboo and draped with a mosquito net as if to protect cherished dreams. A dresser stood against the wall, crowned with photographs and trinkets that whispered of a life once lived elsewhere, their faint scent of nostalgia lingering in the air.

Her older sister had once claimed the room next door, along with her children, before marriage beckoned them away. Yet their presence lingered like echoes waiting to fill the space once more. With dawn's light, we would begin our exploration of the city—my heart buoyant with optimism that nothing could dampen my spirits. Little did I know how profoundly that belief would be challenged.

23

UNEXPECTED CHINESE CULTURE SHOCK

orning light filtered through the blinds, casting shadows across the room. The sound of children's laughter from the parking lot below and the sight of families sharing meals in the neighbouring building's windows roused me from slumber. Steel bars framed each window; clothes hung out to dry, fluttering in the breeze, painting a scene reminiscent of documentaries I had seen about life under Communist rule.

Venturing to the washroom, I walked through the kitchen door and turned right into the washroom. I was met with a sight that stopped me in my tracks. Instead of a familiar toilet, a ceramic slab with a gaping hole lay before me, accompanied by a hose on the wall

—my makeshift shower. Disbelief washed over me as I muttered, "You've got to be kidding me." This was my first encounter with culture shock; Hong Kong's modern amenities had not prepared me for this stark contrast—a toilet that was nothing more than a hole in the ground. It was quite different from even the rudimentary outhouses I had known, where there was at least something to sit upon.

Adapting to this new bathroom ritual—squatting over a hole to relieve oneself—seemed impossible. I found myself avoiding the need for such an encounter, avoiding any dietary choices that might hasten its necessity. The bathroom was a mosaic of buckets and laundry, a testament to the daily handwashing ritual in a space where the heat clung like a second skin, turning my clothes into damp shrouds.

Stepping outside offered no respite; the air was thick and heavy with humidity, leaving me drenched within moments. Yet, amidst this discomfort, there was a semblance of normalcy—Beca's mother returned from her early market visit bearing the gift of Hainanese noodles interlaced with peanuts. The dish was a simple pleasure, its flavours a welcome distraction that satiated my hunger.

Beca and I hopped on the local bus, rumbling towards the heart of Haikou. As we disembarked near a bustling mall shadowed by an overpass, I braced myself to peel back the layers of Beca's past. Yet, the city's rawness jolted me: the ground toilets, the bold brown rats scuttling through the streets, and the sight of children nonchalantly answering nature's call on the sidewalks. It felt like a tumble through time into an era long forgotten, where the line between then and now blurred.

The air was thick, not just with history, but with smoke. It clung to every corner, inside and out, a relentless haze that mocked the very idea of 'no smoking' signs. Men and women alike wielded cigarettes like wands, casting a spell that made my lungs cry out for mercy. Meals became battles for breath, with ashtrays appearing as if by magic and tables of chain-smokers puffing away. It starkly contrasted with the smoke-free havens in Canada, where the air was as Clear as the societal expectations. How quickly one can miss the comforts of home, the simple luxury of a breath of fresh air.

Beca and I collided in the heart of Haikou like two tectonic plates. Our usually harmonious voices clashed like cymbals in a symphony gone awry. It was as if we had been together for years, not weeks. The frustration bubbled up, and I let it spill over, uncaring the curious glances from passersby. "Why can't they just use proper toilets?" I muttered my words, a desperate plea to Beca. The hole-in-the-ground contraptions, remnants of a bygone era, haunted my senses and bowels. And the audacious brown sewer rats scampering through the alleys as if they owned the place.

Beca, my guide through this maze of contradictions, shot back. "If you hate it so much, find a hotel," she retorted, her eyes flashing with defiance. I had just spent a small fortune bringing her back to China, and here we were, locked in a battle of wills. The irony was not lost on me—the clash of cultures mirrored in our heated exchange.

We wandered into the mall; its pristine whiteness starkly contrasted with the chaos outside. Cosmetics and jewelry vendors beckoned from the ground floor, their wares glimmering. Electronics and children's playlands awaited upstairs, a vertical playground for the modern age. And, of course, every mall had its fast-food shrine: KFC or McDonald's, where global flavours mingled with local tastes.

But it was the washrooms that truly baffled me. On each floor, I ventured into the tiled sanctuaries, seeking solace. And there, at the urinals, I discovered a peculiar absence: no doors in the washroom except for the stalls. None. As if privacy had been traded for efficiency. Midstream, a cleaning lady waltzed in, broom in hand, and smiled. "Hi," she chirped as if we were old friends. My discomfort swirled like the water in the porcelain bowl. How awkward, how utterly inappropriate.

At that moment, I realized that Haikou was a city of contrasts—a dance between tradition and modernity, smoke-filled air and sanitized malls. And, just perhaps, it was in these contradictions that the essence of Beca's upbringing lay hidden, waiting for me to unravel it, one awkward encounter at a time.

The bustling rows of buildings, their doorways interwoven like a grand puzzle, beckoned us into a world of knock-off treasures. Clothing, shoes, belts—the vendors peddled their products with the enthusiasm of a good storyteller. I could not resist the allure and soon found myself purchasing a wallet and sunglasses, each item a tangible memory of our thrilling adventure.

Downtown Haikou unfolded like a well-worn map, its streets a patchwork of shopping stores and hidden gems. But the malls on the outskirts held our curiosity —their towering glass facades promising more than mere goods. One mall cradled a secret: hundreds of craft vendors, their stalls brimming with cross-stitch kits. These were not mere patterns but portals to another world, where threads wove tales of tradition and artistry.

"I'll finish this in a month," I declared, pointing to the most elaborate kit. The vendor, her fingers stained with time, chuckled. "Seven months," she corrected, her eyes twinkling. Her unfinished masterpiece lay nearby, a testament to patience and dedication.

And so, we embarked on our shared odyssey. With needles in hand, Beca and I stitched through days and nights. The art piece unfurled—a canvas three feet high, six feet long—thirty-two pages, each a chapter in our shared story. An Asian panorama emerged: a village nestled by a bridge, its timeworn stones echoing with footsteps. People bustled, markets thrived, and boats glided along the ancient rivers. The colours—oh, the colours! They spilled like spilled ink, vibrant and unyielding hues. In this shared creation, we found a beautiful artwork and a bond that would last a lifetime.

As we stitched, we wove more than threads. We wove memories, laughter, and quiet conversations. The purpose was not just to pass the time but to unravel time itself, one delicate stitch at a time. And when we would finally hang our masterpiece on the wall, it wasn't just a scene—it was a testament to our shared journey, a bridge between cultures, and a kaleidoscope of breathtaking Each morning, Beca's father would grace us with his presence at the breakfast table, a subtle reminder of the unconventional family dynamics that unfolded within these walls. He did not reside in the familial abode but at his eclectic establishment—a karaoke tea bar that doubled as a boarding room. Beca often said he needed to safeguard the equipment overnight, yet the unspoken truth hung in the air; it had been ages since he shared a home with Beca's mother.

Despite the distance in their marriage, both parents were devoted to making my stay memorable. They introduced me to the wonders of Haikou, including a dormant volcano that stood as a silent guardian over the island. Ascending its slopes, we reached a summit offering a panoramic view of the island. The crater, now a cradle of life with lush palm trees and dense shrubbery, painted a picture of nature's resilience, transforming what was once a fiery mouth into a serene mountain haven.

Beca's adventurous spirit led us to another hidden gem—the outdoor hot spring baths. These six steaming pools beckoned with the promise of relaxation, complemented by a river-shaped pool adorned with playful slides. The carefree laughter of youth echoed as teenage boys frolicked without a shred of inhibition, their nakedness a testament to the innocence and freedom that the springs seemed to endorse. Adjacent to this Eden was a peculiar pool, a sanctuary for hundreds of tiny fish renowned for their skin-rejuvenating nibbles. A small fee granted access to this natural spa, where one could immerse in the curious sensation of being gently exfoliated by these aquatic therapists.

This oasis of tranquillity lay just before the ocean boardwalk, offering a view of Haikou's bustling port, where majestic cargo ships display a ballet of commerce. As the day waned, the beach transformed into a lively hub of activity. Though tinged with the day's revelry, the waters became a canvas of silhouettes against the setting sun as people from all occupations gathered to savour the evening's salty breeze in the South China Sea.

As dusk settled over Haikou, Beca's father would partake in a nightly ritual that bridged the gap between ancient traditions and the present. We would sit together, the air filled with the day's fading warmth, and he would pour from a colossal fifty-litre carboy he had fermenting for half a year. It was not just rice wine but a potent elixir steeped with medicinal herbs and the curious addition of seahorses swirling within the amber liquid. The alcohol, boasting a formidable fifty-three percent potency, carried a sharp, almost medicinal flavour that lingered on the palate.

With my Irish roots, I was no stranger to the robust world of spirits. Yet, this was different—each gulp from my glass was a nod to tradition, a silent toast to resilience, while Beca's father savoured his share with measured sips from a small shot glass. This ancient brew, we were told, was more than mere alcohol; it was a draught of vitality believed to invigorate the soul and kindle a fiercer flame of passion within men. In those moments, the generational divide dissolved, and we found common ground in the shared experience of a culture's liquid heritage, a testament to the enduring human spirit and the tales it weaves through time.

In the whirlwind of our budding romance, Beca and I found ourselves entwined in a cultural tapestry that was both vibrant and unexpected. Though we had only recently begun our journey together, Beca's desire to capture our love through the lens of tradition led us to the bustling heart of China's wedding photo industry. It is a world where the allure of bridal elegance is not reserved for the betrothed; it is a rite of passage, a celebration of beauty for women regardless of marital status.

The downtown air buzzed with creativity as studios spilled onto the streets and beaches, transforming the cityscape into a living canvas. Couples, adorned in attire that spanned the epochs, became the subjects of timeless narratives captured in a single shutter click. Our chosen package was a treasure trove of memories: two large wall portraits encased in crystal glass, a duo of glossy photo books, and a quaint desktop memento.

Our day unfolded in a series of transformations, each outfit changing a new chapter in our shared story. Beca, usually untouched by cosmetics, was a vision of elegance, her features accentuated by the artistry of the make-up and hair stylists. The transformation was so profound that it felt like I was in a mesmerizing stranger's company. Yet, beneath the layers of makeup and the cascading hair, the essence of the woman I was growing to love shone through. The photoshoot was nothing short of magical, a testament to the skill and dedication of those who immortalized our affection. The decision to embark on this adventure in China rather than Canada proved wise, as the results spoke volumes about the craftsmanship we encountered.

In the end, we could only carry the tangible pieces of this experience that would fit within the confines of our luggage—the photo books and the small frame. The larger, cumbersome frames were left behind, entrusted to Beca's mother. They found a temporary home beneath the dining room table, a space seldom used except to shelter food from the night's embrace. There, they lay like slumbering giants, waiting for the day they could take their rightful place on a wall, a silent witness to the love that bloomed in an unexpected place.

The fleeting nature of time became all too apparent as our month-long sojourn neared its end. With our luggage brimming with souvenirs and hearts heavy with memories, Beca's parents chauffeured us to the airport, marking the beginning of our journey back to Shenzhen. The sun cast a warm glow over my head, a gentle reminder of our cherished days in Haikou.

Beca, ever mindful of family ties, yearned for a few more precious moments with her aunt. We navigated the city's streets, the train carrying us to a rendezvous point etched in familial love. There, amidst the city's hustle, Beca's aunt took us to a grand buffet restaurant, its doors flung open to the world just beyond the hotel's embrace. The vast space was dotted with large round tables inviting conversation and camaraderie.

As we dined, I became an unwitting spectacle, the focus of curious gazes that followed my every move. It was an odd sensation, like the pivot around which their dining experience orbited, their whispers weaving intrigue and speculation. Our meal concluded with the familiar pull of commerce, drawing us back to the shopping center that had become a well-trodden path during our stay. There, I indulged in the luxury of time—encapsulated in the form of another Rolex, a companion to the one I already owned. But this time, I chose a pristine white timepiece for Beca, symbolizing our synchronized hearts and shared moments. More than mere accessories, these matching watches would serve as timeless reminders of our adventures, ticking in unison as we ventured forth on future dates against the relentless march of time.

After an interminable two-hour wait, we finally boarded the train, leaving behind the bustling Shenzhen border as we journeyed back to the heart of Hong Kong. The city welcomed us with its vibrant downtown pulse. We meandered through the streets, our stomachs leading the way, until we stumbled upon a quaint eatery that promised a taste of local flavour.

With thoughts of home tugging at her heartstrings, Beca was trying to find the perfect souvenirs for her aunt and cousin back in Canada. Our quest led us to the famed The One Shopping Centre, nestled on the intersection of Nathan Road and Granville Road. It was a treasure trove of delights, where every turn offered a new temptation.

As dusk darkened the sky in shades of twilight, the realization dawned upon us: the night was ours, but we had no shelter to call our own. With the airport's call looming in the early morning, we surrendered to the allure of the Temple Street Night Market. This ancient Chinese bazaar, alive with the chatter of nightfall, offered sanctuary and the promise of bargains—clothes and gifts that held the essence of tradition, porcelain mirrored the moon's glow, and street foods. Here, among the market's timeless stalls, we found more than good deals; we saw the heartbeat of Hong Kong.

The night we had deepened, and with it, our fatigue. Yet, destitute as we were, the benches of Centenary Garden became our makeshift sanctuary. Nestled near the Tsim Sha Tsui Metro station, they offered a fleeting respite and a strategic spot for our impending journey to the Hong Kong International Airport. Our flight to

Toronto was at dawn, and the city's nocturnal symphony played on.

There I sat, a silent sentinel, as sleep eluded me. My senses were heightened, taking in the nocturnal ballet of passersby—each a story in motion—while Beca found solace in slumber. The garden, a patchwork of shadows and streetlight glow, held us in its embrace as we awaited the call of our early departure, marking the end of our Hong Kong escapade.

As dawn's first light warmed my cheeks, the remnants of the night's chill lingered on my damp attire. We strolled onto the subway, the rhythmic clatter of the train a prelude to our departure. The airport's customs gate gave way to a world of boutique windows and the comforting aroma of breakfast. Our boarding call echoed, summoning us to the Cathay Pacific plane that would carry us home to Toronto. Nestled in my seat, the initial meal was the start of a long nineteen-hour flight.

Awake, I curated a cinematic marathon to while away the hours, punctuated by the occasional cocktail —a bittersweet toast to the uncertainty awaited us. Our possessions lay dormant in Brampton's storage, and our future residence is unknown.

The plane's wheels graced Toronto's tarmac, marking the end of our Chinese sojourn. A Tim Hortons brew was the first familiar comfort in this homecoming ritual. Customs behind us, we embarked on the bus journey to Brampton, our luggage a cumbersome companion. The search for temporary refuge led us to the familiar facade of Knights Inn. There, we secured a week's lodgings—a haven to regroup as we reacquainted ourselves with work's rhythm and embarked on the quest for a new place to call home.

24

BROKEN HEARTS AND SECOND WEDDING

Beca resumed her duties at the store, albeit in a different position than the deli department. The store manager had reassigned her to the cash registers —a role she reluctantly accepted, for any discrepancies in cash would be a deduction from her wages. Meanwhile, I embraced my role in security, working in-house after selling my security company to a firm where my friend Stephen was employed. Being paid in cash suited me well, allowing for tax savings, while Beca's earnings, paid by cheque, contributed to our collective goal of saving for a room.

Our accommodation search led us to a Chinese couple, regulars at the supermarket and acquaintances of Beca. They offered us a lifeline—a furnished room in their house, conveniently located a mere twenty-minute walk from the mall and close to the University. It was a haven within our means at five hundred dollars a month. We settled into our new abode upstairs, adjacent to their daughter's room, while they occupied the main bedroom down the hall. Though the basement housed another tenant in its apartment, it was beyond our reach at the time, but we were content with the arrangement that fate had presented us.

In our quest for autonomy, a car became more than a luxury—a necessity. With its rigid schedules and routes, public transit could not accommodate the spontaneous detours life often demanded. My credit history, marred by indiscretions, would not pave the way. So, we turned to Beca's unblemished credit, a reward for her fresh start in this country. As a new immigrant, her financial slate was clean, and together, we navigated the paperwork, listing me as the co-applicant. It was a strategic move, a chance to rehabilitate my credit alongside hers.

The responsibility of payments fell squarely on my shoulders—a commitment I embraced with pride and trepidation. Insurance policies were penned in my name, a testament to my resolve to shoulder this new chapter. With no driving history, Beca trusted me to steer our course. Our choice of vehicle could not be arbitrary. Beca's heritage, woven into the fabric of who we are, meant that a familiar Honda would not suffice.

We sought a symbol, a chariot that echoed the luxury and ambition that defined our journey. The BMW 218i convertible, cloaked in the sophistication of black, became our unanimous choice.

Yet, this emblem of our aspirations proved to be a fickle companion in the throes of winter. The design, elegant in its complexity, required the windows to lower slightly to free themselves from the embrace of the convertible top—a mechanism utterly defeated by the icy grip of the Canadian cold. Many a morning, I wrestled with the frozen pane, a battle of wills between man and machine, as I struggled to enter our cherished but stubborn steed. It was a reminder that even the most well-laid plans could falter in the face of nature's whims. But it was our car, our symbol of progress, and every triumph over the stubborn window was a small victory in our more significant journey.

The winter beckoned us southward, away from the biting chill and into the embrace of milder climes. During these preparations, Beca, her eyes alight with the future, broached the subjects of marriage and children. Her words stirred a dormant realm of my heart, a chapter I thought closed after my marriage to Margaret. We had danced the dance of parenthood, bringing three vibrant souls into the fold before I chose to close the door on further offspring with a vasectomy. The finality of that decision had seemed absolute.

The road ahead was uncertain, but isn't that the essence of a journey? Whether navigating the icy challenges of a stubborn car window or the complex highways of the heart, the trip promises to be as unpredictable. Indeed, life's crossroads often emerge unannounced, like unexpected bends in the road. As I stood at the juncture of past and future, Beca's hopes shimmered like distant constellations, pulling me toward uncharted territories. The essence of a journey lies not in the well-trodden paths but in the twists and turns that defy our maps and expectations.

Embarking on the delicate subject of reversing time's decree, I delved into the intricacies of vasectomy reversals. The corridors of the internet echoed with statistics and testimonies; each click a step deeper into the realm of possibilities. The stark reality was that the threads of hope grew fainter with each passing year. It had been over five years since Megan took her first breath and laughed, and the sands of time were not known to flow backward.

The financial landscape in Canada presented a daunting mountain—over five thousand dollars, a figure that loomed large against the backdrop of daily life. The journey from consultation to surgery stretched across months, a calendar marked by the silent march of uncertainty. Yet, I stumbled upon a beacon of hope in Oklahoma in a twist divinely scripted. A Christian doctor, David Wilson, whose practice was a testament to faith and science intertwined, offered a ray of light. His clinic, a sanctuary where personal beliefs and medical expertise met, promised a procedure at half the cost.

Beca's journey to the United States was a testament to her determination and the start of a new chapter in her life. As a Chinese citizen residing in Canada, the gateway to her American dream was gated by the need for a U.S. visa. The process was meticulous: an online application to be filled, fees to be paid, and many documents to be gathered.

I remember the crisp Toronto morning we ventured downtown, the city's pulse echoing our nervous heartbeats. The interview at the U.S. Customs office was more than a formality; it was a bridge to Beca's aspirations. She confidently presented her documents, handing over her passport as the last step.

A week of waiting felt like a lifetime, but when we returned to retrieve her passport, it was imbued with more than just a visa; it was the key to a decade of opportunities in the United States. The joy in Beca's eyes was unmistakable. This was not just a travel document—it was the emblem of her excitement and the freedom to explore new horizons that she had yearned for even before our paths crossed.

My heart buoyed by newfound hope, I secured my

reservation with the doctor with a five-hundred-dollar deposit. The following week was set as the threshold between what was and what could be. As the day approached, I prepared to part with the remaining two thousand dollars—a small price for the key to unlock a future once thought unattainable. This decision, weighty with implications, was not just a financial transaction. It was a leap of faith, a testament to the belief in

second chances, and a nod to life's mysterious ways. Standing on the precipice of change, I could not help but marvel at the journey that had led me here.

Our BMW was polished and ready—a sleek chariot that would ferry us through the heart of America. The engine hummed with anticipation, its oil freshly changed, as if whispering secrets of the open road. We did not alter our winter tires as we only went for a week and were unsure about the weather coming home. Our route traced a poetic arc: from the windswept plains of Oklahoma to the tornado alleys of Kansas, then Texas unfurled before us, vast and varied—a symphony of deserts, canyons, and cowboy tales.

The road to Oklahoma unfolded like a novel, each mile a chapter of anticipation and determination—twenty-two hours of relentless driving, fueled by the urgency of my noon surgery appointment. We embarked on this odyssey at dawn, the sun barely peeking over the horizon as we left Toronto behind.

Our first stop was the majestic Niagara Falls, where the mist and the roar of cascading water drowned out the ticking clock. Crossing the Rainbow Bridge into the United States, we wanted to step into a new chapter of our lives; American Flags waved overhead, and we passed the Welcome to the United States sign. Beca's passport, scrutinized at the border, held the promises of adventure for her.

The customs agent's questions were routine, but their answers carried weight. Why Oklahoma? Why now? We explained the purpose of our journey—the surgery that would alter the course of my life. The agent nodded, glimpsing the courage in Beca's eyes, and stamped our passage.

The transition from the lush greenery of Niagara Falls to the gritty streets and highways of Buffalo, NY, was like turning a page in a novel. The sun pursued us relentlessly, casting elongated shadows across the asphalt. And amidst the urban decay stood our beacon: the iconic red-and-brown sign of Tim Hortons. It was not merely a pit stop but a pilgrimage—a way to hold onto our Canadian identity as we ventured deeper into the heart of America. We sipped our double-doubles, the warmth seeping into our hands, and savoured Boston Cream donuts. Beca's eyes held excitement and wistfulness; we both knew this was the last taste of Canada and the last Tim Horton's for the week.

Asphalt stretched before us, faded billboards, their once-bold letters now weathered and worn. The cracked pavement bore the weight of countless journeys—a roadmap of resilience, but all my trips to the United States were my first time to Oklahoma. Buffalo City, with its gritty façade, retreated in the rearview mirror. Its steel skeletons and forgotten alleys blurred into abstraction, and into Pennsylvania, a quilt of rolling hills embraced us. We passed through towns with names like Scranton, Allentown, and Harrisburg. Each exit held a story—a diner where lovers met, a gas station where truckers swapped tales. Beca's eyes, wide as saucers, drank it all in. For her, this was a canvas waiting for her imprint.

Ohio unfurled like a patchwork quilt of Americana. We cruised through Cleveland, where the Rock and Roll Hall of Fame stood like a sentinel to rebellion. Then came Columbus, its skyline a blend of glass and green. Beca pressed her palm against the window as if absorbing the essence of each state. Her wonder was contagious, infecting me with curiosity. And there, on the horizon, lay more States in our and beyond. The road was our ballad, and we sang it together—two souls chasing the sun, leaving tire tracks across borders. As the miles ticked, I realized this journey Was not just about surgery or geography. It was about unfurling, about becoming. And Beca, with her eyes wide open, was my compass, guiding me toward a future where every mile held a promise.

Around Springfield, Missouri, the sun dipped below the horizon, casting a warm glow on the rolling hills. Exhausted from a day of driving, we pulled into a dimly lit truck stop. Beca, my adventurous companion, stretched her legs and marvelled at the vastness of the open road. She did not have a driver's license, leaving me with the daunting task of steering our trusty car through the night.

The truck stop buzzed with life—a symphony of clinking coffee mugs, distant laughter, and the low hum of engines. We ordered greasy burgers and fries, savouring the taste of freedom. Beca gazed out the window, always the dreamer, tracing constellations with her finger. I envied her ability to lose herself in the stars while I grappled with the road ahead.

As the clock ticked past midnight, we settled back into the car. The seats, warm and familiar, cradled our tired bodies. The highway stretched before us like an uncharted path, its asphalt roads leading us deeper into the heart of America. We were not just driving but creating memories that will never be forgotten.

Our final truck rest stop for the night was a lonely, desolate darkness. The air smelled of pine and diesel fuel, and the distant rumble of passing trucks lulled us into a fitful sleep. Beca curled up in the passenger seat, wrapped in her oversized hoodie, while I kept watch in a light sleep. The night—the rustling leaves, the distant hoot of an owl, the soft patter of rain on the windshield finally, I fell into a deep sleep, resting my swollen feet from the twenty-hour drive.

In the morning, we rubbed our eyes, stiff from the makeshift slumber, and resumed our journey. Coffee in hand, not Tim Horton's, Oklahoma City beckoned—an hour away so we could relax and enjoy the remaining drive. The navigation system, our digital guide, played tricks on us. It led us down winding backroads, past collapsed barns and plowed over fields. We laughed, half-delirious, as we recalibrated our route. Beca held the phone, squinting at the screen, while I navigated the maze of streets using the car and phone navigation together.

Finally, we stood outside the doctor's office—a nondescript building in a commercial strip plaza with only a unit number on the door. The Doctor met us inside, had me fill out some waiver forms, and collected the rest of the two-thousand-dollar payment for the surgery. Beca squeezed my hand, her excitement contagious. We had conquered the night, wrestled with uncertainty, and emerged victorious.

The waiting room smelled of antiseptic and hope.

The doctor, kind-eyed and gentle, listened to our story. My appointment held promise—a chance for answers, for second chances. Side by side, in the serenity of the pre-op room, Dr. Wilson's voice broke the silence with a gentle request to offer a prayer for us—a tradition he honoured with every patient. It was a moment of shared humanity before the clinical precision of surgery. In the adjacent operating room, the reality of the procedure awaited. I reclined on the sterile table, the cool air brushing against my skin as I adjusted my clothing to the knees.

Dr. Wilson administered a local anesthetic, its numbing promise starkly contrasting the warmth in his eyes. Beca offered a seat with a view and could witness the meticulous preparation of surgical instruments—a symphony of steel that seemed to overshadow the procedure itself, the vasectomy, in its complexity. The doctor told me I could watch on the monitor during the procedure, but somehow, the strength of the anesthetic knocked me out, and I awoke to the procedure being completed.

Curious and slightly nervous, I asked Beca, 'Did you watch?' She shook her head, revealing that she had opted for the waiting room during the procedure. Meanwhile, I had this surreal moment—there I was, post-surgery, with a tiny straw protruding from my scrotum sac. The doctor assured me it was for draining blood and would be removed after twenty-four hours. 'It'll heal on its own,' he said, as if discussing a minor inconvenience. Three months later, I would have to get my sperm checked, but the doctor's confidence in success was contagious.

"Where to next?" I asked Beca as we contemplated our journey home. Her eyes sparkled with wanderlust—she was eager for more adventures. With winter's chill, I proposed a detour to Miami, Florida. "Let's chase the sun," I said, picturing the iconic South Beach and the scenic coastal drive that awaited us in our convertible.

I programmed our BMW's navigation for Florida, and it calculated a twenty-three-hour odyssey from Oklahoma. The return trip would take us another twenty-something hours back toward Canada. But the adventure and experience for Beca and building new memories made the miles ahead seem trivial.

Our route covered seventeen States of American landscapes: Interstate 40 through Arkansas, a brief homage to the King of Rock 'n' Roll in Memphis, Tennessee—Elvis Presley, my middle school idol—and then a southern sojourn through Mississippi and Alabama. Each state is a chapter, and each mile is a story waiting to unfold. We chased lightning storms along the ocean side, the Atlantic's salty breath mingling with our lips. Florida's palms waved us closer, inviting us to dip our toes in warm Gulf waters.

Georgia welcomed us with open arms, and as the soft top of our car unfurled, we transformed our ride into a sun-kissed convertible. The wind tousled Beca's hair, and the warmth of the air enveloped us. Our destination? Miami, Florida—the promise of South Beach boardwalks and endless ocean waves pulling us southward.

But before we reached the neon-lit streets of Miami, I veered off the highway. A quaint orchard field beckoned, its citrus-scented breeze luring us in. I plucked a bag of Florida Navel Oranges, their vibrant hues like miniature suns. Beca's eyes widened as she bit into the juicy fruit, savouring the sweet taste of sunshine.

Stepping into South Beach for the first time, I was immediately swept up in its electrifying atmosphere. This was not just a beach but the pulsing heart of fashion and artistry. Renowned artists mingled with the crowd, designer boutiques flaunted the latest trends, and the legendary Villa Casa Casuarina, once the illustrious Versace Mansion, was a monument to luxury and history, bringing me back to my times in Milan, Italy, at Club Hollywood.

Tucked away in an artsy diner brimming with local charm, we savoured a coffee and dessert across the vibrant boardwalk strip. As we prepared to journey northward, a surprise awaited us at our car—two tickets clung to the windshield, a quirky souvenir from the city for my clear plate cover and unconventional parking orientation. The local custom was to park nose-first, not tail-in. Being a foreigner to these shores, you can imagine the fate of those tickets.

From Miami, our adventure continued north, and we cruised down the iconic Daytona Beach strip, renowned for its pulse-pounding Daytona 500 speedway. The mercury soared into the thirties, turning our winter tires into a gooey mess on the scorching asphalt and sand. It was not long before our trusty bimmer found itself trapped in the Sam embrace of the beach, halting our progress and inadvertently creating a roadblock. In a stroke of luck, a merry band of beachgoers, spirits high and inhibitions low, rallied to our aid. With their help, we broke free from the Sam trap, and I floored the accelerator, eager to rejoin the flow of the main road.

As we bid farewell to the action-packed shores and students coming to Florida for Spring Break, we finally stopped beneath the towering "Welcome to Daytona Beach" sign. There, we indulged in the flavours of the South at Popeyes Louisiana Kitchen, fueling up for the next chapter of our Floridian escapade. Our last stop in Florida unfolded in the sun-drenched streets of Ft.

Lauderdale. I strolled with Beca along the bustling main beach; we meandered to the Dania Beach Fishing Pier, where the horizon stretched endlessly, a canvas of blues and greens. Ah, and how could I forget the infamous 'lobster sunburn'? While my memories of this city were tinged with the discomfort of that fiery souvenir, for Beca, it was an exhilarating first. Each step in the Floridian sands marked her delightful discovery of America's diverse states.

We bid farewell to Florida's sunny borders and paused at a quaint roadside stand to fuel up for the long haul. There, we selected sun-ripened oranges, their zest promising a burst of sunshine with every bite. A tiny orange sapling also caught my eye—a living memento destined to flourish back home, a leafy echo of our southern vacation.

With the convertible's top retracted, we embraced the open road, the wind our companion as we departed Georgia for another fourteen-hour drive. Our destination: Washington D.C.—a treasure trove of history and heritage. Beca's eyes sparkled with anticipation at the thought of witnessing the grandeur of the White House, the sprawling expanse of the National Mall, the stoic presence of the Lincoln Memorial, the myriad wonders within the Smithsonian National Museum, and the imposing United States Capitol Building.

Our time in the capital was a whirlwind of awe and

inspiration, but the journey beckoned us onward. Northward, we ventured back to the familiar embrace of New York. Yet, no odyssey through the Empire State could ever be complete without succumbing to the magnetic allure of New York City—the city that never sleeps, a pulsing kaleidoscope of ambition, welcomed us with its neon embrace. Skyscrapers reached for the heavens, their glass facades reflecting our aspirations. We parked at an above-ground lot near Battery Park. The wind was so cold I had to buy a couple of hats and gloves to keep us warm after returning from the sunny south.

Beneath the city's pulsating rhythm, Beca and I navigated the underground veins of New York by subway. Emerging at Penn Station, we ascended to the urban oasis of Madison Square Gardens. There, nestled among the entrance, a familiar beacon of comfort greeted us—a Tim Hortons. It was a divine revelation amidst the biting chill, coffee's warmth, and being Canadian.

We meandered past the storied walls of the New York Times, each headline a whisper of history in the making. Our journey led us to the ferry, where we sailed across the waters to salute the Statue of Liberty from afar. The island remained an elusive gem, its access a relic of the past, so we embraced the scenic detour to Staten Island and back.

We strolled over to Wall Street to take pictures with the famous Charging Bull to remind those of the 1987 Wall Street crash. From there, we went to Canal Street in Lower Manhattan to eat in a Chinese restaurant and shop for replica merchandise. It felt like we were still in Shenzhen, China.

The heart of the city beckoned, and we answered its call at Broadway and Times Square, the world's crossroads. Ascending the heights of the Empire State Building, we stood atop the cityscape, the horizon stretching beyond dreams and ambition and the Grand Central Station. Our final act took us on a train to Brooklyn, to the nostalgic shores of Coney Island. Though silent for the season, its charm was undiminished as we strolled amidst echoes of laughter and joy. With memories etched in our hearts, we returned to our car, the city's lights guiding us homeward.

And finally, the last eight-hour drive home, as the Niagara Falls roared its ancient song, we crossed back into Canada. The mist clung to our skin, baptizing us anew. Like love itself, the falls tumbled ceaselessly, defying gravity and reason. Once a mere machine, our BMW had become a witness to our odyssey—a silent companion in our shared narrative.

As the miles blurred and the seasons shifted, I pondered Beca's hopes—the marriage she envisioned, the children she longed for. Could I rewrite my story and add new chapters to a life already etched in ink? The road ahead shimmered with uncertainty, but isn't that the beauty of it all? We are travellers, not just passengers, and every detour, every icy window thawed, becomes part of our legacy.

So, with Beca by my side, I embraced the unpredictable—the twists, the turns, the uncharted highways. Our BMW carried more than just our bodies; it cradled our dreams, doubts, and the promise of an unwritten future. As we hurtled toward the horizon, I realized that sometimes, the most profound journeys are the ones that lead us back to ourselves.

In the soft glow of the storefront, I knelt before Beca, my heart in my hands. With a ring, a symbol of eternal commitment, I asked her to start a life with me. On February 14th, 2012, we intertwined our souls, embarking on the odyssey of marriage and nurturing the roots of our new family. Yet, as one chapter closes, the pages rustle with the promise of more. Is this the finale of my saga or merely the prologue to a more significant journey? Forty years of wandering, a pilgrimage through trials and tribulations, have led me to this sanctuary of love. The shadows of my past—abuse, addiction, the quest for fidelity—do they dissolve in the light of this new dawn?

This tale pauses here, but the narrative of life is unending. As I step into the future with Beca, the echoes of my experiences serve as a beacon, illuminating the forgotten corners of history. The legacy of the Catholic Children's Aid Society and the foster homes of yesteryears remains etched in time, a testament to resilience and the unyielding hope for change.

And so, with a heart full of dreams and eyes set on the horizon, I close this memoir. Not with a period, but with an ellipsis…

THE END

EPILOGUE

As I pen down the final words of this book, I find myself standing at the crossroads of my past and the uncertainty of the future. I hope my life's narrative will inspire empathy, urging readers to look beyond the surface of a child's behaviour and recognize that their actions may be a cry for help.

I have often wondered why God chose this path, leading me through a wilderness of experiences. Yet, I have learned not to question His wisdom. Like Paul, who bore his thorn with grace, I, too, carry my burdens, waiting for the day God deems fit to lift them. Throughout my journey, I have encountered both protectors and predators. Protectors who shielded me from harm and guided me away from destructive influences. Predators who sought to drain my spirit, leaving me lost in the wilderness.

Now, it is time for a new beginning. It is time to sever ties with those who have hindered my spiritual growth and strained my relationships with family and God. It is time to rid myself of parasitic friendships that drain my moral strength, leaving me isolated and lonely.

Unless I leave my past behind, my future risks becoming a lonely existence, reduced to a man begging for change on a street corner, unnoticed by the world. I am committed to ending my self-centeredness, focusing instead on how I can enrich others' lives without expecting anything in return.

I seek God's forgiveness for all the people I have wronged, especially those genuine souls who went out of their way to improve my life. I also forgive those who hurt me, shaping me into who I am today. Their actions have given me the strength to help others who bear emotional scars from their past. The Catholic Children's Aid Society has seen too much abuse—physical, sexual, and emotional—over the generations. It is time they acknowledge their failures and strive to protect today's children better. These children are our future.

As I conclude, I am reminded of a verse from

Romans 8:37-39, "No, in all these things we are more than conquerors through him who loves us...". This journey is far from over. It is merely a pause, a moment of reflection before I continue my path.

9 781069 097125